International Nietzsche Studies

Richard Schacht, series editor

Editorial Board

Ruediger Bittner (Bielefeld)
Eric Blondel (Paris-Sorbonne)
Maudemarie Clark (Colgate)
David Cooper (Durham)
Arthur Danto (Columbia)
Kathleen Higgins (Texas-Austin)
R. J. Hollingdale (London)
Bernd Magnus (California-Riverside)
Wolfgang Mueller-Lauter (Berlin)
Alexander Nehamas (Princeton)
Martha Nussbaum (Brown)
Joerg Salaquarda (Vienna)
Gary Shapiro (Richmond)
Robert Solomon (Texas-Austin)
Tracy Strong (California-San Diego)
Yirmiyahu Yovel (Jerusalem)

A list of books in the series appears at the back of this book.

International Nietzsche Studies

Nietzsche has emerged as a thinker of extraordinary importance, not only in the history of philosophy but in many fields of contemporary inquiry. Nietzsche studies are maturing and flourishing in many parts of the world. This internationalization of inquiry with respect to Nietzsche's thought and significance may be expected to continue.

International Nietzsche Studies is conceived as a series of monographs and essay collections that will reflect and contribute to these developments. The series will present studies in which responsible scholarship is joined to the analysis, interpretation, and assessment of the many aspects of Nietzsche's thought that bear significantly upon matters of moment today. In many respects Nietzsche is our contemporary, with whom we do well to reckon, even when we find ourselves at odds with him. The series is intended to promote this reckoning, embracing diverse interpretive perspectives, philosophical orientations, and critical assessments.

The series is also intended to contribute to the ongoing reconsideration of the character, agenda, and prospects of philosophy itself. Nietzsche was much concerned with philosophy's past, present, and future. He sought to affect not only its understanding but also its practice. The future of philosophy is an open question today, thanks at least in part to Nietzsche's challenge to the philosophical traditions of which he was so critical. It remains to be seen—and determined—whether philosophy's future will turn out to resemble the "philosophy of the future" to which he proffered a prelude and of which he provided a preview, by both precept and practice. But this is a possibility we do well to take seriously. International Nietzsche Studies will attempt to do so, while contributing to the understanding of Nietzsche's philosophical thinking and its bearing upon contemporary inquiry.

❧ Richard Schacht

Nietzsche
and the Problem of Sovereignty

Nietzsche

and the Problem of Sovereignty

❧ *Richard J. White*

University of Illinois Press

Urbana and Chicago

© 1997 by the Board of Trustees of the University of Illinois
Manufactured in the United States of America
1   2   3   4   5   C   P   6   5   4   3   2

This book is printed on acid-free paper.

Library of Congress Cataloging-in-Publication Data
White, Richard J. (Richard John), 1956–
Nietzsche and the problem of sovereignty / Richard J. White.
p.   cm. — (International Nietzsche studies)
ISBN 0-252-02300-5 (alk. paper). — ISBN 0-252-06603-0
(pbk. : alk. paper)
1. Nietzsche, Friedrich Wilhelm, 1844-1900. I. Title. II. Series.
B3317.W454   1997
193—dc20   96-25212
                               CIP
ISBN 978-0-252-06603-0 (pbk. : alk. paper)

Contents

Acknowledgments   ix

Abbreviations   xi

Introduction: Reading Nietzsche   1

1. On the Value of the Individual   13

2. The Genealogy of Sovereignty: St. Paul, Kant, Schopenhauer   28

3. The Individual and the Birth of Tragedy   54

4. Against Idealism   78

5. Zarathustra and the Teaching of Sovereignty   100

6. The Return of the Master   124

7. *Ecce Homo,* or the Revaluation of Values   150

8. Nietzsche and the Philosophy of the Future   174

Afterword   189

Notes   195

Index   207

Acknowledgments

This book could not have been written without the intellectual and spiritual support of my friends and colleagues in Omaha, San Diego, New York, England, and elsewhere. In particular, I would like to thank Deborah Chaffin, philosopher and friend, who sustained and encouraged this project over a number of years. Thanks also to David Allison, Hugh Silverman, and Tom Altizer, who originally inspired me to think about Nietzsche and the philosophy of sovereignty; and to Patrick Murray, Jeanne Schuler, Clarinda Karpov, and numerous students and colleagues over the past few years who were interested in my work and challenged me to think through the subject of this book. Dick Schacht has been a very thoughtful and supportive editor—his excellent comments have helped to give this book its focus.

Part of this book was written with the assistance of an NEH summer stipend. The Graduate School at Creighton University also provided some support. I owe a special debt to Peggy Troy, who helped so much with the final editorial process.

Earlier versions of some sections of this book appeared in the following publications:

"Art and the Individual in Nietzsche's *Birth of Tragedy*," *British Journal of Aesthetics* 28 (Winter 1988): 59–67. Used by permission of Oxford University Press.

"Autobiography against Itself," *Philosophy Today* 35 (Fall 1991): 291–303. Used by permission of DePaul University.

"Autonomy as Foundational," in *Questioning Foundations: Truth, Subjectivity and Culture*, ed. Hugh Silverman (London: Routledge, 1993), pp. 79–97. Used by permission of the publisher.

"The Return of the Master: An Interpretation of Nietzsche's *Genealogy of Morals*," *Philosophy and Phenomenological Research* 48 (1988): 683–96. Used by permission of the publisher.

"Zarathustra and the Progress of Sovereignty: From the Overman to the

Eternal Recurrence," *International Studies in Philosophy* 26, no. 3 (1994): 107–15. Used by permission of Scholars Press.

✧

Special thanks to my son, Adam White, for keeping me cheerful. I would like to dedicate this book to my parents, Jack and Margaret White of Exmouth, England.

Abbreviations

In citing Nietzsche's writings, I use the following abbreviations, providing the title, chapter name or essay number (wherever appropriate), and section number, if there is one:

A   *The Antichrist,* trans. W. Kaufmann, in *The Portable Nietzsche* (London: Chatto, 1971)

BGE   *Beyond Good and Evil,* trans. W. Kaufmann (New York: Random House/Vintage 1966)

BT   *The Birth of Tragedy,* trans. W. Kaufmann (New York: Random House/Vintage, 1967)

D   *Daybreak,* trans. R. J. Hollingdale (Cambridge: Cambridge University Press, 1982)

EH   *Ecce Homo,* trans. W. Kaufmann (New York: Random House/ Vintage, 1967)

GM   *On the Genealogy of Morals,* trans. W. Kaufmann (New York: Random House/Vintage 1967)

GS   *The Gay Science,* trans. W. Kaufmann (New York: Random House/Vintage 1974)

HH   *Human, All Too Human,* trans. R. J. Hollingdale (Cambridge: Cambridge University Press, 1986)

TI   *Twilight of the Idols,* trans. W. Kaufmann, in *The Portable Nietzsche* (London: Chatto, 1971)

TSZ   *Thus Spoke Zarathustra,* trans. W. Kaufmann, in *The Portable Nietzsche* (London: Chatto, 1971)

UM   *Untimely Meditations,* trans. R. J. Hollingdale (Cambridge: Cambridge University Press, 1983)

WTP   *The Will to Power,* trans. W. Kaufmann and R. J. Hollingdale (New York: Random House/Vintage, 1967)

Introduction: Reading Nietzsche

There are many paths through the thought of Nietzsche; and one of the chief criticisms of Nietzsche's philosophical enterprise is that his thought permits an extreme diversity of conflicting interpretations. In different ways and with different ends, Nietzsche's work has been appropriated by Nazism, analytical philosophy, postmodernism, and the libidinal politics of recent French thought. This has inevitably called his philosophical rigor and integrity into question, for such apparent ambiguity is not usually reckoned as a philosophical virtue. The problem is that Nietzsche presents us with various figures, ideas, and themes—such as the eternal recurrence, the overman, and the will to power—and while these may be compelling or even seductive, they are not straightforward philosophical doctrines that bear a univocal meaning and that are consistently maintained through all of his writings. In Nietzsche, the "meaning," the constellation, and the priority of these figures changes from one work to the next and even from one part of a text to another part of the same text. In this respect, they are *overdetermined* and resist every attempt at paraphrase or critical appropriation. Perhaps it is not surprising, then, that in the absence of any fixed concepts some commentators may decide that Nietzsche does not have any final "message," since he is not saying anything determinate at all. Nietzsche is still appreciated as a poet and as a master stylist of the German language, but on this reading his genius would be limited to inspiration as opposed to philosophical illumination.

The problematic status of Nietzsche's writing has contributed to the reading of him as a "poet-philosopher" who is apparently more concerned with matters of style than substance.[1] More recently, though, it has also led to the appropriation of his thought by the supporters of deconstruction.[2] The latter interpret Nietzsche's onslaught against traditional philosophical categories as deconstruction *avant la lettre.* They claim that his apparent refusal to occupy a determinate position within the traditional problems of philosophy is actually an attempt to overcome the fixed oppositions—between mind and body, the "true" world and the apparent, free will and determinism, and so on—that structure and constrain all of our philosophical thinking. Indeed, his use of a "mobile" set of terms and concepts seems deliberately intended to challenge every substantial unity and every fixed determination and belief, concepts that deconstruction has diagnosed as the prejudice of our "logocentric" tradition.

There is much to be learned from this kind of approach. Certainly, Heidegger was right to emphasize the *rigorous* nature of Nietzsche's thinking, in opposition to the simplistic portrait of the poet-philosopher. But it is also obvious that the *style* of Nietzsche's writing is actually inseparable from his philosophical argument. For this reason, any good reader of Nietzsche must approach his texts with a keen sense for his *strategy* in both the immediate and the overall context of his concerns. Jaspers and others have discovered that Nietzsche's arguments in one place may flatly contradict what he says somewhere else.[3] But if we bear in mind his particular purpose at any given point of the text, it is likely that we will discover a rigorous and consistent argument.

To take just one example: Nietzsche often criticizes "idealism" for ignoring the claims of the body and completely neglecting the impact of physiological factors upon our apprehension of the world. In *Ecce Homo*, for instance, he argues that philosophers should discuss the influence of diet and the weather, and elsewhere he speculates about the effects of "alcohol-poisoning" upon the fortunes of German philosophy; in commenting upon Schopenhauer he suggests that all philosophical pessimism is ultimately the product of a bad digestion. At first glance, this could be interpreted as the statement of a crude materialist position. And yet, this seems to fly in the face of Nietzsche's frequent attacks upon the mechanistic reduction of the world that he viewed as the overall tendency of contemporary science.[4] Once we discard our usual philosophical preconceptions, however, we will realize that Nietzsche's arguments against idealism are so excessive, the points he raises so extreme, that this can only be regarded as the caricature of a materialist position. Nietzsche attacks idealism, and he makes us aware of what idealism has forgotten; but at the same time, his materialist stance is so overblown that we cannot remain on either side of the materialism/idealism debate. Through such a strategy, his most immediate goal is to force us beyond this traditional opposition of thought.

By citing examples like this, I want to show that an appreciation of what has often been dismissed as the "literary" dimension of Nietzsche's texts is really essential to an understanding of the overall nature of his philosophical task. And if we are aware of his use of comedy, caricature, *reductio ad absurdum,* and other literary devices, this will help us to realize the respect in which he is primarily a *performative* writer. This means that Nietzsche is not simply content to offer us an illuminating analysis of modern culture, or to describe the basic forms of nihilism, the prejudices of philosophers, or the logic of the "death of God." For in addition to his profound diagnoses of modern life, his primary intention is actually to effect a cure, using his own writing as a means of *forcing* us to confront nihilism and to make us think through the death of God so that we may escape the sickness that he describes. It is in this active and affirmative sense that Nietzsche is a "performative" writer—for he seeks a transformation of the individual soul. One of the primary concerns of the present work will be to clarify this aspect of Nietzsche's writing by showing that ideas like the eternal recurrence may appear inconsistent on the "theoretical" level, but follow a rigorous and compelling logic when viewed in a performative light.

An attunement to Nietzsche's style and strategy is therefore essential for an adequate involvement with his philosophy. Having said this, however, there is an obvious question that must now be asked: What, if anything, *is* the positive goal of Nietzsche's writing? Is there a final point to all of his strategic maneuvers, some ultimate *intention* that might be articulated? Or is his writing primarily "critical," insofar as it seeks to disabuse us of accepted attitudes and ideas, without proposing any alternative ideals? An exclusive emphasis on Nietzsche's style will probably not help us at this point. Deconstruction, for instance, has been very useful in making explicit the ways in which Nietzsche's texts turn traditional categories and conceptual oppositions against each other in order to undermine the philosophical edifice from within. But since deconstruction is enacted at this *transcendental* (or *ultra-transcendental*) level, it is constitutionally opposed to any unitary interpretation that seeks to discover a single overriding project beneath the "play" of the text.[5] Deconstruction has taught us to appreciate Nietzsche's dancing, but it has subordinated the material concerns of his philosophy—his emphasis on history, the body, and above all, individual experience—to the free play of the text. I think this represents a misconstrual of Nietzsche's project, and in the present work I will suggest that there *is* a fundamental concern, which informs and directs all of his writing, and which allows us to view categories as diverse as eternal recurrence, will to power, master and slave, and Apollo and Dionysus as the shifting manifestations of a singular project.

In his book on Nietzsche, Heidegger argues that every philosopher is inspired by a single "guiding question" that informs the whole of that philosopher's work. And while I disagree with Heidegger's particular interpretation of Nietzsche, I think that this suggestion is both illuminating and correct;

for in reading through Nietzsche systematically, one cannot fail to be impressed by the persistence of certain thoughts and basic concerns that survive every change in style and strategy or the manifest content of the text. Nietzsche, we might say, is generally preoccupied with the problem of "higher humanity"—and so he asks, How are we to reverse the decline of modern culture and regain something like the spiritual condition of ancient Greece? What are we to think about contemporary education and institutional arrangements, which seem to suppress creativity and difference? And how are we to foster the philosopher, artist, and saint, who celebrate life and justify it for us? Sometimes Nietzsche frames his question in terms of "higher" and "lower" moralities, and sometimes he thinks in terms of "the overman" and his nemesis, "the last man." The basic problem is to understand how creative individuals can come to terms with their tradition and those everyday forces, like morality, politics, and even pity, that may promote oblivion and the abandonment of their creative task. And given the absolute importance of self-overcoming, how does one become what one is? Or, in the alternative language that he sometimes uses, what is "sovereignty," and what does it mean to be a sovereign individual? If we follow the lead of traditional philosophy, then we might expect that such an ideal could be legislated or prescribed in terms of a specific formula. Or could it be that the creative soul, or the higher type of "man," is simply a "gift" that emerges suddenly as an unprecedented fulguration of nature?

In the *Twilight of the Idols,* Nietzsche emphasizes that individuals as such are nothing apart from the culture to which they belong. "Every individual," he writes, "may be scrutinized to see whether he represents the ascending or the descending line of life. Having made that decision, one has a canon for the worth of his self-interest." He goes on to make it clear that the problem of the individual is ultimately inseparable from the broader issues of culture and the need to achieve a "higher humanity":

> If he represents the ascending line, then his worth is indeed extraordinary—and for the sake of life as a whole, which takes a step farther through him, the care for his preservation and for the creation of the best conditions for him may even be extreme. The single one, the "individual" as hitherto understood by the people and the philosophers alike, is an error after all: he is nothing by himself, no atom, no "link in the chain," nothing merely inherited from former times; he is the whole single line of humanity up to himself. (*TI* "Skirmishes" sec. 33)

In this respect, of course, Nietzsche's thinking is "aristocratic" in the extreme. With his concern for the higher and lower types of humanity—or masters and slaves—and his emphasis on genealogy and *blood,* Nietzsche affects himself as the final opponent of democratic values and modern nihilistic culture. And yet, with Nietzsche things are never so simple; for at the same time as he rejoins the tradition that he believes is being destroyed, he also accepts that it is the Western tradition itself, and specifically its Christian manifestations, that has created the conditions of its own destruction. From this perspective, his genealogical method is *not* concerned with heredity and the claims of natural right, but with forging another history that would best account for the way things are and force us to reflect upon an alternative future than the one we have hitherto imagined. Likewise, "blood" is not to be grasped in any essentialist or crudely naturalistic sense, for if Nietzsche's philosophical activity is itself a creative exercise of sovereignty—in rejecting and reshaping the genealogy that he has been given—we must understand his appeal to "blood" as part of a revolutionary impulse that uses traditional forms in order to loosen their familiar hold upon us.

In this book I aim to address the general issue of Nietzsche's thinking concerning the problem of higher humanity. What is the nature of higher humanity, who are its exemplars, and how are they to be invoked? Nietzsche uses a number of different models and approaches, but in what follows I will focus more specifically on the problem of individual *sovereignty,* since I think that it is this theme, more than any other, that links Nietzsche to the modern philosophical tradition, at the same time as it allows us to grasp his continuing relevance to contemporary debates. To be sure, Nietzsche does not have an explicit "theory" of sovereignty that is sustained and developed throughout his texts. But it is a theme that he returns to over and over again, from *The Birth of Tragedy* to *Ecce Homo.* And at key points in his writing he presents the image of the "sovereign individual"—or the imperative of sovereignty—in ways that leave no doubt as to its importance. Most famously, in the second essay of *On the Genealogy of Morals,* he writes as follows:

> If we place ourselves at the end of this tremendous process, where the tree at last brings forth fruit, where society and the morality of custom at last reveal *what* they have simply been the means to: then we discover that the ripest fruit is the *sovereign individual,* like only to himself, liberated again from morality of custom, autonomous and supramoral (for "autonomous" and "moral" are mutually exclusive), in short, the man who has his own independent, protracted will and the *right to make promises*—and in him a proud consciousness, quivering in every muscle, of *what* has at length been achieved and become flesh in him, a consciousness of his own power and freedom, a sensation of mankind come to completion. (*GM* II sec. 2)

Here the sovereign individual is depicted as the very fulfillment and justification of nature. But it is also clear from the overall context of *On the Gene-*

alogy of Morals that this is *not* to assert that the sovereign individual is the preordained goal of history, or the final purpose of "Nature" in any straightforward sense. The sovereign individual is sovereign because he is capable of self-commandment, and this implies that he is capable of gathering the various threads of his own existence in order to pledge and control himself for the future.[6] Thus sovereignty is a product and an outcome, but at the same time it represents a new beginning and a meaningful appropriation of the fundamental powers of life. In this respect, the sovereign individual actually *creates* a retrospective justification for the indifferent accumulation of history. And he transfigures nature by bestowing meaning where none had existed before, or creating new meaning in place of old.

Let us say, then, that "sovereignty" is the condition of the individual *as an individual*, or the determination of the individual *as such*. For Nietzsche, however, the latter is not the individual who is determined by the various codifications of class, race, sex, and so on, and thus subjected to the herd. The sovereign individual is a "free spirit" who possesses the strength to will his own will, and who thereby appropriates his own proper selfhood. The summons to individual sovereignty appears throughout Nietzsche's writings as the original imperative of the individual life. Most dramatically, in *Schopenhauer as Educator*, for example, there is an expression of sheer astonishment at the fact of individual existence, and an urgent proclamation of the call to sovereignty that this evokes. "Even if the future gave us no cause for hope," he writes,

> the fact of our existing at all in this here and now must be the strongest incentive to us to live according to our own laws and standards: the inexplicable fact that we live precisely today, when we had all infinite time in which to come into existence, that we possess only a shortlived today in which to demonstrate why and to what end we came into existence now and at no other time. We are responsible to ourselves for our own existence; consequently we want to be the true helmsman of this existence and refuse to allow our existence to resemble a mindless act of chance. (*UM* III sec. 1)

Nietzsche later described *Schopenhauer as Educator* as his most personal work, in which "my innermost history, my *becoming*, is inscribed" (*EH* "The Untimely Ones" sec. 3). It is significant, then, that in this essay the question of the individual is always forcefully maintained, as Nietzsche seeks to articulate the absolute singularity of the individual life. "Each of us bears a productive uniqueness within him as the core of his being; and when he becomes aware of it, there appears around him a strange penumbra which is the mark of his singularity" (*UM* III sec. 3). Thus Nietzsche seems to bring his vision of the individual to the very threshold of the sacred. To focus upon sovereignty is to focus upon the point at which life is transfigured and redeemed from its own "nausea" and distress. I will show how this urgent concern for the individual, with the consequent demand for sovereignty, suggests a possible basis for all evaluation and critique.

In the earlier passage from *On the Genealogy of Morals* quoted above, Nietzsche's account of the sovereign individual possesses all the connotations of self-mastery and self-legislation that we would typically associate with the ordinary ideal of autonomy. In fact, his ideal of "sovereignty" is closely related to Kant's notion of "autonomy"; for according to the latter, there is a significant sense in which individuals can resist all *heteronomous* forces and desires to take charge of themselves and live according to their own law. Kantian autonomy implies self-determination in the sense that one may be both the sovereign and the subject of the same self-given law. It also implies that such an ideal of self-appropriation must be absolutely original and self-justifying since it cannot be regarded, without contradiction, as the "effect" of anything else. And yet, Nietzsche's discussion of sovereignty is significantly different from the Kantian ideal. Like so many other terms and concepts that he uses, Nietzsche appropriates the thought of sovereignty for his own ends. He uses an idea that has a certain popularity and even a tradition behind it. But while this is his point of departure, in his work he goes on to develop a sustained critique of the very idea of sovereignty—not rejecting it, as some commentators would have us believe, but challenging it and rethinking it, so that all the problems associated with it are made completely apparent. In effect, he attempts to think through the paradox of an embodied conception of sovereignty, as an outcome of nature that is somehow creative and spontaneous in itself.

The goal of individual sovereignty seems to direct much of Nietzsche's philosophical strategy and helps us to find relations between associated figures and ideals, like the free spirit, the artist, or the very idea of a higher humanity, that inhabit all of his texts. Nietzsche affirms the priority and the urgency of individual sovereignty, and it is significant that in his most antagonistic works he apparently criticizes or repudiates all existing ideals except this one. This is not to say that the issue of sovereignty represents "the secret of Nietzsche"; but I do believe that the pursuit of this particular theme will give us a very full interpretation of his work, and it will help us to follow the trajectory of his thinking on "higher humanity" in a very determinate way.

But even if this is a reasonable account of Nietzsche's philosophy, there are still some immediate problems that must be dealt with, at least in a preliminary way. First, there is an obvious problem in that Nietzsche does not seem to offer an explicit or detailed account of individual sovereignty any-where in his writings. Unlike Kant, who painstakingly determines the nec-essary and sufficient conditions of autonomy (as opposed to heteronomy), Nietzsche's discussions of sovereignty seem to be much less "precise," and they are evocative and inspirational rather than didactic. My suggestion is that this is in fact a deliberate tactic on his part. Since sovereignty is a matter of self-commandment it appears to follow that any attempt to *specify* its nature may actually destroy the sovereignty of the individual by circumscribing it in advance. As the singular project of the individual as such, sovereignty resists all conceptual determination. And this means, for example, that while Zar-athustra could be regarded as an exemplar of the sovereign ideal, he cannot simply be a model to be imitated, since that would imply the abandonment of the very sovereignty that he is seeking to inspire. In this way we can un-derstand the message that he gives to his disciples (and hence to all of us): "I bid you lose me and find yourselves; and only when you have all denied me will I return to you" (*TSZ* I "On the Gift-Giving Virtue").

The dialectic of individual sovereignty therefore *requires* an oblique ap-proach, and this returns us to the performative dimension of Nietzsche's work. In fact, there are *some* general claims about sovereignty that can be deduced from his texts; but going beyond any straightforward description and analysis, one of his primary aims is to confront us with our own will-lessness, and literally to provoke us into sovereignty.

A second objection may be raised at this early point that it is a very con-servative interpretation of Nietzsche that aligns him with "the tradition" and stresses his preoccupation with individuality and self-determination. On this reading, Nietzsche appears to be an apologist of bourgeois indi-vidualism, in the same nineteenth-century tradition of self-reliance and self-discipline as Samuel Smiles or Thomas Arnold. But such a response would be mistaken. By comparing Nietzsche's discussion of sovereignty to that of Kant and the rest of the tradition, we shall be able to measure the distance that separates their thinking. Moreover, even though there is a definite ideology of the individual that prevails in much of nineteenth-century thought, Nietzsche was quite aware of the dangers of rampant in-dividualism, and his meditation upon sovereignty is simply not a eulogy to "the great man." In fact, as we shall see, he realized that the sovereignty of the individual must include both the moments of self-appropriation *and* self-abandonment. He recognizes that sovereignty entails an absolute "openness" to the world—an attunement to the ecstatic impulses of life, or the "Dionysian"—and a consequent refusal to be limited by any kind of fixed identity. Perhaps his account of sovereignty *begins* with the thought of the individual and with ordinary ideas about autonomy and self-commandment. But in the very unfolding of these ideas within the text it becomes apparent that this is only a partial perspective. Thus, in *Thus Spoke Zarathustra,* the doctrine of the overman eventually gives place to the thought of eternal recurrence, which shatters the identity of the subject in the horizon of eternity; likewise in his final meditations upon sovereignty, the heroic project of the self is placed within the total context of nature, and the forces that subtend the individual as such.

Ironically, then, in recent years Nietzsche has often been interpreted as a kind of existentialist, for whom the ultimate challenge is one of "authenticity," "commitment," and taking responsibility for one's life.[7] Perhaps the earlier quotations from *Schopenhauer as Educator* seem to support this suggestion. But if this reading was correct, then all of Nietzsche's talk about sovereignty and "becoming what one is" would presuppose a very nonhistorical and even an empty account of the individual self. For the absolute emphasis upon personal freedom entails that the subject must somehow remain separate from all the determinations of instinct, tradition, or class. This interpretation emphasizes the role of individual decision in determining the will, but it completely underplays Nietzsche's obvious awareness of history and material necessity—the body—which shapes our understanding and our will in the first place. Nietzsche's thought is much more complex than such a philosophical individualism would suggest. And in what follows we will see how he consistently thinks beneath the level of the individual to uncover those impersonal determinations of nature and history—including the idea of the will to power itself—that shape us as subjects in the world. Nietzsche is not a humanist in any traditional sense, but an "antihumanist" who remains deeply suspicious of every conventional assertion of freedom, subjectivity, and the will.

Probably in response to this first reading, there is now a tendency in recent poststructuralist writing to uphold the absolute rejection of the metaphysical subject and to conclude that this must also entail the abandonment of anything like "autonomy" as a meaningful ideal. Thus sovereignty is viewed as an impossible goal, and it cannot even be recognized as a coherent concept. I will argue that this is a mistake. For even if the grand theological conceptions of the subject must now be abandoned, explicitly in the light of Nietzsche's critique, it does not follow that every account of sovereignty or every attempt to apprehend the individual is necessarily mistaken. Nietzsche attacks the subject and traditional ideas about free will, while at the same time he tries to think through the possibility of sovereignty as a valid ideal even within the overall context of history and nature. The poststructuralist reading concentrates on Nietzsche's dissolution of the subject. But the imperative of sovereignty is equally strong and equally important in his work.

Indeed, this is why Nietzsche's philosophy is still so relevant to the present age, for it offers an account of the individual that fills a significant aporia in contemporary thought. We may live in an age that valorizes "the death of the subject," after the original celebration of the death of God; but in spite of this, much of recent Continental philosophy is still directed by the unspoken thought of sovereignty that Nietzsche's work can help us to apprehend. And this is not "simply" a philosophical issue. For if the rise of postmodern culture is associated with the oblivion of the individual and the demise of the sacred, then the thought that wrestles with sovereignty and tries to understand it may finally evoke and inspire the subject that it describes. At the end of book four of *The Gay Science* Nietzsche writes, "We, however, *want to become those we are*—human beings who are new, unique, incomparable, who give themselves laws, who create themselves" (*GS* sec. 335). While the philosophical articulation of this sovereign ideal may be fraught with difficulty and may even be inconclusive in a strong theoretical sense, in the *performative* dimension of his writing sovereignty is still projected as an imperative.

❧

Nietzsche was a classical scholar, and so it is customary to compare his thought most closely to the values and ideals of ancient Greece. His first book is an extended meditation upon Greek tragedy, while several commentators have suggested that his discussion of the overman is basically derived from Aristotle's account of the great-souled man.[8] Leaving these particular debates to one side, what I would like to suggest in this work is that Nietzsche is in fact a thinker who belongs most essentially to the *Christian* tradition. This is *not* to say that Nietzsche was secretly a Christian, whether he realized it or not; and this is not an attempt to minimize his savage attacks upon Christianity and its pernicious influence upon the history of culture and the individual soul. There can be no mistaking Nietzsche when he refers to Christianity as "the one great curse, the one great innermost corruption . . . the immortal blemish of mankind" (*AC* sec. 62). What I want to suggest here is that the central concerns and issues that Nietzsche faced in his own writing are in many respects the same issues that have traditionally ordered Christianity. Thus, Nietzsche is no Christian, but at the same time it is instructive to understand him as someone who is inspired and directed by a particular momentum of thinking whose origins must be sought in Christianity, as opposed to classical thought.

I have suggested that Nietzsche was inspired by the question of individual sovereignty. Such a concern is surely an echo or a final manifestation of the original Christian concern for the salvation of the individual soul. Certainly, it is Christianity, and St. Paul in particular, that first poses the drama of the individual life as the most urgent concern of all; and although Nietzsche abandons the religious context of salvation he preserves the same focus and the same intensity of expression when he deals with the issue of individual existence. For this reason, I will begin the present work by considering Nietzsche's idea of sovereignty within the total context of a certain tradition of thought that begins with Christianity and achieves its most systematic and articulate expression in the writings of Kant. My aim is not to offer a complete history of ideas, or to show how he is simply another representative of the tradition. Rather, what I want to do in the first part of this work is to uncover three decisive moments in the history of thought that will help to illuminate Nietzsche's discussion of sovereignty by comparison. Specifically, I will show how St. Paul, Kant, and Schopenhauer bring us to the philosophy of Nietzsche.

Having established this "genealogy of sovereignty," I will discuss Nietzsche's texts in a more or less chronological order. Given what I have said about the importance of grasping Nietzsche's philosophical strategy, it would seem to follow that the best way of coming to grips with him is to examine his ideas within the particular context in which they are embedded. Thus I will approach his philosophy for the most part through the discussion of individual texts, rather than through the isolation of major themes. Each chapter will be relatively self-contained and will offer a reading that uses the optic of sovereignty to follow the basic direction of his thought. I do not purport to offer an exhaustive interpretation of Nietzsche; and in order to keep my argument focused I will not dwell at length on every work that he wrote. Instead I will examine one of the most central aspects of Nietzsche's overarching reflection on culture and higher humanity, and I will show how this thread—the problematic of individual sovereignty—allows for a sustained reading of his work. I am not about to reconstruct an explicit theory of sovereignty that Nietzsche himself did not produce; but I will show how his reflection on the problem of sovereignty illuminates his thinking from the outset.

Finally, I will explicitly address the contemporary importance of Nietzsche, although of course, this issue is bound to raise itself at every moment. In writing this book, my aim is to show that Nietzsche's discussion of sovereignty fills an important void in recent philosophy, which urgently requires an alternative philosophy of the individual if its attack on "humanism" and individualism is not to issue in the denial of all individual agency. In fact, it could be argued that the ideal of sovereignty manifests itself through its very absence: for to the extent that it has not been a theme of recent thinking, sovereignty now makes its claims upon us. At this juncture, perhaps the most important issue is to decide whether the whole tradition of "sovereignty" and "autonomy" must simply be abandoned as the expression of a pernicious "philosophy of mastery"; or whether Nietzsche's evocation of the individual—even though it never reaches the level of an explicit theory—can still illuminate sovereignty as a valid and empowering goal.

Nietzsche proclaimed himself an "untimely" thinker. I would argue that in many respects he is *our* contemporary. Indeed, I would go further: to my mind he is the one philosopher that our own age must learn to read and to come to grips with if it is ever to understand itself or secure a meaningful direction for the future. It is this belief in the continuing *relevance* of Nietzsche that has inspired the present study.

1 ❧

On the Value of the Individual

In our culture, it is customary to speak of the absolute value of the individual. We are very much concerned with "being true to ourselves," and if unfortunate circumstances should prevent an individual from achieving "true potential," we regard this as a tragedy and a waste. Thus we consider the discovery and achievement of one's "true" self to be a fundamental project of existence. "You must become who you are!" "You must try to be yourself!" This does not mean that the individual must simply follow an appropriate path in life, but that the individual must live a life that testifies to the unique and unrepeatable character of his or her own existence. Negatively, it is sometimes said that our culture is informed by an extreme individualism, such that any duties that we do have to the community are regarded as necessary evils that ultimately protect our own selfish goals. More positively, however, this means that there is at least a "discourse" of human rights and some concern for individual liberty as the necessary condition for any individual fulfillment.

It is important to remember, though, that not every culture has valued the individual in this way or even distinguished the individual as such from the role or place in life that the individual happens to occupy. Perhaps we are encouraged to think of the value of the individual as if it were an absolute; but it would be more correct to say that concern for the individual has a definite history and appears in a particular culture at a particular period of time. In most "primitive" societies, which are bound by ritual and the recurrent rhythms of nature, an individual's place is effectively marked out in advance. He or she will receive the name of a dead ancestor and for the most part will live exactly the same kind of life as those who lived before. In this way, individuals may live and die, but the society as a whole remains the same. In these "cold" societies, as Lévi-Strauss calls them, individuals can only possess a separate identity insofar as they accept their place within the community. To stand in opposition, or outside of the social order, is literally unthinkable. The community reproduces itself through its members, and along with the absence of any stress upon the individual, there is also an absence of "history" or "progress," as opposed to the cyclical return of nature.

It is also important to remember that even Western culture has not always valued true individuality. The Greeks and the Romans had their heroes and their ideal "models" of existence, which were exemplified by the likes of Achilles and Alexander, Socrates, Cicero, and Caesar. But what the Greeks and the Romans sought to emulate was the model itself. They were not concerned to express their own unique existence, but to live the life of the philosopher, or live up to the heroic ideal embodied by Achilles and the others. Success might be gauged in terms of how far the individual life could be brought to coincide with the ideal; while the remainder, or that which belonged purely to the individual as such, was considered irrelevant and unworthy of consideration. Thus, even though the Greeks and Romans did pay tribute to the individual and commemorated individual virtue and achievement, it was not the unique and unrepeatable existence that concerned them but the public persona or model.[1]

The Iliad, for example, is full of individual heroes, like Ajax, Achilles, and Hector. In spite of their different personalities, however, it might be more accurate to say that they are all embodiments of a single ideal, since they are essentially indistinguishable from each other. The valorization of this heroic model imposes an imperative upon the individual since it celebrates a particular "script" for life. Yet in following such an example, individuals would not be acting in their own name or giving the law to themselves, since the goal would be to fulfill a set of prescriptions and expectations that impose themselves from without. As one recent commentator concludes, "The self becomes what it is in heroic societies only in and through its role; it is a social creation not an individual one."[2]

Thus even though he is the greatest of all the Greeks, Achilles himself never initiates action in any deep sense. Nor is he anxious to impress his own unique nature upon the people around him. When all is said and done, the one thing that motivates Achilles is *shame* and the desire not to fail in the eyes of others. In spite of his own love of life, for example, Achilles is determined to revenge his lover Patroclus by killing Hector, although it was prophesied that after Hector he would be the next to die. His basic motivation, however, is not his determination to do the right thing, but his desire to follow the heroic ideal. "Let me die forthwith," he says, "when I have requited the villain, rather than remain here by the beaked ships to be mocked, a burden on the ground." And with this he follows his father's general policy: "To be always among the bravest and to hold my head above the others."[3]

Similarly, in classical Greek philosophy, the proper task of the individual is not the original and free creation of the self, but an attunement to the total order of things. In Plato's *Republic*, the search for justice is related to the achievement of a proper self-mastery, in which reason as one part of the soul rules legitimately, while the appetitive and spirited aspects are supposed to obey. But such a conception implies that any specific "virtue" of the individual must derive from an ideal model that is already given. In the *Republic*, Plato describes the just man as follows: "He doesn't let each part in him mind other people's business or the three classes in the soul meddle with each other, but really sets his own house in order and rules himself; he arranges himself, becomes his own friend, and harmonizes the three parts, exactly like three notes in a harmonic scale, lowest, highest, and middle."[4] This suggests that the individual is nothing more than a configuration of given principles. Reason, supported by spiritedness, seeks to tame the wild beast of our desires, and the individual only emerges as the specific outcome of this struggle. Once again, it is not we who choose between good and evil principles, for such principles actually choose us insofar as reason or desire is predominant. According to Plato, reason directs us toward the compelling power of the good; and this means that evil can only be understood as a kind of "error," while individual choice in defiance of reason—the possibility of *akrasia*—is formally impossible. In Plato it is clearly impersonal reason itself, or *nous*, that gives the orders to the soul; this means, however, that he cannot support a metaphysics of the self in any genuinely individual sense.

Aristotle rejected the excessive rationalism of Plato's ethics and sought to account for the obvious existence of "incontinence," in which the good is known but not adhered to. In the *Nicomachean Ethics*, he accordingly recognized *proairesis* as a faculty of deliberate choice, which would allow for some mediation between the claims of reason and the promptings of desire. Aristotle defines *proairesis* as "an appetite guided by deliberate choice for things within our power," and he writes that as "desiderative reason or rational desire," it is "a principle that the human being is the source and origin of his actions."[5] In his ethics it is precisely this that first brings human action within the domain of morality itself. But while it may be argued that *proairesis* is the forerunner of later conceptions of "the will," it is also clear that as a mediating concept between reason and desire it is in no way creative. *Proairesis* is the faculty of practical reasoning that allows us to deliberate between the different means of achieving ends that are inherent in human nature and are the same for everyone. It does not establish a genuine possibility of self-determination, and since it is supposed to follow the determinations of *boulesis* ("a rational desire for what is good and beneficial"), it once again implies that the ultimate foundation of reason, or *nous*, is the true locus of selfhood.[6]

Finally, much the same would be true of the later Stoics' appropriation of *proairesis*. The growth of Stoic and Epicurean ideals in later antiquity brings about a focus upon the self as an object of improvement and inquiry. In one respect, as Foucault has recognized, this preoccupation with the self signifies the emergence of subjectivity as a specific problematic and domain of inquiry. Even so, the Stoics' attempt to use *proairesis*, in order to master nature within the self and to live according to the requirements of reason, entails an impersonal ideal of "reason" or "nature," which remains oblivious to the specific manifestations of the individual.

Epictetus, for example, seems to identify *proairesis* with the inner personal self: "The tyrant says, I will put you in bonds," to which the Stoic replies, "Put *me* in bonds? You will fetter my leg, but not even Zeus can conquer my *proairesis*."[7] Epictetus certainly goes beyond Plato and Aristotle's account of the rationally ordered and hence impersonal self. *Proairesis* in Epictetus is something like the individual's personal identity. And yet, in Epictetus, as with all the Stoics, the goal of individual choice is nothing other than complete conformity to the will of nature, or "God." In fact, Epictetus argues that our *proairesis* is nothing other than "a part of God" that he has given to us. Hence the self must not assert itself, but only accept its place in the ultimate order of things. And in this respect the ideal sage is one who suppresses any truly "individual" impulse and models himself after the ideal. For Epictetus, the purpose of philosophy is simply to achieve some measure of tranquillity by overcoming the self's impotent refusal of pain and death. This is to be achieved not through apathy or indifference, but through an active approval and assent to whatever must happen anyway. "In every case I want what God wants," he comments, "I simply share his will."[8]

What this brief survey suggests is that our concern for the individual, and our celebration of the unique singularity of each individual life, is a comparatively recent event. And if Foucault and other contemporary thinkers who have argued for the "death of the subject" are correct, then such an ideal is about to disappear "like a figure marked on the sand."[9] I will consider the possible future of the individual later, and I will also leave in suspense the question of whether individual sovereignty is a valuable or a pernicious ideal. Here I only want to establish that the value of the individual is not universal, but has a definite history and a genealogy, which is reflected in the work of thinkers from St. Paul to Nietzsche and beyond.

Much of this is in fact confirmed by the history of autobiography. Since an essential condition of autobiography is the appropriation of one's existence as something valuable and worth recalling to others, autobiography will not exist if one regards one's own life as irrelevant or beside the point.[10] And in this respect it is not a coincidence that the emergence of autobiography is associated with early Christianity and that St. Augustine's *Confessions* is generally accepted as the first true autobiography. Certainly, in the classical world, famous individuals sought to immortalize themselves by recording their conquests and the full extent of their public acts. But apart from such memoirs of public life, there is simply no desire to record the inner history of one's own particular existence. In his *Commentary on the Gallic Wars*, Julius Caesar may show that he is an embodiment of the heroic type, but he only writes about his career and whatever else is a matter of public record.

In fact, Christianity makes autobiography possible because it announces that every soul is uniquely valuable, and because it makes the drama of individual salvation absolutely crucial. With Christianity, moreover, the *intentions* that motivate one to act are just as important as the actions themselves. Saint Augustine writes the *Confessions* to examine himself before God and to uncover the true motivations for his actions. He is relentless in his self-scrutiny because he knows that God will know if his self-examination is deficient. Thus, Christianity deepens the nature of the self; as Nietzsche himself points out, the whole thematics of conscience and guilt, which Christianity emphasizes, only intensifies subjectivity by turning individuals against themselves. And with the issue of eternal life in the balance, the project of individual existence becomes the most urgent issue of all. In accordance with this, the very nature of the autobiographer's task obliges the individual to affirm the complete singularity of his or her own existence. Rousseau, for example, justifies his autobiography precisely on the grounds that no one like him has ever existed before. "I am like no one in the whole world," he says, "I may be no better but at least I am different";[11] while even St. Augustine, who proclaims his own unworthiness and discovers his sinful motivations everywhere, implicitly affirms his own existence as a useful example to others.

The conceptual significance of Christianity is supported by recent scholarship in the history of ancient philosophy. It is now generally accepted that a distinct concept of the will, in opposition to both reason and desire, was actually unknown to the classical mind.[12] As we have seen, Aristotle had a weak concept of choice and an account of voluntary action that was later appropriated by Stoicism. But in Aristotle there are several loosely related concepts—*proairesis, boulesis,* and the idea of a "voluntary" action (*hekousios*)—that are not themselves supported by a unitary concept of the will; similarly, for Epictetus and later Stoicism, our power to "will" is limited to our ability to assent to whatever must happen anyway. The idea of the will as an absolutely original principle of action—and hence the seat of individuality—is apparently original to Christianity. It may be found in emergent form in St. Paul's *Letter to the Romans,* and it is the focal point of St. Augustine's self-understanding in the narrative of the *Confessions.*

In book eight of the *Confessions,* for example, Augustine reflects upon the strangely gradual process of his own conversion, and he explains his spiritual progress in terms of the conflict between his "old" and "new" will: "The new will which had come to life in me and made me wish to serve you freely and enjoy you, my God . . . was not yet strong enough to overcome the old, hardened as it was by the passage of time." And hence, "these two wills within me, one old, one new, one the servant of the flesh, the other of the spirit, were in conflict and between them they tore my soul apart."[13] Within this account of the divided self, however, the new will that St. Augustine describes is nothing other than the true self that he had abandoned for so long. "I had deserted even my own self," he writes, "I could not find myself, much less you."[14] In this respect, the final moment of his conversion is also the final recovery of his own true self; and it suggests the total empowerment of his new will in being able to take charge of himself. But given the inevitable resistance of the will to the will's own commands, an experience that St. Augustine dwells upon in some detail, this point of sovereignty can only be achieved through the grace and favor of God.

What is most decisive here, however, is not the elaboration of a new concept of the will, but the "phenomenological" account of willing and resistance, or a split within the will itself that testifies to the imperative of self-commandment or sovereignty as an urgent project of the individual life. And in this respect it is perhaps in the writing of the *Confessions* themselves that St. Augustine achieves his own self-mastery. For in this work he effects a complete revaluation and reappropriation of the previous stages of his life so that everything now culminates in the final "rest" with God.

Thus, if the will is specifically "Christian," at least in origin, then it follows that the will to will, or the autonomous assertion of the individual, derives from the same source. God commands us, and the only appropriate response is not understanding, but obedience and a decisive commitment of the whole person, which St. Paul and later St. Augustine, struggle to achieve. The imperative of sovereignty summons each of us to the task of self-appropriation. It commands us to take command of ourselves and to make our existence our own. And were it not for this possibility of acting in our own name, the individual could never emerge as a specific or singular individual in any significant sense. Hence the importance of the will, and more specifically of the *will to will,* which expresses the sovereign self-assertion of the individual as such. For if it is legitimate to speak of the individual in this strong sense then it is also necessary to refer to the will as the locus of every original choice, and to "autonomy" or "sovereignty" as the true achievement of individuality through the will's determination to will itself. Hence the issue of the individual is finally tied to the problem of sovereignty, and in this work I will focus on the latter as a way of attending to the first.

✿

In this discussion so far I have used a number of basic concepts whose meaning can now be made clearer. The will, for example, is the principle of choice; it is that which selects between different principles and desires, and in this respect it would be true to say that it is not on the same level as those desires themselves. Early thinkers about the will thus identified it as the locus of the individual self. And this makes sense, for I may find myself desiring things that I do not *want* to desire; and such a conflict can only happen if I can identify "myself" with one particular impulse, instead of simply accepting myself as the outcome of the inner struggle, regardless of what it might be. Thus, like St. Augustine or St. Paul, I will experience my will as an "unfree" will if it is not capable of controlling the inner manifold and effecting what it wants. This failure—or weakness—of the will is experienced as a failure of sovereignty, insofar as I am unable to take charge of myself.

From the will, we move to "the will to will," which involves choosing oneself as a being who wills. This means that one has the power to maintain oneself as a singular or individual being instead of being "willed" or conditioned by principles that determine one from without. In this sense the will to will involves a continual activity of self-gathering and self-appropriation. And the "sovereign" individual who thereby emerges is an individual in the strong sense. Not merely an empty identity—in the obvious respect that "everyone is an individual"—but an individual who has achieved self-commandment as a separate and self-determining being.

Within this general context, we can now look ahead to Nietzsche's discussion of the individual and sovereignty. In his concern for the free spirit and the overman, for what it means to be a master and the ideal of becoming what one is, Nietzsche is clearly preoccupied with the issue of sovereignty and its claim upon the individual. But as I have already said, he does not offer a single "theory" of sovereignty, since that would be to destroy sovereignty by ordering it in advance. Even though he conducts an intense meditation upon the *nature* of sovereignty that lasts from *The Birth of Tragedy* to the final published works, his discussion remains fragmentary and is *theoretically* inconclusive. In fact, Nietzsche's final goal is to evoke sovereignty and to charge the individual with the task of self-commandment. In this book I will read Nietzsche's texts primarily (though not exclusively) in the light of this issue. My aim is to offer a sustained reading of his philosophy, and for reasons that I have already given, I think that the best way to do this is by paying particular attention to his evocation of sovereignty and his reflection upon the individual life.

Now there can be little doubt that for Nietzsche, sovereignty involves self-appropriation, which he variously describes as "giving style to one's character," cultivating one's life as an "aesthetic phenomenon," or "becoming what one is." This is not a marginal theme in his work, but a focal point that allows us to understand much of his rhetorical strategy. In Nietzsche, such self-appropriation involves the ability to maintain oneself as a separate and self-determining individual who can resist those "external" forces and principles that would otherwise condition the will. Thus in *Twilight of the Idols,* Nietzsche comments that "All un-spirituality, all vulgar commonness, depend on the inability to resist a stimulus: one *must* react, one follows every impulse. In many cases, such a compulsion is already pathology, decline, a symptom of exhaustion—almost everything that unphilosophical crudity designates with the word 'vice' is merely this physiological inability not to react" (*TI* "What the Germans Lack" sec. 6). In contrast to this, he specifies that true strength of will, in learning how to see, for example, is characterized by an ability *not* to react, and to endure as a separate and self-legislating being. "Learning to see," he continues, "is almost what, unphilosophically speaking, is called a strong will: the essential feature is precisely *not* to 'will'—to be able to suspend decision." From this perspective, self-appropriation seems to involve a "heroic" stance toward life, in which individuals are bound by the imperative of autonomy and must somehow withstand and even recuperate every accident and arbitrary moment of existence in order to demonstrate their own particular sovereignty. This suggests that the individual is not a given, but a canvas that we create in the very act of living our lives; and hence the final verdict on our existence must come from an aesthetic perspective, which evaluates the individual in terms of the "integration," "coherence," and "harmony" that has been achieved.

Once again, in the *Twilight of the Idols,* Nietzsche uses the example of Goethe as a creative individual who was able to achieve such a measure of self-appropriation. "What he wanted," Nietzsche comments, "was *totality;* he fought the mutual extraneousness of reason, senses, feeling and will (preached with the most abhorrent scholasticism by Kant . . .); he disciplined himself to wholeness, he *created* himself" (*TI* "Skirmishes" sec. 49). In this regard, Goethe had the strength of will to will himself. Nietzsche would say that he became a free spirit, and this implies that he followed the basic imperative of life insofar as he felt himself commanded to take charge of himself.

It is this aspect of his meditation that connects Nietzsche to the Christian tradition of sovereignty and individual self-concern that I have described. And yet sovereignty—at least in its Christian and Kantian formulations—is very much a relationship that the self has to itself. It is a matter of conforming the self to its higher rational nature or incorporating the will of God as if it were one's own; and this seems to involve a strict self-mastery and self-discipline that sets the individual *apart* from the world as the one who must maintain the self exactly as it is. In Nietzsche, however, the sovereignty of the individual definitely involves a relationship to the cosmos, or the outside, and that which is "other." Not as something "out there," to be used and appropriated or organized in terms of the categories of the self, but as the Dionysian order of "life" that supports and subtends the individual, who belongs to it completely. In this sense, Nietzsche's insistence upon materialism and remaining faithful to the earth reflects his concern to think about the individual, not in opposition to the world, but as an integral aspect of the world and as something embedded within it.

Thus, in apparent opposition to the imperative of self-appropriation, Nietzsche also argues that the concept of the self is a fiction. He condemns the error of free will and he says that the very idea of the ego is really a "fable, a fiction, a play on words" (*TI* "The Four Great Errors" sec. 2). At first it might seem that this second perspective, which emphasizes the destruction and dispersion of the self, stands completely opposed to the initial project of self-appropriation. For if there is no free will, and the self is just a product and an outcome, then how could it be possible for individuals to take charge of their own existence in any meaningful way? Indeed, the whole discussion of self-appropriation must turn out to be illusory if the self is really not in control of itself. From this we may conclude that Nietzsche is simply inconsistent; or we can try to understand how the tension between self-dispersion and self-appropriation may actually lead us to a deeper understanding of sovereignty and the meaning of the individual life. This book is an attempt to achieve the latter.

In distinction to the "Apollinian" realm of individual purposes and projects, then, Nietzsche also elaborates a Dionysian order of "life." And this is the realm of the sacred, which can only be encountered and experienced once one has abandoned every self-regarding concern. To achieve a complete involvement with life the individual must be willing to encounter existence on its own terms without all the categories and projections of selfhood that usually keep existence at bay; and in this sense, the Dionysian demands the death of the self as the necessary condition for entering its sacred realm. For most of the time, we might say, we *do not* live in the moment, but always project ourselves ahead to some particular goal. Thus we work in order to get money, in order to buy a car, in order to go to work, in order to get more money, and so on, but in all of this we are never coincident with the moment itself, which means that we never accept the moment—or life—on its own terms, but always and only as a means to an end.

According to Nietzsche, it is therefore necessary to shatter the subject and all of its claims to fixity and a substantial existence. For it makes sense to say that we can only be completely attuned to life once we abandon such self-assertion and are able to experience a total participation, or abandonment, in this "sacred" order of being: in the passion of eros, for example, or drunkenness, or the experience of tragedy, when the moment is celebrated and life is finally valued for what it is. This is the "deep eternity" of the present moment that Zarathustra describes, and it is also the perspective upon existence that the eternal recurrence is meant to bring about. Such a complete attunement to existence allows the Dionysian surge of empowerment. When one is "*oneself* the eternal joy of becoming, beyond all terror and pity," Nietzsche writes, one must experience that deep and total joy, "which included even joy in destroying" (*TI* "What I Owe to the Ancients" sec. 5). This is the tragic wisdom that describes the illusory character of all individual purposes and goals; while it also suggests a deeper community of existence that underlies our separation as individual selves.

For Nietzsche, then, true sovereignty involves self-appropriation, though it also requires an absolute "openness" to the forces of life; and for this to be possible, true sovereignty must involve self-dispossession and a continual self-overcoming that refuses any final determination. Thus he emphasizes, in *Ecce Homo*, that individual sovereignty is *not* simply a subjective accomplishment of the will; indeed, he argues by implication that self-appropriation *presupposes* an openness to the world that allows the individual to encounter itself in the first place. "I never even suspected what was growing in me," he writes, "and one day all my capacities, suddenly ripe, *leaped forth* in their ultimate perfection. I cannot remember that I ever tried hard—no trace of *struggle* can be demonstrated in my life; I am the opposite of a heroic nature. 'Willing' something, 'striving' for something, envisaging a 'purpose,' a 'wish'—I know none of this from experience" (*EH* "Why I Am So Clever" sec. 9). Here, and quite unequivocally, Nietzsche challenges the heroic model of sovereignty as simple self-assertion. Such comments are significant, since they come from Nietzsche's final discussion of "How One Becomes What One Is." Following this, we may conclude that sovereignty is not an end or a fixed state of being but a continual movement of the self that yokes together the Apollinian urge to self-cultivation and form with the Dionysian urge to self-abandonment.

In Nietzsche's writing, the sovereign individual is clearly someone who treats his own existence as some kind of an experiment and wager with life. Such an individual is forever open to new possibilities of experience, and in this sense is ready to "risk" individual identity at every moment. As Nietzsche comments in *The Gay Science:* "The wish to preserve oneself is the symptom of a condition of distress, of a limitation of the really fundamental instinct of life which aims at the expansion of power and, wishing for that, frequently risks and even sacrifices self-preservation" (*GS* sec. 349). Indeed, such an "openness" toward existence constitutes the most supreme generosity of being, insofar as it manifests a refusal to hold on to life or to hold anything back for oneself. At the same time, however, this individual also creates an identity within the flux, like an artist whose material is the movement of existence itself—like Nietzsche, when he creates his own autobiography, or like the "philosopher of the future," who forges the genealogy of his own society and thereby acquires the right to command.

It is probably in the very nature of such claims that they must remain both vague and fragmentary. But can we now make any sense out of them? And can we relate such an a priori framework to the details of our own life? I think this is where Nietzsche's discussion ends and the reader's work begins. For even though Nietzsche offers us *Ecce Homo* as his own classic example of "How one becomes what one is," that text may never function as a model for imitation. Sovereignty, we might say, only emerges in the active encounter with oneself and the world; it is a *movement* that has determinate moments and a definite shape of its own—and beyond this it cannot be specified or constrained, but only "evoked" through the workings of the text.

Nietzsche is clearly preoccupied with the question of the individual, and he sought to provoke the individual to sovereignty, so that sovereignty can be grasped as a basic imperative of life. On the other hand, he also denies every ordinary doctrine of alienation and authenticity, and there is no sense in his work of an implicit or original self that could be the real individual that he seeks. As he remarks in passing, "Your true nature lies, not concealed deep within you, but immeasurably high above you, or at least above that which you usually take yourself to be" (*UM* III sec. 1). This suggests that sovereignty is not a given, but something that follows from the creative act of the will that wills itself; it is an experiment with life, through which the individual transfigures nature by working on the self.

At the same time, however, Nietzsche also insists that the sovereign individual is really an outcome and the product of nature, or history, and the training of millennia. "If we place ourselves at the end of this tremendous process," he writes, "where the tree at last brings forth fruit, where society and the morality of custom at last reveal *what* they have simply been the means to: then we discover that the ripest fruit is the *sovereign individual* like only to himself, liberated again from morality of custom, autonomous and su-pramoral" (*GM* II sec. 2). Nietzsche is ambiguous here, for even if the sover-eign individual is just a product and an outcome, it must be allowed that in this case nature has finally created a being who is "free" and self-determin-ing. Even if Nietzsche affirms that in the end everything is necessary, he also defines the sovereign individual as one who creates his own will. Elsewhere, he argues that the will must be forced to will itself again, but this would make no sense if the will were completely determined. Once again, we could sim-ply conclude that Nietzsche is inconsistent. But it also makes sense to under-stand Nietzsche as a philosopher who writes from both the "human" and the "cosmic" perspectives. He accepts the validity of the sovereign ideal, though he also attempts to describe the ultimate place of the individual within the cosmos itself. It is in the creative tension between these two perspectives that a higher and more complete version of sovereignty may finally emerge.

Thus, in opposition to contemporary thinkers like Foucault, who have proclaimed the "death of man" and the impossibility of individual agency, Nietzsche's position is much more nuanced. Yes, the individual is a "subject" created by the various codes and structures of existence—such as family, class, and gender—but in the movement beyond these determinations it is still possible for the individual to create his or her own life. This does not mean that we are all free to do whatever we want; but it does suggest that even if we are conditioned by these codes we can still achieve some distance from them. In such transcendence lies the possibility of sovereignty, even if the latter must also be viewed as the final achievement of nature.

From *The Birth of Tragedy* onward, Nietzsche was aware of these conflict-ing aspects of sovereignty, and it might be said that much of his philosophy is an attempt to think through the proper relationship between them—which is not to *reconcile* Apollo with Dionysus, but to articulate their creative ten-sion with each other. It is not clear whether he achieved an account of sov-ereignty that would finally settle the issue. But each of his major themes and writings can now be viewed as an embodiment of this conflict. Thus, in his "free spirit" trilogy—*Human, All Too Human, Daybreak,* and *The Gay Sci-ence*—Nietzsche vehemently condemns the error of free will, though in the same works this theme is balanced by the achievement of the "free spirit" that is taken as a kind of ideal. Likewise, in *Thus Spoke Zarathustra*, the eternal recurrence is presented as a single thought that expresses *both* the imperative of self-appropriation (with its focus upon the individual within eternity) and the ecstasy of self-abandonment (which leads to the final affirmation of everything that is). In fact, there is a strong sense in which Nietzsche's philosophy is an experiment that encounters the issue of sovereignty as a question that must be *experienced* in order to be known. Perhaps it would not be completely correct to say that Nietzsche has a determinate philosophy of sovereignty; but he raises the issue of sovereignty in all of his writings as the most urgent problem that the reader is forced to address. Nietzsche problematizes sovereignty. He probably goes further than anyone to reveal the paradoxical nature of the sovereign ideal. Insofar as we can follow his meditation, we are also directed toward sovereignty itself.

๛

Earlier in this chapter I argued that for various reasons a full-blown ideal of sovereignty first became possible with Christianity and the emergence of "the will." In the next chapter I want to outline the possibility of a "tradition" of individual sovereignty, which begins with Christianity and culminates with Nietzsche, even though Nietzsche himself is not a Christian philosopher. In short, I want to propose a genealogy of sovereignty to situate Nietzsche and the guiding question that orders his thought.

But first, there should be no misunderstanding about my use of the word "tradition." Quite often a "tradition" is thought of as a "common stream" that precedes and maintains all of us. The individual thinker is supposed to be supported by this stream, and thus enabled to make a contribution to the tradition, which is thereby nourished by what it has produced. And yet, such a model is blind to the dynamic and dialectical relationship that exists between the individual and tradition itself. Following this reading, every tradition becomes a dead tradition, and the individual thinker is nothing more than a cipher. Likewise, there is also a problem of how the course of any tradition could ever be changed, since the latter is viewed as a unity that envelops and controls everything.

In the famous section on "The Three Metamorphoses" in *Thus Spoke Zarathustra*, Nietzsche offers a more dynamic reading of the relationship between the individual thinker and tradition; indeed, he points to three essential moments, symbolized respectively by the camel, the lion, and the child, in which the true thinker must first "carry" and incorporate the tradition, then find the strength to challenge it, and finally, through the achievement and incorporation of the previous stages, create a new perspective. The nature of the individual's relationship to tradition is an abiding problem in

Nietzsche's thinking, and it gives rise to a complex commentary on his own predecessors—St. Paul, Kant, and Schopenhauer, for example—who are at one and the same time both furthest from him and nearest to him. As Nietzsche comments rather ambivalently, "I honor, I distinguish by associating my name with that of a cause or person: pro or con that makes no difference to me at this point" (*EH* "Why I Am So Wise" sec. 7). We should therefore beware of using the concept of tradition so as to destroy, in advance, everything that is original to Nietzsche's philosophy.

I have said that I will offer a "genealogy" of sovereignty that seeks to recover the most decisive moments of Nietzsche's intellectual patrimony. Genealogy, however, is not an attempt to recover origins. It begins with the present and seeks to understand the present and to place it in a proper perspective by locating the most decisive moments of thought that help to orient our understanding of it. Genealogy is always retrospective: in *Ecce Homo*, for example, Nietzsche constructs his own genealogy, with his parents "on the highest and the lowest rung on the ladder of life" (*EH* "Why I Am So Wise" sec. 1), in order to explain how it is that he has the right to revalue all values. Likewise, in *On the Genealogy of Morals*, he unsettles our contemporary moral perspectives by recalling the *double* origin of value through the assertion of the master and the revenge of the slave. Following his own warrant, I will propose a specific genealogy that will help us to understand his own orientation in thinking.

Even before St. Augustine, St. Paul is perhaps the first to raise the issue of individual sovereignty when he describes the agony of self-laceration that he endures in trying to follow God's law. Eventually, however, St. Paul comes to believe that the goal of self-possession is an illusory one, and he throws himself upon the grace of God. This self-denial sets the tone for Christianity and perhaps Western culture as a whole; and this is why St. Paul remains one of the most consistent targets of Nietzsche's attack.

Similarly, Kant valorizes the individual subject as the one who lays down the conditions of all possible experience, while in his ethical writings he formalizes a doctrine of autonomy and makes it the basis of his ethics, and consequently of his entire philosophical system. In his many criticisms of Kant, however, Nietzsche argues that Kant's doctrine of the categorical imperative is precisely that which destroys the individual as such, so that Kantian autonomy finally betrays the ideal of sovereignty. By examining Kant's account of autonomy, and Nietzsche's critique, it will therefore be possible to clarify and delineate Nietzsche's own discussion of sovereignty.

Finally, Schopenhauer is probably the most decisive influence on Nietzsche's own philosophical development. Of course, Schopenhauer does not readily fit into this "Christian" tradition that focuses upon the question of the individual. In fact, he denigrates individual existence as a curse and he argues that our lot is "tragic" in every way. Even so, a profound contradiction runs through Schopenhauer's work: while he despises the individual and relates all our projects to the pointless striving of the one primordial Will, he also suggests the possibility of a salvation from the Will through individual renunciation. In this way the individual becomes the salvation of nature. Nietzsche was aware of this essential contradiction in Schopenhauer's position, and in *The Birth of Tragedy* and other works, he pushes Schopenhauerian pessimism to the very point at which it transforms itself into a doctrine of sovereignty.

These three thinkers, St. Paul, Kant, and Schopenhauer, are frequently cited by Nietzsche, and would have to be included in any ordinary "history of influence." Even so, it is not the strict continuity of intellectual influence that unites St. Paul, Kant, Schopenhauer, and Nietzsche into a single genealogy. Certainly, the former does exist—with the Lutheran elevation of St. Paul, or Nietzsche's deep involvement with Schopenhauer, both directly and through the intermediary of Wagner. But in the end these are "external" considerations. Here, it is not decisive whether Nietzsche actually read the second *Critique*, or whether Kant was impressed by the teachings of St. Paul. For quite apart from all these historical details is the fact that all of these figures have similar priorities in their thinking. They share a common problematic that focuses upon the issue of "individuality," "sovereignty," and "will," and hence they share a tradition insofar as they are all inspired by the same general problems. The "tradition" that I refer to is thus constituted by a kindredness of priorities and themes, and while it is supported by an actual historical filiation, the filiation is secondary. Nietzsche's work represents a fulfillment of this particular tradition of sovereignty, and it remains profoundly relevant, not simply because it is historically or philosophically "interesting," but because it suggests an empowering ideal that challenges nihilism and the self-abandonment of contemporary life.

2 ❧

The Genealogy of Sovereignty: St. Paul, Kant, Schopenhauer

Christianity intensifies the experience of the individual. By directing attention toward the most urgent issue of salvation and the immortality of the soul it engenders self-consciousness to an extent that had not previously existed. The summons to Christ is addressed to every individual as an individual; and once this summons has been incorporated, or taken seriously, it inevitably issues in the guilty reflection of the self that knows itself to be sinful and lacking. Through this consciousness of sin, Nietzsche writes, "life again became *very* interesting: awake, everlastingly awake, sleepless, glowing, charred, spent and yet not weary—thus was the man, 'the sinner,' initiated into *this* mystery" (*GM* III sec. 20). Both St. Paul and St. Augustine make it very clear, for example, that no one "deserves" salvation, and that the self cannot justify itself by simply observing the law. On the contrary, the way of the spirit that Christ demands calls for a total self-commandment and a commitment that is apparently more than anyone can possibly achieve. The awareness of failure—that "though the will to do good is there the deed is not"—leads to a despair that is finally overcome when the individual forswears the principle of sovereignty and seeks abandonment in the grace of God. As Nietzsche realized, the paradox here is that the very selfhood that is first called forth by Christianity must ultimately deny itself in order to achieve an eternal life.

I have suggested that the will, and more specifically the possibility of "sovereignty," embodied in the will to will, is linked to the beginning of Christianity. Perhaps in this respect the seventh chapter of St. Paul's *Letter to the Romans* has a paradigmatic status and can serve as the focal point for the self-understanding of this tradition as a whole. In the seventh chapter, St. Paul first describes the experience of willing, self-appropriation, frustration, and self-denial that is outlined above. The law is given, and he finds himself commanded to obey. But even more decisive than the specific content of the command is his realization that such an imperative always presupposes and preordains the sovereignty of the individual as a condition of its fulfillment. In its very pronouncement, the law calls upon one to take charge of one's own life and to gather one's whole being in readiness to obey. As St. Paul realizes, however, there is always a part of the self that resists this command. "I do not even acknowledge my actions as mine," he writes, "for what I do is not what I want to do but what I detest." And it is the inevitable failure of self-appropriation that directs the seventh chapter as a whole.

The seventh chapter later became a focus of St. Augustine's own meditations upon the will, and it was a decisive text for the self-understanding of Christians throughout the Middle Ages and the Reformation.[1] An enormous amount of theological commentary has been written on the *Letter to the Romans,* and the seventh chapter has also been the subject of continued philosophical interest, since it seems to offer a classic formulation of the problem of *akrasia,* or weakness of the will.[2] I will examine this text as an original articulation of the will to sovereignty that is first attempted and then repudiated. The "autobiographical" or "phenomenological" reading that I offer is certainly not the only possible one, but I think it is consistent and psychologically compelling, and it seems to offer the most appropriate point of departure for our eventual understanding of Nietzsche's discussion of sovereignty.

Here is the complete text from St. Paul:

You cannot be unaware, my friends—I am speaking to those who have some knowledge of law—that a person is subject to the law so long as he is alive, and no longer. For example, a married woman is bound by law to her husband while he lives; but if her husband dies, she is discharged from the obligations of the marriage law. If, therefore in her husband's lifetime she consorts with another man, she will incur the charge of adultery; but if her husband dies she is free of the law, and she does not commit adultery by consorting with another man. So you, my friends, have died to the law by becoming identified with the body of Christ, and accordingly you have found another husband in him who rose from the dead, so that we may bear fruit for God. While we lived on the level of our lower nature, the sinful passions evoked by the law worked in our bodies, to bear fruit for death. But now, having died to that which held us bound, we are discharged from the law, to serve God in a new way, the way of the spirit, in contrast to the old way, the way of a written code.

What follows? Is the law identical with sin? Of course not. But except through law I should never have become acquainted with sin. For example, I should never have known what it was to covet, if the law had not said, 'Thou shalt not covet.' Through that commandment sin found its opportunity, and produced in me all kinds of wrong desires. In the absence of law, sin is a dead thing. There was a time when, in the absence of law, I was fully alive; but when the commandment came, sin sprang to life and I died. The commandment which should have led to life proved in my experience to lead to death, because sin found its opportunity in the commandment, seduced me, and through the commandment killed me.

Therefore the law is in itself holy, and the commandment is holy and just and good. Are we to say then that this good thing was the death of me? By no means. It was sin that killed me, and thereby sin exposed its true character: it used a good thing to bring about my death, and so, through the commandment, sin became more sinful than ever.

We know that the law is spiritual; but I am not: I am unspiritual, the purchased slave of sin. I do not even acknowledge my own actions as mine, for what I do is not what I want to do but what I detest. But if what I do is against my will, it means that I agree with the law and hold it to be admirable. But as things are, it is no longer I who perform the action, but sin that lodges in me. For I know that nothing good lodges in me—in my unspiritual nature I mean—for though the will to do good is there, the deed is not. The good which I want to do, I fail to do; but what I do is the wrong which is against my will; and if what I do is against my will, clearly it is no longer I who am the agent, but sin that has its lodging in me.

I discover this principle, then: that when I want to do the right, only the wrong is within my reach. In my inmost self I delight in the law of God, but I perceive that there is in my bodily members a different law, fighting against the law that my reason approves and making me a prisoner under the law that is in my members, the law of sin. Miserable creature that I am, who is there to rescue me out of this body doomed to death? God alone, through Jesus Christ our Lord! Thanks be to God! In a word then, I myself, subject to God's law as a rational being, am yet, in my unspiritual nature, a slave to the law of sin.[3]

Here, St. Paul accepts the burden of individual responsibility as something that is both irreducible and urgent. The law—as the Torah, the law of Israel—commands its own fulfillment. But through its very proclamation it provokes a resistance and an aversion to the law that had not existed before. Paradoxically enough, it is therefore the law that first creates the awareness of sin, and Paul laments that this has been the death of him: "There was a time when, in the absence of law, I was fully alive; but when the commandment came, sin sprang to life and I died." Accordingly, in this chapter St. Paul describes his own sinfulness and his complete inability to accomplish what the law has commanded. He *wants* to follow God's commands, but he discovers that his will is simply not strong enough.

At the start of the seventh chapter, St. Paul describes how a woman commits adultery if she consorts with another man while her husband is still alive, though if her husband is dead she is no longer bound by such a law. He then argues that by identifying ourselves with the body of Christ we have also "died" to the law, or been "discharged" from it, in order to serve God in a new way, which is the "way of the spirit, in contrast to the old way, the way of a written code." Now it is clear from what follows that even though Christ is supposed to "end" the law, this does not mean that the law must simply be abandoned as an erroneous conception. Instead, it makes sense to say that in this passage St. Paul relates the irrelevance of a written code for one who is justified by faith and who has incorporated the "spirit of Christ" as the guiding principle of existence. The passage relies upon the general distinction between a legal righteousness and the deeper justification that is achieved through faith.

This is confirmed in the next paragraph, where Paul explicitly denies that the law is to be identified with sin, even if it is through the law that sin has entered the world. "Is the law identical with sin? Of course not. But except through law I should never have become acquainted with sin"; and again, "There was a time when in the absence of law, I was fully alive; but when the commandment came, sin sprang to life and I died." How are we to understand this? How does the law, a good thing in itself, lead to sin and death? Perhaps the most obvious response is to suggest that the law leads to death because it is too difficult to fulfill. At some time or another everyone is bound to commit a transgression, and hence "justification" through the law is ultimately impossible. The law makes me aware of my obligations, which I then find that I cannot fulfill. The problem with this reading is that there is evidence elsewhere that St. Paul had no problem in meeting his legal obligations. In the *Letter to Philippians,* for example, he describes himself as "faultless" in legal rectitude. And presumably there were many others, and just as many today, who can quite easily follow a written code and do their appropriate duty.

It is significant, then, that when St. Paul gives an example of how the law has incited sin, he does not refer to unlawful actions, but to unlawful thoughts and desires that the very pronouncement of law has evoked from his own sinful nature. "I should never have known what it was to covet," he says, "if the law had not said, 'Thou shalt not covet.' Through that commandment sin found its opportunity and produced in me all kinds of wrong desires." Thus St. Paul is overwhelmed by the law precisely because he takes it so seriously that he wants it to become the guiding principle of his entire life. For him, it is simply not enough to "go through the motions"; any hypocrite can act in accordance with duty, but the true zealot, and the most righteous, is one who incorporates the law as the principle determination of their own will.

Significantly, in his most sustained discussion of St. Paul, Nietzsche dwells upon St. Paul's encounter with the law as the key to his whole development. "He suffered from a fixed idea," he comments, "or more clearly from a *fixed question* which was always present to him and would never rest: what is the Jewish *law* really concerned with? And in particular, what is *the fulfillment of this law*?" (*D* sec. 68). From this perspective, the complete incorporation of the law would represent the most sublime achievement and a final release from torment. In effect, Paul wills that his own will shall be completely identical to the will of the law, for only in this way is the law fulfilled in the deepest sense. Thus he desperately needs to take charge of himself, to become the complete master of his own individual nature. And yet it is here that he experiences failure, for he finds that he cannot will what he wants to will. The law provokes a resistance to itself. "Thou shalt not covet" creates a covetousness that had not existed before, and unlawful desires and questionable motives finally prevent him from achieving self-appropriation in the spirit of the law. The result is complete alienation and division within the self. As he writes a little later, "When I want to do the right, only the wrong is within my reach. In my inmost self I delight in the law of God, but I perceive that there is a different law, fighting against the law that my reason approves and making me a prisoner under the law that is in my members, the law of sin."

In describing this failure of sovereignty, St. Paul dwells upon the divided nature of his own will. Every time the commandment is given, a counter-will is created that resists the command; and for Paul this is nothing other than the self-assertion of sin: "sin found its opportunity in the commandment, seduced me and through the commandment killed me." But we should consider this closely, for there is another respect in which St. Paul's project of self-righteousness is impossible and self-canceling; and it may actually be an *essential* aspect of this project that he will never be able to free himself from the sinful part of his nature that opposes God's law. The problem is that self-righteousness demands that one maintain a will that is absolutely pure. But how is one to determine this? As the full promoter of the law, St. Paul is compelled to submit himself to the most subtle self-scrutiny. To ensure that his whole being has accepted the principle of the law, he is obliged to question the ground of all his actions, and to consider in every case whether it might not be pride or fear or another evil motive that really inspires his good behavior. For the sake of the law, he must call himself into question at every moment, being merciless and even malicious in suggesting a sinful motive where none had existed before. And if, after examining his conscience, he still cannot find anything to doubt, then he would have to question his own self-righteousness and the sinful self-regarding impulse on which it must be based. In short, the more seriously he takes this project, the more he must be aware of his own failure, as the sheer brilliance of the law seems to illuminate sinful motives that were previously hidden. Self-examination leads to self-laceration, so that sovereignty and self-justification are formally impossible.[4]

If sin constantly multiplies itself in the way described above, and if the sinful will must always assert itself against the rule of law, then the commitment to the law will forever be inadequate. Paul describes how in total guilt the self is forced into an awareness of itself as an individual yet divided being. And the emergence of this guilty self-consciousness is an awareness that is so "lacerating" that the "I" can only experience itself as "not-I": "The good which I want to do, I fail to do; but what I do is the wrong which is against my will; and if what I do is against my will, clearly it is no longer I who am the agent, but sin that has its lodging in me." We must be careful, however, not to argue that St. Paul is insisting upon his own innocence, as a passive victim who simply cannot do what he is supposed to. Calvin, for example, held that "Paul here denies that he is wholly possessed by sin. Nay, he declares himself to be exempt from its bondage."[5] This is wrong, because Paul is clearly anguished over his inability to incorporate the law, and it is the profundity of his guilt and sense of responsibility that finally leads him to abandon self-reliance.

In fact, it is more reasonable to assume that Paul's experience, though presented as a total loss of agency, is actually the record of a self that endures its own impotence when it cannot command itself. It is a variation of the classical problem of *akrasia,* except that here it is not the will that cannot restrain its unlawful actions, but the will that cannot compel itself to will. On the one hand, Paul wants to incorporate the law; there is no reason to believe that he is lacking in self-knowledge, or that this is not his deepest wish: in this respect we may say that he *wills* to follow the law. On the other hand, he remains beset by unlawful desires, he does not always will for the sake of the law; and so we may also say that he does *not* will to follow the law. How can this contradiction be explained? Or how is it, to repeat St. Augustine's later formulation, that the will can refuse to follow the very command that it promulgates to itself?

St. Augustine's meditation on the weakness of the will occurs in the *Confessions* at the point where he is trying to understand why he does not simply accept Christ when he knows in his heart of hearts that this is exactly what he wants to do. St. Augustine explains the conflict within his soul as a struggle between two competing principles, and he argues that the will to follow Christ, which is his *own* will, has not yet triumphed because it is still not strong enough to overcome his old sinful will that has been strengthened by habit. "The reason then why the command is not obeyed," he says, "is that it is not given with the full will. For if the will were full it would not command itself to be full, since it would be so already."[6] By resolving this issue in terms of the strong (or full) will and the weak will, St. Augustine implies that the will that must choose between competing desires may find itself constrained and impotent. In this regard, it makes sense to say that his will is not a free will; and insofar as he identifies *himself* with this will he experiences the failure of sovereignty. Perhaps the alternative to this would be to suggest that his self is merely a passive observer whose decisions always follow, but never determine, the outcome of the struggle within. But such a model fails to explain the reality of inner conflict and the possibility of *akrasia,* when one wishes or wills to have other desires than the ones one has.

St. Paul identifies himself with one particular will when he says that, "in my inmost self I delight in the law of God," although "I perceive that there is in my bodily members a different law, fighting against the law that my reason approves and making me a prisoner under the law . . . of sin." Here also, it can hardly be denied that St. Paul's commitment and resolution has some bearing upon the success of his project; for if his "inmost self" or good will is to gain command then it must be affirmed or *willed* by the individual Paul himself. This "will to will" oneself is the essential project of sovereignty.

In the end, St. Paul despairs of ever being able to achieve sovereignty through his own efforts. Autonomy is commanded, but it belongs to the very nature of freedom that it will always exceed whatever control is imposed upon it. For Paul, the only possible resolution becomes the complete surrender of his own life to God: "Miserable creature that I am, who is there to rescue me out of this body doomed to death? God alone, through Jesus Christ our Lord!" And now as a Christian he relies upon God's grace instead of his own inadequate power. The original imperative of self-appropriation is thus superseded by the stronger demand for a total self-denial. At the beginning of *Romans,* chapter eight, Paul experiences this conversion as the final end of self-assertion, and the triumph of that which is not-I:

> The conclusion of the matter is this: there is no condemnation for those who are united with Christ Jesus, because in Christ Jesus the life-giving law of the Spirit has set you free from the law of sin and death. What the law could never do, because our lower nature robbed it of all potency, God has done: By sending his own son in a form like that of our sinful nature, and as a sacrifice for sin, he has passed judgment against sin within that very nature, so that the commandment of the law may find fulfillment in us, whose conduct, no longer under the control of our lower nature, is directed by the spirit.

Similarly, in *Galatians,* chapter two, Paul writes: "I have been crucified with Christ: the life I now live is not my life, but the life which Christ lives in me;

and my present bodily life is lived by faith in the son of God, who loved me and gave himself up for me.'"

How are we to understand this conclusion? Speaking cynically, we might say that such self-abandonment in the glory of God represents the easiest solution to the agony of a divided consciousness. For in this way the burden of individual sovereignty is finally avoided, as the suppression of the individual becomes the only way of atoning for a sinful, guilty nature. Thus, even if St. Paul is the first to raise the issue of sovereignty, he never resolves the issue but actually betrays it when he calls for the crucifixion of our sinful nature as the condition of our unity with Christ. This is certainly how Nietzsche understood the progress of Christianity, and it accounts for his violent polemics against St. Paul. In *Daybreak,* for example, he offers an extended meditation on St. Paul as "the *first Christian . . .* the inventor of Christianness! Before him there were only a few Jewish sectarians" (*D* sec. 68). Nietzsche views St. Paul as the avatar of the Christian priest who uses every ruse and strategy to turn the self against itself, by revaluing self-affirmation as the simple expression of sin. In *On the Genealogy of Morals* and *The Antichrist,* Nietzsche diagnosed the self-suppression of religious asceticism as the origin of contemporary nihilism and the will-lessness of modern life; and as an heir to the project of sovereignty, he sought to restore the autonomy of the individual through his *own* strategies, like the eternal recurrence and the proclamation of the death of God.

On the other hand, it could also be urged that it is precisely this stress on "taking charge" of oneself and willing one's *own* will that stands behind the spiritual failure of the modern age. It may well be that such willfulness is itself our greatest danger, for it leads to the domination and dehumanization of modern technology, and it prevents the possibility of a genuine relation to the Other, as one who is necessarily beyond the circle of my own self-concern. From this perspective, what the seventh chapter suggests is that any form of self-assertion, self-cultivation, or preoccupation with the self must inevitably lead to "death" or the final dispersion of the self in the agony of self-laceration. Conversely, self-denial, or even self-abandonment in the grace of God, leads to life and the possibility of individual fulfillment. St. Paul viewed sovereignty in terms of a strict self-discipline and self-assertion; and in this respect he grasped that self-commandment and self-destruction are reciprocal terms that imply and fulfill each other. Hence, he understood the danger of individualism in its narrow and selfish sense.

In short, the general thematic of sovereignty underlies the seventh chapter of St. Paul's *Letter to the Romans.* At this point, sovereignty still remains an obscure ideal. But it seems tied to the self-empowerment of the individual, or the will that wills itself. In St. Paul, as in St. Augustine, there remains the idea of a "true" self that may be hidden under layers of self-deceit. The project of sovereignty then becomes a matter of the true self securing total command; and this leads to a model of sovereignty that is ordered in terms of strict self-discipline. But perhaps this is not the only possible conception of sovereignty, and in the following chapters we will see how Nietzsche embraces the sovereign ideal *without* accepting a fixed and substantial conception of the self.

～

In his moral philosophy, Kant sought to provide an independent warrant for the ethical precepts of Christianity and to establish the rational basis of our ordinary moral truths. At the same time, however, a reconstruction of Kant suggests that all of our ethical obligations are ultimately founded upon the imperative of autonomy. In Kant, morality follows from the need to reclaim our own higher nature, and in this respect Kant's ethics is actually the most systematic articulation of the project of sovereignty itself. The following discussion will focus on Kant's conception of morality and his account of self-determination, or self-mastery, which finds expression in the positive freedom of autonomy. When this doctrine of sovereignty is viewed as a discussion of "how one becomes what one is," it may finally be evaluated in the light of Nietzsche's interpretation and critique.

According to Kant, the reality of moral obligation is both absolutely basic and yet inexplicable, for while it exists as a pure and indisputable "fact," it cannot be comprehended within the horizon of material necessity, since it is precisely this necessity that obligation requires us to transcend. Certainly, in the *Foundations,* Kant still looked forward to a theoretical argument that would justify the moral law, and so silence all of those skeptics for whom morality is "but a phantom of the brain." But even here Kant concludes with a perplexed admission of our final ignorance in these matters, that, while "we do not indeed comprehend the practical unconditional necessity of the moral imperative; yet do we comprehend its incomprehensibility."[7] Later, in the *Critique of Practical Reason,* Kant renounced the very possibility of a transcendental deduction of morality as something entirely problematic. Now the moral law is to be accepted as an ultimate fact of experience that cannot be further explained: "The objective reality of the moral law can be proved through no deduction, through no exertion of the theoretical, speculative, or empirically supported reason." "Nevertheless," he concludes, "it is firmly established of itself."[8] Thus we experience the fact of obligation; as rational creatures we find ourselves commanded by a moral imperative, and in the decision to obey or disobey we first discover the possibility of our freedom.

It follows that there is an element of paradox at the very heart of our moral experience. On the one hand, moral obligation is grasped as the most obvious fact, the familiar experience of the common man that in no way requires the confirmation of philosophy. At the beginning of the second *Critique,* for example, Kant condemns anyone who would propose or invent alternative moral principles from those that have hitherto been accepted. Throughout his work, Kant insists that the moral wisdom of the common man is unassailable, and only requires philosophical reconstruction to systematize the basic order of its beliefs. On the other hand, moral obligation is also the uncanniest of all experiences; for in prompting us to our duties, obligation seems to reveal the possibility of overcoming all selfish inclinations, and hence of transcending the realm of natural law. The experience of obligation, our inevitable "reverence" for the moral law, cannot be comprehended from the empirical standpoint; for it is not simply the urging of another desire, and to reduce it to the status of a material determination would violate all our intuitions concerning it.

Kant argues, then, that as an a priori "fact of pure reason," obligation is both insistent and inescapable, making even "the boldest sinner tremble." In demanding our respect, it forces us to acknowledge the comparative worthlessness of our own sensible existence. It follows that moral obligation is most typically experienced as a painful burden that is imposed upon us, and as a task that we are called to, though without threats or the promise of reward. This completely distinguishes it from every determination of desire that issues from our self-love.

In his famous "Hymn to Duty," Kant makes all of this especially clear when he meditates upon the ultimate origin of the moral command:

> Duty! Thou sublime and mighty name that dost embrace nothing charming or insinuating but requirest submission and yet seekest not to move the will by threatening aught that would arouse natural aversion or terror, but only holdest forth a law which of itself finds entrance into the mind and yet gains reluctant reverence (though not always obedience)—a law before which all inclinations are dumb even though they secretly work against it: what origin is there worthy of thee, and where is to be found the root of thy noble descent which proudly rejects all kinship with the inclinations and from which to be descended is the indispensable condition of the only worth which men can give themselves?

To which the answer is given: "It cannot be less than something which elevates man above himself as a part of the world of sense, something which connects him with an order of things which only the understanding can think and which has under it the entire world of sense, including the empirically determinable existence of man in time, and the whole system of all ends which is alone suitable to such unconditional practical laws as the moral" (*CPR* pp. 89, 86).

According to Kant, our "wonder" at obligation—Where does it come from? What supports it? Why and how does it exist?—is really the wonder at another realm that the experience of obligation discloses to us. What humbles us is the presentation of a higher "intelligible" world, where actions are not conditioned by inclinations and where the will is accordingly free. "The moral law," he says, "does provide a fact absolutely inexplicable from any data of the world of sense . . . and this fact points to a pure intelligible world" (*CPR* pp. 44, 43). Through the experience of obligation we are recalled to this "intelligible" or "noumenal" order; and it turns out that the imperative to recover such a world is necessarily inescapable since it is at root the summons to a recollection of our own higher self. Rather than any alien or "heteronomous" principle, it is the intelligible or rational part of the self that seeks to subject its phenomenal counterpart to the principle of its own higher law. "Since the intelligible world contains the ground of the world of sense and hence of its laws," Kant argues,

> the intelligible world is (and must be conceived as) directly legislative for my will, which belongs wholly to the intelligible world. Therefore I recognize myself qua intelligence as subject to the law of the world of understanding and to the autonomy of the will. That is, I recognize myself as subject to the law of reason which contains in the idea of freedom the law of the intelligible world, while at the same time I must acknowledge that I am a being which belongs to the world of sense. (*F* p. 72; 453)

Thus from one perspective we are rational creatures who are affected by our natural inclinations, while from another perspective we are intelligible, rational beings whose autonomous will is expressed in the legislation of rational principles or "the *a priori* commands of pure practical reason." The moral imperative arises in the gap between our two natures, and it expresses nothing other than the need to reclaim our higher self from all the disruptions of sensibility. This means that for Kant, morality is not a restriction upon our freedom but freedom's guarantee and the very expression of its fulfillment. Similarly, in acting for the sake of the moral law we are most completely "ourselves," for only here are we free from the rule of sensuous nature that would otherwise lure us into self-abandonment.

In the second *Critique*, Kant therefore claims that the "fact" of the moral law must serve as the principle of the deduction of freedom. For in distinction to the actual *feeling* of freedom, which is easily explicable in terms of natural causes, it is the moral imperative that first evokes a will that realizes the possibility of rejecting all sensuous determination. The implication here is that without this constraint of obligation we could never have become aware of our capacity for authentic freedom; and, even more radically, that without the moral law we could never even have grasped ourselves as separate and individual beings. Kant often insists upon the "priority of practical reason" over theoretical or speculative reason; but perhaps the most essential aspect of this priority is that individual identity is first brought into being through the commandment of the moral law.

According to Kant, the moral law must be expressed as a categorical imperative since it commands us unconditionally, without regard for the possible consequences of its fulfillment. The categorical imperative, however, requires a will that is capable of complete self-mastery and independence from the determination of nature—for if it were conditioned by inclination, it could never accept such an unconditional duty as its own. Thus morality implies freedom, but more particularly the most complete freedom of autonomy, in which the rational will commands itself by requiring us to follow the law of our own higher nature.[9] As he comments, "What else, then, can the freedom of the will be but autonomy, i.e., the property of the will to be a law to itself?" (*F* p. 65; 446).

We can now appreciate the crucial place of autonomy within Kant's system, for the concept of autonomy provides the only possible synthesis between the negative freedom from nature and the total unconditional necessity that is demanded by the order of law. Kant holds that autonomous individuals act as both "sovereigns" and "subjects," insofar as they obey the very law that they promulgate to themselves. With respect to the determination of the will this means that in autonomy, "The will is . . . not only subject to the law but subject in such a way that it must be regarded also as self-legislative and only for this reason as being subject to the law (of which it can regard itself as the author)" (*F* p. 49; 431). In short, the autonomous will does not submit to anything beyond itself; it is not lured by the voices of inclination or determined by religious hopes. For in autonomy it is the will itself that issues the commandment for its own existence. By contrast, the *heteronomous* will is a will that allows itself to be governed by some preestablished impulse or principle, such as "happiness," "physical desire," or "the will of God." The heteronomous will is thus a will that actively surrenders itself, for even though some of these principles may be praiseworthy, they effectively limit the freedom of the will by ordering it in advance.

In the "Analytic of Practical Reason," Kant concludes this discussion with the following theorem: "The *autonomy* of the will is the sole principle of all moral laws and of the duties conforming to them; *heteronomy* of choice, on the other hand, not only does not establish any obligation but is opposed to the principle of duty and to the morality of the will" (*CPR* p. 33; 33). In the second *Critique*, Kant's argument is a negative one, to show that no heteronomous principle can serve as the proper basis for morality, and that consequently, morality presupposes autonomy. In the preceding account, I have suggested that the *positive* argument would show how for Kant autonomy is also the *sufficient* condition of morality, since moral obligation is nothing more than the imperative of autonomy when "reason" is taken as the principle of our own higher self.

In fact, once we have grasped this absolute priority of autonomy, our ordinary understanding of both morality and freedom must inevitably be changed. First, it is clear that the moral imperative is nothing other than the imperative of autonomy. It is the command that first calls the self into existence and that sets it the task of taking charge of itself. In this respect, autonomy or sovereignty must now be regarded as the underlying intention of morality itself: action for the sake of the moral law is really action that derives from the incentive of willing one's own highest nature as a person. "For it is then not to be wondered at," Kant comments, "that man, as belonging to two worlds, must regard his own being in relation to his second and higher vocation with reverence and the laws of this vocation with the deepest respect" (*CPR* p. 90; 87). And elsewhere he writes: "The moral law with the respect which is inseparable from it . . . is personality itself."[10] In other words, moral obligation follows from the compulsion of our own higher nature, which according to Kant is our rational part; and hence, morality is not primarily a "debt" that we owe to others, but a relationship that we have to our own higher self. Thus Kant condemns those who believe that morality is based on the welfare of others, in exactly the same way that he condemns those who believe that it is based on self-love. We should seek the happiness of others, but only because this conforms to the claims of autonomy. "The law that we should further the happiness of others," he writes, "arises not from the presupposition that this law is an object of everyone's choice but from the fact that the form of universality, which reason requires as condition for giving to the maxim of self-love the objective validity of law, is itself the determining ground of the will" (*CPR* p. 35; 35).

In the end, morality is nothing other than the explication or "exegesis" of autonomy, insofar as the principles of morality describe the conditions for self-appropriation. Through the intermediary of the categorical imperative, the self comes to realize which of its maxims are in accordance with the principle of its own higher nature and which of its maxims are not. Indeed, the very concepts of "good" and "evil" are now to be understood as subsequent to these determinations. "The moral law," Kant says, "is that which first defines the concept of the good . . . and makes it possible" (*CPR* p. 66; 64). This is Kant's so-called Copernican revolution in ethics, according to which "the good" is not something that exists outside of ourselves, as a final end that commands us, but is rather a product of our own willing, insofar as this conforms to the principle of autonomy.

In a similar way the proper meaning of freedom has also been changed. Freedom can no longer be thought of as a blind, chaotic striving that is without law, for such a precarious power would undermine and destroy itself. In fact, the only real freedom is freedom that constantly renews and recovers itself, because it is directed by the principle of its own self-possession. And Kant says that it is through the activity of such freedom that we come to approximate to the ultimate self-sufficiency and self-mastery of God; the laws of morality are different from the laws of nature, insofar as the former are the products of our free willing, whereas the latter impose themselves upon us whether we want them to or not. Thus it may be said that in moral activity we spontaneously create a realm of freedom (and reason) in exactly the same way as God himself created and sustains the world. And by analogy, this activity of pure *sovereignty* must be the highest activity of which we are capable.[11]

In the first *Critique*, Kant condemned speculative metaphysics because he realized that access to a higher realm of being could not be achieved through simple contemplation: our knowledge of the world is subject to the categories, and *these* are limited to the conditions of our sensibility, space and time. In the second *Critique*, however, Kant insists that the noumenal realm can be grasped through active participation that affirms the being of this realm in the very act of making it real.[12] Once again, as a will that wills itself, autonomy is the highest form of activity; and more than participation, it must be understood as the very principle of creation itself.

So far, I have tried to abstract a certain moment from the Kantian system, to consider Kantian autonomy in isolation from the rest of Kant's project. While avoiding the whole issue of Kant's metaphysical context, I have suggested that our ordinary understanding of both morality and freedom must be transformed in light of our recognition of autonomy as the basic value. From all of this, two essential points now emerge. The first is the foundational role of sovereignty in Kant's system. The imperative of autonomy is the basic commandment of existence from which the whole of ethics is consequently derived. For Kant "autonomy" is both a necessary *and* a sufficient condition for morality and every possible system of value, and it also represents the fulfillment of our freedom. Thus, although it must be reconstructed and literally unearthed from the foundations of the metaphysics of morals, Kant has a doctrine of sovereignty that is really the focal point of his whole metaphysical scheme.

On the other hand, it must also be admitted that all of Kant's discussion takes place within the context of an overarching "metaphysics of reason," in which reason is our "truth" and the locus of our fulfillment. The project of autonomy consequently involves the oblivion of our particular nature, for in Kant I am most "myself" when I set aside whatever individual qualities or goals I may have and follow the moral law as if I were an impersonal agent of reason. In *The Gay Science*, Nietzsche comments specifically on this paradox:

> What? You admire the categorical imperative within you? This "firmness" of your so-called moral judgment? This "unconditional" feeling that "here everyone must judge as I do?" Rather admire your *selfishness* at this point. And the blindness, pettiness, and frugality of your selfishness. For it is selfish to experience one's own judgment as a universal law; and this selfishness is blind, petty and frugal because it betrays that you have not yet discovered yourself nor created for yourself an ideal of your own. (*GS* sec. 335)

This passage helps us to understand Nietzsche's essential ambivalence toward Kant. For while Kant celebrates the project of sovereignty, and makes it the focus of his philosophical project, he also betrays sovereignty—or so Nietzsche complains—when he conflates sovereignty with the simple fulfillment of our rational nature. The requirements of morality are one thing, but "sovereignty" expresses the individuality of the individual or the fulfillment of the individual as such. Nietzsche claims, however, that the categorical imperative finally destroys sovereignty by subsuming it under the "universal" and "necessary" principles of reason. This is a charge that can now be considered in light of Nietzsche's general perspective on Kant.

In *The Birth of Tragedy* Nietzsche praises Kant, along with Schopenhauer, as the one who determined the necessary limitations of our scientific understanding of the world and so encouraged the self-overcoming of such a perspective. In this work, he celebrates Kant as the opponent of all illusion and prejudice, and he claims that Kant's critical labors have prepared the way for the eventual return of "tragic wisdom." Elsewhere, Nietzsche uses Kant's critique of the limits of human understanding in order to destroy the traditional problems of philosophy—like "truth," "personal identity," or "the real versus the apparent world"—and to show them incapable of resolution. Especially in his "scientific" period, Nietzsche effects a *reductio ad absurdum* of such academic questions in order to focus our attention upon the problem of the individual as one of the most urgent philosophical problems. Likewise, when Kant criticized traditional metaphysics he had a similar strategy in mind: to curtail all the claims of metaphysical knowledge in order to make room for faith, and more importantly, the possibility of autonomy through the legislation of our own higher nature.

If we look at Nietzsche's later work, however, it becomes much more difficult to maintain any kind of continuity between the two thinkers. Nietzsche repeatedly attacks the categories of "freedom," "will," and "responsibility" that subtend Kant's description of autonomy. In *Twilight of the Idols* he celebrates Goethe as the affirmative spirit who unified all of his powers and instincts, in opposition to Kant's decadent demand for a strict separation of the faculties; while later he writes, "What could destroy us more quickly than working, thinking, and feeling without any inner necessity, without any deeply personal choice, without *pleasure* as an automaton of 'duty'? This is the very recipe for decadence, even for idiocy. Kant became an idiot. And this man was the contemporary of *Goethe!*" (*AC* sec. 11). Perhaps the change in Nietzsche's attitude to Kant is directly related to a deepening awareness of the nature of his own philosophical mission. Kant's philosophy may have enabled the resurgence of tragic wisdom. But it soon became clear to Nietzsche that while his own philosophy was also concerned with the sovereignty of the individual, Kantian solutions, like the categorical imperative, must entail the complete oblivion of the individual as such.

In *The Antichrist*, for example, Nietzsche describes the categorical imperative as a typical metaphysical ploy. He views it as an attempt to escape or redeem individual existence by directing it after a law that is both "universal" and "necessary." "The fundamental laws of self-preservation and growth demand that everyone invent *his own* virtue, *his own* categorical imperative," he writes. "Nothing ruins us more profoundly, more intimately than every 'impersonal' duty, every sacrifice to the Moloch of abstraction" (*AC* sec. 11). We might say that for Kant we are only moral (and hence autonomous) agents insofar as we disregard the particularities of space and time to consider ourselves the embodiment of universal law. Arguing from the perspective of sovereignty, Nietzsche asserts that the categorical imperative is therefore an "immoral" concept since it suppresses the singularity of individual existence within the monotonous rule of "law."

In fact, Nietzsche realized that reason by itself, or through the mediation of the categorical imperative, may never be used to direct or determine the nature of individual sovereignty. This conclusion is in keeping with our basic understanding of what sovereignty means. If sovereignty really is the celebration of the individual, or that mode of being in which the individual achieves some kind of self-possession, the legislation of any specific formula for sovereignty actually denies individuality by attempting to order it in advance. The paradox here is that no one may simply "legislate" sovereignty, since sovereignty is precisely the commandment one has over oneself. Thus, in *Ecce Homo* Nietzsche celebrates his own life and the project of self-appropriation, but he deliberately frustrates all imitation when he warns about the dangers of *all* books, or when he counters the heroic portrayal of himself as the champion of impossible causes with a warning to beware of all great poses (*EH* "Why I Am So Clever" sec. 10). Clearly, he understood that to *prescribe* the specific content of sovereignty is ipso facto to destroy it; and he was therefore bound to reject Kant's circumscription of autonomy and sovereignty in the formula of the categorical imperative.

In the end, Nietzsche's criticism of Kant is really a critique from within. For it is an attempt to radicalize Kant that is still guided by the same sovereign ideal that is common to both of them. And perhaps for this reason, Nietzsche's invective against Kant is so relentless and impassioned; for in this way he emphasizes the essential *difference* between their respective projects. In fact, Nietzsche's meditation on Kant's doctrine of sovereignty suggests the paradoxical nature of Nietzsche's own philosophical goal. In all of the passages quoted above, Nietzsche criticizes Kant because the latter has abandoned the individual to the rule of an impersonal law. Clearly, Nietzsche's goal is somehow to *rescue* individuals from whatever values, institutions, or moralities constrain them and encourage self-oblivion. But if sovereignty is to be identified with the affirmation of the individual as such, then it follows that sovereignty can *never* be conceptually appropriated; the individual is that which cannot be analyzed, reduced, or repeated in language: *individuum ineffabile est.* In this sense, however, a "philosophy of sovereignty" is bound to express that which can never be said. Hence it must remain deeply problematic and will require every kind of ruse and strategy if it is ever to succeed.

◌

Schopenhauer is not a Christian philosopher in any obvious sense. One of the distinctive features of his work is his sympathetic appropriation of Hindu and Buddhist texts as alternative articulations of his own philosophical claims. Even more decisively, Schopenhauer completely rejects the idea of God or the possibility of any final purpose to human life. He is insistent upon the miseries of existence, and in a series of gloomy passages he describes all of our most cherished ideals and projects with the utmost contempt and disdain. "It is really incredible how meaningless and insignificant when seen from without, and how dull and senseless when felt from within, is the course of life of the great majority of men." He continues, "Every time a man is begotten and born the clock of human life is wound up anew, to repeat once more its same old tune that has already been played out innumerable times, movement by movement and measure by measure, with insignificant variations."[13] These claims are typical, and they only serve to emphasize Schopenhauer's complete estrangement from every Christian sentiment and belief. Thus, even if Schopenhauer sometimes refers to his philosophy as the "only true Christianity," he *also* argues that religion is bad metaphysics. While he accepts that Christianity has grasped the fundamental character of life as a "vale of tears" and a period of inevitable suffering, he rejects its otherworldly dream of "heaven" as a mendacious fantasy that obscures the full horror of existence and seduces us into life.

Despite all of this, however, Nietzsche had no doubt that Schopenhauer was still firmly within the Christian tradition of thought. In notes published in *The Will to Power*, Nietzsche begins a discussion of "the extent to which Schopenhauer's nihilism still follows from the same ideal that created Christian theism" (*WTP* sec. 17), and in several passages he dismisses Schopenhauer's morality of pity as another expression of Christian neighbor-love that derives from the same urge to *self*-abandonment.[14] Nietzsche's final verdict on Schopenhauer clearly follows from his own identification of Christianity with nihilism and his recognition of "will-lessness" as the most fundamental expression of the latter. By promoting the denial of the will, Schopenhauer's thought expresses the same spirit of asceticism and hostility to life that Christianity has also embodied. In this respect, Nietzsche's comparison of Schopenhauer and Christianity is an ironic comment upon how little Schopenhauer understood about the ultimate motivation of his own philosophy.

In fact, Nietzsche's critique of Schopenhauer seems to confirm the possibility of a "Christian" tradition in philosophy that would be more than just a list of thinkers who have accepted the truth of the Christian religion. I have argued above that the original Christian concern for individual salvation is reflected within the history of philosophy as an intense preoccupation with the problem of individual existence. Through Christianity the issue of the individual achieves a certain momentum and focus, which later thinkers, regardless of their religious affiliation, have responded to or denied. As a general guiding theme this can now help us to understand the very interesting position that Schopenhauer occupies in the history of thought.

In *The World as Will and Representation*, Schopenhauer insists upon the "illusory" character of individual purposes and goals. He describes the individual as a phenomenal manifestation of the one primordial will, which alone possesses being in the fullest sense. He argues that even space and time, the very principles of individuation, are projections of this will; so that nature as a whole, including all human activity, represents nothing more than the will's perpetual striving. And since the striving of the will is without purpose and without end, Schopenhauer concludes that the individual life, which is empowered by it, must be doomed to continual dissatisfaction and misery. "Such a life, by its whole tendency and disposition, is not capable of any true bliss or happiness," he writes, "but is essentially suffering in many forms and a tragic state in every way" (*WWR* 1:323).

In fact, throughout *The World as Will and Representation*, Schopenhauer argues that nature only cares about the continuation of the species. The struggle for existence is chaotic and blind. While individuals strive intensely for the preservation and enhancement of their own life, the accident of individual existence is absolutely irrelevant when considered from the perspective of eternity. "For it is not the individual that nature cares for," he comments, "but only the species; and in all seriousness she urges the preservation of the species, since she provides for this so lavishly through the immense surplus of the seed and the great strength of the fructifying impulse. The individual, on the contrary, has no value for nature, and can have none, for infinite time, infinite space, and the infinite number of possible individuals therein are her kingdom" (*WWR* 1:276).

Now it is certainly true that in Schopenhauer the individual human being is accorded some respect as the highest level of the objectification of will. As opposed to the brute or the stone, the human being is the only creature in which nature may achieve consciousness of itself and of its final end or endlessness. Far from being a blessing, however, such a distinction actually makes our situation as painful as possible: for it means that we are not only doomed to a life of pointless unhappy striving and activity, but also doomed, if we look deeply enough, to become aware of the complete absurdity of our situation.

In his ethical writings Schopenhauer proclaims the complete freedom of the will. Nevertheless, he denies that this entails the possibility of an authentic self-determination, for it means that the character of the individual is in fact a *necessary* manifestation of the *will to live,* insofar as the latter achieves objectification in each particular instance. Thus Schopenhauer asserts that the good man is *born* good, while "the wicked man is born with his wickedness as the snake is born with its poison fangs and its sac of venom, and the one can as little change his nature as the other."[15] It is quite impossible to change the kind of people that we are, and we are brought to the unhappy conclusion that we are not in charge of our lives in the way that we once thought.

For even though we experience ourselves as freely pursuing particular goals and projects, it is really only the will that pursues them through us, relentlessly and without cease, and throughout the course of our lives.

Thus the will acts through the conduit of nature and each individual is "played out" by the objectification of the will to which he or she corresponds. What this means, however, is that individual existence can never achieve satisfaction or happiness since the will's incessant striving must always force the individual from one objective to the next. The will to live can never allow the individual to rest on any particular triumph since its goal is *only* to strive, and this apart from all particular ends. In the final analysis, to exist is to suffer. "For all striving springs from want or deficiency," he writes, "from dissatisfaction with one's own state or condition, and is therefore suffering so long as it is not satisfied. No satisfaction, however, is lasting; on the contrary, it is always merely the starting-point of a fresh striving. We see striving everywhere impeded in many ways, everywhere struggling and fighting, and hence always as suffering. Thus that there is no ultimate aim of striving means that there is no measure or end of suffering" (*WWR* 1:309).

Schopenhauer describes a grotesque and malicious world that, if anything, appears especially contrived to torment and punish its inhabitants. This is, as he says, the worst of all possible worlds. The universe has no order, and nature surges forward toward nothing in particular. So that if we see deeply enough we must accept that all human purposes are illusory, while at the same time we are bound to participate in them. The inevitable result is despair. And, as Schopenhauer says, the more we become aware of this situation the more painful it will become.

Thus it is clear that Schopenhauer labors to establish the wretched character of human existence. And yet, as I will argue, such pessimism is eventually forced to overcome itself. For even though Schopenhauer attacks our ordinary conception of individuality, in his system it is the individual, the original curse of nature, who finally emerges as the very possibility of nature's own transfiguration.

In the latter part of *The World as Will and Representation*, Schopenhauer considers the problem of suicide. Given the task of philosophy—to free us from all the claims of life—we might have expected that Schopenhauer would affirm suicide as the most obvious and legitimate response to the suffering of life. Here, however, Schopenhauer argues that suicide really changes nothing for the individual concerned; and he claims that the will to suicide—to remove oneself from life when it has become too painful—is actually a manifestation of the will to live. Thus, "far from being denial of the will," he comments, "suicide is a phenomenon of the will's strong affirmation. For denial has its essential nature in the fact that the pleasures of life, not its sorrows, are shunned. The suicide wills life, and is dissatisfied merely with the conditions on which it has come to him. Therefore he gives up by no means the will-to-live, but merely life, since he destroys the individual phenomenon" (*WWR* 1:398). Here Schopenhauer distinguishes between the affirmation of the will to death, which is still a manifestation of will, and the denial of the will to live, which is described, significantly enough, as the only *salvation* available to us.

We can leave aside the obvious question of Schopenhauer's consistency on this point. If individuation is the greatest evil, then it is not entirely clear how the act of self-destruction could ever leave matters as they are, or even make things worse for the individual concerned.[16] Schopenhauer condemns the will to suicide because he sees it as a *passive* response to the misery of life, in which the individual, though seeking death, is still directed by the cravings of the will to live. He argues that such a response does not solve anything because it preserves the complete priority of the will, even if it does destroy the "individual phenomenon."

In fact, Schopenhauer argues that the only authentic way in which one *can* escape from this situation is through an *active* effort of will—in which one would renounce the claims of the world by suppressing, within oneself, the very striving of the will to live. In effect, the individual will must turn upon itself to destroy the very same impulse by which it is empowered. This means that, in opposition to the gloomy acceptance of pessimism, Schopenhauer's position actually directs us toward a stance of willful self-denial, and even self-mortification, as the means by which the individual may finally overcome the dominion of the will. The ascetic who has gained complete self-mastery now becomes the individual ideal:

> every suffering that comes to him from outside through chance or the wickedness of others is welcome to him. . . . He gladly accepts them as the opportunity for giving himself the certainty that he no longer affirms the will, but gladly sides with every enemy of the will's phenomenon that is his own person. . . . Just as he mortifies the will itself, so does he mortify its visibility, its objectivity, the body. He nourishes it sparingly, lest its vigorous flourishing and thriving should animate afresh and excite more strongly the will, of which it is the mere expression and mirror. Thus he resorts to fasting, and even to self-castigation and self-torture, in order that, by constant privation and suffering, he may more and more break down and kill the will that he recognizes and abhors as the source of his own suffering existence and of the world's. (*WWR* 1:382)

The paradox of all of this, however, is that such an assertion of will *against* will points ahead to a final goal of self-affirmation and strength. For in the very act of denying the will the individual is forced to take charge. In effect, the abolition of the will is achieved by an individual *act of will,* a will not to have to will any more, which seems to presuppose the very same power that it is seeking to destroy.

As we have seen, Schopenhauer insists upon the complete necessity of all events that occur in space and time. But he also believes in the possibility of the individual will freely destroying the very power that should direct it. In the end, such an eruption of freedom in its *phenomenal* manifestation is something that Schopenhauer can only describe in religious terms as a "miracle" or an act of "grace":

> For just what the Christian mystics call the *effect of grace* and the *new birth,* is for us the only direct expression of the *freedom of the will.* It appears only when the will, after arriving at the knowledge of its own inner nature, obtains from this a *quieter,* and is thus removed from the effect of *motives* which lies in the province of a different kind of knowledge, whose objects are only phenomena. The possibility of the freedom that thus manifests itself is man's greatest prerogative, which is for ever wanting in the animal, because the condition for it is the deliberation of the faculty of reason, enabling him to survey the whole of life independently of the impression of the present moment. . . . *Necessity is the kingdom of nature; freedom is the kingdom of grace.* (WWR 1:404)

It is significant that at this decisive point Schopenhauer feels obliged to resort to the traditional categories of Christianity in order to express his insight. Nietzsche had no doubt that in spite of his professed atheism and pessimism Schopenhauer was basically a Christian apologist; for here Schopenhauer's philosophy reproduces the moment of individual *redemption,* which can be viewed as a hallmark of Christian thinking. Let us add that in terms of our initial problematic, Schopenhauer's "Christianity" is apparent in his final insistence upon the possibility of human freedom and in his depiction of the individual who is first evoked by the need to overcome the "evil" forces of will.

In spite of everything, then, Schopenhauer's system eventually overcomes itself as the sovereign individual appears as the apogee and only salvation of nature. It is precisely this aspect of Schopenhauer's philosophy that Nietzsche is heir to: in Schopenhauer, the individual's relationship to nature is fundamental. The individual is a product of nature and another manifestation of the one primordial will; but he or she is also the conduit through which nature may eventually overcome itself, as the sovereign individual transfigures the world.

To conclude this discussion, and by way of a transition, we can finally consider some ways in which *The Birth of Tragedy,* and other writings, can help us to understand the real issue of Schopenhauer's thought. In a later preface, called "An Attempt at Self-Criticism," Nietzsche acknowledged that his first major work, *The Birth of Tragedy,* was profoundly influenced by the language and thematics of Schopenhauer's thought. Indeed, in *The Birth of Tragedy,* Nietzsche describes the "Dionysian" heart of being in straightforward Schopenhauerian terms, as "the primordial unity," whose dissolution and individuation is understood to be the cause of all suffering. It is significant, however, that according to Nietzsche this "horror" at the heart of existence is eventually overcome by the radiance of Apollo, and by the projection of an ideal Olympian realm of deities who *justify* existence in the very act of living it themselves. As he puts it, "the figure of Apollo, rising full of pride, held out the Gorgon's head to this grotesquely uncouth Dionysian power" (*BT* sec. 2).

Clearly, Nietzsche recognized the power and even the truth of Schopenhauer's pessimistic vision of existence. But he also saw, like Schopenhauer, that such *nihilism* might be overcome—might be challenged and surpassed— through the affirmation of an ideal mode of individuality *that it effectively summons forth.* In this respect, the celebration of individual sovereignty is the remedy of nature, although such a remedy would not be possible without the most complete awareness of nature's "wound"—all the horror of existence—which demands an overcoming. "Man has often had enough," Nietzsche writes, "there are actual epidemics of having had enough . . . but even this nausea, this weariness, this disgust with himself—all this bursts from him with such violence that it at once becomes a new fetter. The No he says to life brings to light, as if by magic, an abundance of tender Yeses; even when he *wounds* himself, this master of destruction and self-destruction—the very wound itself afterward compels him *to live*" (*GM* III sec. 13). Elsewhere, in *Beyond Good and Evil,* he comments explicitly:

> Whoever has endeavored with some enigmatic longing, as I have, to think pessimism through to its depths and to liberate it from the half-Christian, half-German narrowness and simplicity in which it has finally presented itself to our century, namely, in the form of Schopenhauer's philosophy; whoever has really, with an Asiatic and supra-Asiatic eye, looked into, down into the most world-denying of all possible ways of thinking—beyond good and evil and no longer, like the Buddha and Schopenhauer, under the spell and delusion of morality—may just thereby, without really meaning to do so, have opened his eyes to the opposite ideal: the ideal of the most high-spirited, alive, and world-affirming human being who has not only come to terms and learned to get along with whatever was and is, but who wants to have *what was and is* repeated into all eternity. (*BGE* sec. 56)

What remains implicit in Schopenhauer, and what Nietzsche later realized, is that in its most abysmal and world-denying form, nihilism is actually transformed into its opposite. Likewise, the final issue of Schopenhauerian pessimism is affirmation and "an abundance of tender Yeses."

Thus, if *absolute* nihilism is closest to the denial of nihilism, it makes sense to confront humanity with the full horror of its situation so that it can endure the passage into *life*. In Nietzsche, the doctrine of eternal recurrence is clearly intended in this respect, and is alluded to in the passage above; for by focusing upon the horror of existence, magnified within the perspective of eternity, it forces us either to affirm our existence or else to die of despair. Here is the original statement of eternal recurrence as it appears in *The Gay Science:*

> *The greatest weight.*—What if some day or night a demon were to steal after you into your loneliest loneliness and say to you: "This life as you now live it and have lived it, you will have to live once more and innumerable times more; and there will be nothing new in it, but every pain and every joy and every thought and sigh and everything unutterably small or great in your life will have to return to you, all in the same succession and sequence. . . ." Would you not throw yourself down and gnash your teeth and curse the demon who spoke thus? Or have you once experienced a tremendous moment when you would have answered him: "You are a god and never have I heard anything more divine." If this thought gained possession of you, it would change you as you are or perhaps crush you. (*GS* sec. 341)

The eternal recurrence presents a situation of the most complete meaninglessness, or as Nietzsche would have it, it is the most extreme form of nihilism ever envisaged. As Schopenhauer had already divined, however, a situation like this cannot really be avoided by an immediate act of suicide, since the infinite wheel of existence inevitably brings one back to the same condition again. On the contrary, according to *The World as Will and Representation* the only possible response to this horror is one of resolution and self-transformation, in which individuals would finally destroy their absolute bondage to nature by seizing hold of their own existence and directing themselves anew. In this way, pessimism destroys itself, and Schopenhauer's own thinking directs us to Nietzsche's affirmative position and the necessity of the second response: "You are a god, and never have I heard anything more divine".

By means of stratagems like the eternal recurrence Nietzsche seeks to direct us toward individual sovereignty. I have argued that Schopenhauer's account of the individual issues in a similar conclusion, so that in this respect, Schopenhauer's philosophy prefigures Nietzsche's own thematic of sovereignty. Since nihilism is inherently unstable, his own pessimism must finally destroy itself. Schopenhauer *is* therefore in the same "Christian" tradition that we described above. For despite everything else in his system, he finally affirms the possibility and the goal of individual "salvation."

↶

So far, I have argued that three moments in the history of thought, summarized by St. Paul, Kant, and Schopenhauer, can help to illuminate the essential nature of Nietzsche's own philosophical project. This genealogy of sovereignty was intended neither to be either exhaustive nor exclusive, but the encounter with these three thinkers does serve to distinguish Nietzsche's philosophy and place it in stark relief. Thus, in St. Paul, Nietzsche discovers the avatar of every priest and his own greatest enemy, who revalued the values of the classical world for the sake of self-abandonment in the glory of God. According to Nietzsche, St. Paul is the originator of Christianity as an organized movement and as a system of basic values; and he claims that it is these very values that have diminished the soul and directed the "taming" of the human animal over the past two thousand years. But Christianity has achieved all this through an intensification of individual existence and a summons to accountability—even to sovereignty—that can only end in failure. Through Christianity, then—and this is already manifest in St. Paul's *Letter to the Romans*—there issues a consciousness that is grounded in guilt and a deep awareness of its own impotence and sinful nature. It is this that Nietzsche seeks to overcome with his own "revaluation of values."

At the beginning of the modern age, Kant's emphasis on the absolute priority of autonomy provides the theoretical basis of contemporary individualism and every later doctrine of self-reliance. For just as the French revolutionaries had originally sought to legislate the order of society, instead of having it dictated to them by the force of custom and arbitrary decree, so also in Kant it is the subject who determines the limit of all possible experience, and this is the basis of his Copernican revolution in philosophy. We have seen, however, that for Kant the constitutive activity of the theoretical subject depends upon the original constitution of the self as practical, which follows, in turn, from the imperative of autonomy and the claim of our own higher self. Kant rationalizes the priority of autonomy; he shows how autonomy is foundational for the establishment of any ethics or value system that requires the accountability of the subject and the possibility of self-determination. Even so, Nietzsche vehemently rejects the metaphysical model that Kant uses, since it figures sovereignty in terms of the purely rational self that commands its own phenomenal counterpart. And while Hegel and others would draw our attention to the emptiness of this legislation by reason, I have suggested that Nietzsche's critique is really a critique from within. It accepts the priority of sovereignty, but challenges Kant's rational model of autonomy as one that testifies to whatever is universal and necessary and so finally *ignores* the individual as such. All of Nietzsche's critical comments on Kant bring us back, then, to the absolute singularity of the individual existence and the need to remain true to this sovereignty. And the latter is thus revisioned as a goal that must be evoked, even if it can never be prescribed.

Finally, Schopenhauer views life as meaningless, and he never ceases to call individual existence absurd. But his absolute nihilism cannot be maintained, as the individual is ultimately charged with self-affirmation in the need to deal with this miserable situation. In Schopenhauer, the individual is both an integral part of nature and the means of nature's salvation from itself. Nietzsche condemns Schopenhauer's pessimism as just another form of nihilism, and he attacks the will-lessness that such a position seems to endorse. On the other hand, his whole philosophy continues Schopenhauer's attempt to figure the place and the value of the individual vis-à-vis the cosmos as a whole; and he shows how sovereignty can also follow from the provocation of the abyss and the effective transfiguration of all the horrors of life.

We might say that Nietzsche's encounter with St. Paul underlies the "cultural" and historical dimension of his philosophy of sovereignty. His encounter with Kant clarifies his insistence upon the absolutely irreducible character of individual existence. And his encounter with Schopenhauer helps to illuminate the relation between the individual and the cosmos itself. Obviously, there are many other "influences" to be reckoned with, but in terms of the issue of sovereignty that I want to address, this is the philosophical genealogy that illuminates the thinking of Nietzsche.

We can now turn to Nietzsche's own philosophy of sovereignty; first, as this develops in *The Birth of Tragedy* and the original posing of the problem; then in the so-called scientific writings, in which he completes his disavowal of traditional philosophy and its inherent idealism; and then in *Thus Spoke Zarathustra*, in which a positive sense of his own philosophical mission first becomes clear. In this regard, the next three chapters will correspond to the three stages of Nietzsche's own metamorphosis. After this, the two chapters on his later writings will come to grips with his mature discussion of sovereignty and prepare us for a discussion of Nietzsche's relevance today.

3 ❖

The Individual and the Birth of Tragedy

<hr>

Tragedy lies at the very core of the Greek experience, for tragedy seems to condense and epitomize the spirit of ancient Greece. Thus, in order to understand the Greeks, let alone to appropriate their greatness, it is first of all necessary to understand the mechanism of tragedy and how it empowered Athenian culture. In *The Birth of Tragedy,* Nietzsche reconstructs the history of Greek tragedy and shows how it emerged from the creative tension of the Apollinian and Dionysian art impulses. Beginning with the earliest "age of the Titans," Nietzsche describes how each of these impulses gained ascendancy in turn, until the decisive moment of their unity was achieved in tragedy, when "Dionysus speaks the language of Apollo; and Apollo, finally the language of Dionysus; and so the highest goal . . . of all art is attained" (*BT* sec. 21). Nietzsche goes on to discuss the breakdown of tragedy, and the abandonment of tragic wisdom, which he associates with the triumph of Socrates and the "theoretical" perspective. Finally, in the latter half of *The Birth of Tragedy,* he continues his genealogy of art into the present. He claims that in modern opera, where the Dionysian and Apollinian tendencies have never been more absent, the possibility of a reversal has suddenly appeared. So now we may contemplate the *rebirth* of tragedy from out of German music, and specifically through the operas of Wagner.

When Nietzsche first published *The Birth of Tragedy* in 1872 it was greeted with much critical contempt and disappointment. From a scholarly perspective, Nietzsche is absolutely right to call this an "impossible" book, "very convinced and therefore disdainful of proof, mistrustful even of the *propriety* of proof," and "a book for initiates" (*BT* "Attempt at a Self-Criticism" sec. 3). With its concern for the origin of tragedy, the place of the chorus, or the development of Greek mythology, *The Birth of Tragedy* certainly appears to be a typical exercise in philology. But it must also be said that Nietzsche *uses* all of the procedures of traditional scholarship and the investigation of the past in order to *provoke* the present and to invoke a particular vision of the future. Nietzsche writes at a spiritual crossroads, whose possibilities suggest either the resurgence of tragic wisdom or the continuation of decline. Thus his final goal in *The Birth of Tragedy* is not to recover the past or to justify a particular reading of the origin of tragedy itself. In fact, he claims that the meaning of the past can only be appropriated by the one who uses it to promote a certain vision of the future; and for the purposes of "life," history must be read as an oracle that illuminates the way forward. "When the past speaks it always speaks as an oracle," he comments in the later essay on history, and "only if you are an architect of the future and know the present will you understand it" (*UM* II sec. 6).

In this respect, Nietzsche's entire discussion of Dionysus, Apollo, and Socrates suggests a new genealogy and a different perspective on the triumph of contemporary scientific culture, one that successfully challenges the fixed horizons of our thought. For he realized that we must first pass beyond the essential optimism and self-satisfaction of our own culture if we are ever to recollect the possibility of a deeper "tragic wisdom." Nietzsche claims that every society requires a set of unifying myths, a site of the sacred, which forms the framework for all self-understanding and creative activity. "Only a horizon defined by myths completes and unifies a whole cultural movement," he writes, and, "Myth alone saves all the powers of the imagination and of the Apollinian dream from their aimless wanderings" (*BT* sec. 23). In *The Birth of Tragedy* he accordingly provides us with a new mythological perspective on Socrates and scientific reason, which we can neither completely affirm nor reject. For as our own rational-scientific culture is breaking down, we are fast reaching the point at which we must accept the impenetrable depth of things. This means that when instrumental reason has reached its limits, the return of tragic wisdom will finally become possible; and Nietzsche's perspective justifies itself in provoking the future that it describes.

Thus, I think it is important to remember that Nietzsche's discussion and diagnosis of modern culture may still be valid, even though he later rejected Wagner as a universal panacea and condemned his own longing for "metaphysical comfort" as the very worst kind of escapism. Likewise, Nietzsche's analysis of tragedy remains relevant, even if contemporary scholars are divided over the historical accuracy of his basic claims.[1] At its deepest level, *The Birth of Tragedy* is concerned with the spiritual health of the culture as a whole. But more significantly for us, *The Birth of Tragedy* also suggests a preliminary philosophical account of the sovereign individual, in the experience of the spectator of tragedy who is transformed by the energies of Apollo and Dionysus.

Admittedly, Nietzsche's reflections upon the individual are not completely worked through in *The Birth of Tragedy* itself; and it must be allowed that in one respect he explicitly celebrates tragedy because it affirms the *overcoming* of the ordinary individual self. But at the same time he also comments at several points in *The Birth of Tragedy* that life is eternally justified as an "aesthetic phenomenon" and that "we have our highest dignity in our significance as works of art" (*BT* sec. 5). This distinguishes the life of the individual and it requires us to scrutinize the relation between the individual and the forms of the dominant culture. In this chapter, I want to suggest that Nietzsche's discussion of tragedy—as the highest form of art—suggests a corresponding model of individual sovereignty, as the highest project of the individual life. In effect, the dynamics of the Apollinian and the Dionysian inaugurate Nietzsche's philosophical reflection upon the individual. And since the latter *includes* the moment of self-dispossession, it can be argued that his account testifies to the priority of the individual life while it also implies a rejection of all selfish or one-sided forms of individual*ism*.

At a couple of significant places in *The Birth of Tragedy* Nietzsche relies upon the critique of Kant and Schopenhauer to suggest that modern theoretical culture has reached its limits, where logic "coils up . . . and bites its own tail" (*BT* sec. 15). Schopenhauer's influence on Nietzsche's work is especially obvious when Nietzsche uses Schopenhauerian language to describe the Dionysian heart of the world as a region of "primordial suffering," which is transfigured by the Apollinian order of appearances. It must be emphasized, however, that in *The Birth of Tragedy* Nietzsche marks his absolute difference from previous philosophical positions. First, his repeated claim that life is only justified as an aesthetic phenomenon stands in strict opposition to Kant, for whom the only justification is a *moral* justification and for whom the essential task of life is to act as an embodiment of moral law. Nietzsche argues that art, and not morality, is the highest metaphysical activity, which is to say that individuals do not achieve their highest fulfillment as the expression of an impersonal principle, but only insofar as their existence is itself a unique and unrepeatable work of art. Similarly, as we have seen, even though Nietzsche uses a Schopenhauerian vocabulary to develop his insights, his final position is completely opposed to Schopenhauer's *explicit* pessimism and life denial. For Nietzsche, the individual achieves the transfiguration of nature. Likewise, in opposition to Schopenhauer, Nietzsche's Dionysian is not "the bottom line," but a point of departure that is itself transformed, from terrible to benign, in the actual movement of *The Birth of Tragedy*.

Nietzsche's most obvious intention in *The Birth of Tragedy* is to prepare and legitimate the rebirth of the spirit of tragedy from out of German music. After reconstructing his basic strategy and argument, however, I will show that behind this explicit purpose there is an implicit conception of the individual that inspires and directs much of his later thinking, though it finds its first, elliptical expression in *The Birth of Tragedy*. The discussion of the individual in *The Birth of Tragedy* will help us to understand the problematic basis of Nietzsche's mature philosophical position, one essential aspect of which is his proximity and distance from his philosophical predecessors, Schopenhauer and Kant. Finally, I want to suggest that Nietzsche's account of the individual, and his understanding of the power of art, is profoundly relevant to anyone who is concerned with the anonymous character of human existence in contemporary society, and its frequent development into selfish individualism.

٭

According to Nietzsche, Dionysus and Apollo are the two artistic powers that continually incite each other and ultimately give rise to tragedy. They are also symbolic representations of nature itself, insofar as they express the infinite productivity of life and the stability of enduring forms.

In Greek mythology, Dionysus is associated with the primordial energies of nature, and so he is present at every moment of frenzy and abandon, when individuals lose themselves in the rapture of dispossession. Thus he is the god of drunkenness and sexual passion, for it is precisely in such experiences that the stable and substantial self is shattered by natural impulses that overwhelm it. Dionysus is the name for that explosive surge that destroys the conventional boundaries between individuals and between the individual and the rest of nature. Speaking of the early Dionysian festivals, for example, Nietzsche writes that, "in nearly every case these festivals centered in extravagant sexual licentiousness, whose waves overwhelmed all family life and its venerable traditions" (*BT* sec. 2). Such an experience is terrifying, since it represents the collapse of every ordinary project and value and the destruction of individual control; and yet, it is also liberating and empowering, since it returns the individual to the primordial energies of nature and the sheer creativity of life. As Nietzsche comments: "I believe the Greek man of culture felt himself nullified in the presence of the satyric culture; and this is the most immediate effect of the Dionysian tragedy, that the state and society and, quite generally the gulfs between man and man give way to an overwhelming feeling of unity leading back to the very heart of nature" (*BT* sec. 7).

With regard to Apollo, who comes later and who temporarily fixes the Dionysian flux, Dionysus therefore has a certain priority. He is the truth of our condition; he is the underlying movement of life that drives and supports all of our individual projects and goals, before life itself finally destroys us in its relentless creation and destruction of forms. But this is not to say that the

Dionysian represents a noumenal realm that lies beyond all appearances.[2] Nietzsche's examples of the Dionysian phenomenon—the Babylonian Sacaea, the St. Vitus dancers of the Middle Ages, or the Greek worshipers of Bacchus—are all drawn from *within* historical experience and do not point toward some "other" realm of being.

Instead, it would be better to say that the *original* Dionysian impulse in *The Birth of Tragedy* is simply a provisional starting point and a convenient philosophical fiction that allows us to follow a particular development from this point. "Under the charm of the Dionysian," Nietzsche writes,

> not only is the union between man and man reaffirmed, but nature which has become alienated, hostile, or subjugated, celebrates once more her reconciliation with her lost son, man. Freely, earth proffers her gifts, and peacefully the beasts of prey of the rocks and desert approach. The chariot of Dionysus is covered with flowers and garlands; panthers and tigers walk under its yoke. Transform Beethoven's "Hymn to Joy" into a painting; let your imagination conceive the multitudes bowing to the dust, awestruck—then you will approach the Dionysian. Now the slave is a free man; now all the rigid, hostile barriers that necessity, caprice, or "impudent convention" have fixed between man and man are broken. Now, with the gospel of universal harmony, each one feels himself not only united, reconciled, and fused with his neighbor, but as one with him, as if the veil of *māyā* had been torn aside and were now merely fluttering in tatters before the mysterious primordial unity. (*BT* sec. 1)

In this very lyrical passage, the "Dionysian" seems to signify the point at which life achieves its own celebration. In fact, we could say that for Nietzsche the Dionysian realm is the realm of the *sacred*. For it is the creative and empowering dimension of life, which we briefly glimpse in sex, drunkenness, even terror, and every time we lose possession of ourselves and our self-regarding concerns. And it is this that is both threatening and reassuring, like Dionysus himself. It is threatening because it illuminates the insubstantial character of all our selfish projects; and it is reassuring because it allows us to experience a more basic *community* with everything that is.

In a later passage, Nietzsche comments further on this experience of participation and community that lies at the heart of the Dionysian ecstasy. "We are really for a brief moment," he writes,

> primordial being itself, feeling its raging desire for existence and joy in existence; the struggle, the pain, the destruction of phenomena, now appear necessary to us, in view of the excess of countless forms of existence which force and push one another into life, in view of the exuberant fertility of the universal will. We are pierced by the maddening sting of these pains just when we have become, as it were, one with the infinite primordial joy in existence, and when we anticipate,

in Dionysian ecstasy, the indestructibility and eternity of this joy. In spite of fear and pity, we are the happy living beings, not as individuals, but as the *one* living being, with whose creative joy we are united. (*BT* sec. 17)

Dionysus is the sacrificial victim who was torn apart by the Maenads; and now he demands *our* sacrifice—which means the destruction of every particular interest and personal goal—as a condition for entering the realm of the sacred in which we can become attuned to the absolute power of nature. In this respect, the Dionysian ecstasy is a joyful, though mediated, anticipation of our own death, when "the spell of individuation" will be broken. We might call this"joyful," but it is also terrifying, for from the ordinary perspective it portends the absolute oblivion of all that we hold most dear.[3]

By contrast, Nietzsche describes Apollo as the principle of measured harmony and form, and "the god of individuals and just boundaries" (*BT* sec. 9). Whereas drunkenness seems to epitomize the Dionysian experience, Nietzsche suggests that the essential Apollinian activity is that of dreaming. "The beautiful illusion of the dream worlds," he writes, "in the creation of which every man is truly an artist, is the prerequisite of all plastic art, and, as we shall see, of an important part of poetry also. In our dreams we delight in the immediate understanding of figures; all forms speak to us; there is nothing unimportant or superfluous" (*BT* sec. 1). In dreaming it is possible to delight in the pure forms of appearance without the intrusion of our everyday investment in these forms. Likewise, the Apollinian releases us from the craving of our everyday desires and interests by endowing ordinary reality with the illusion—or the image—of the beautiful appearance. In this way, Apollo transfigures the horror of the Dionysian. Through beauty he makes life bearable, and he offers us a calm detachment from the ordinary struggles of life. "And so in one sense," we are told,

> we might apply to Apollo the words of Schopenhauer when he speaks of the man wrapped in the veil of *māyā*: "Just as in a stormy sea that, unbounded in all directions, raises and drops mountainous waves, howling, a sailor sits in a boat and trusts in his frail bark: so in the midst of a world of torments the individual human being sits quietly, supported by and trusting in the *principium individuationis*." In fact, we might say of Apollo that in him the unshaken faith in this *principium* and the calm repose of the man wrapped up in it receive their most sublime expression; and we might call Apollo himself the glorious divine image of the *principium individuationis*, through whose gestures and eyes all the joy and wisdom of "illusion," together with its beauty, speak to us. (*BT* sec. 1)

If there is a sense, then, in which, from the Dionysian perspective, individuals are only an illusion, through the magic of Apollo individuals are able to maintain themselves as separate beings against the flux of becoming. In creating themselves they create a perspective that was not simply given and that recreates the world as a realm of significance and beauty. Along these lines, Nietzsche comments that the Delphic imperatives, "Know Thyself" and "Nothing in excess," are really strategies for self-cultivation and self-refinement that hold the Dionysian at bay.

Apollo is the power that overcomes the horror of life and the suffering of Dionysus. But he does not achieve this victory by turning away from life: he faces it, he overcomes it, and he transfigures it through art and beauty. This is what Nietzsche describes in his discussion of Raphael's "Transfiguration":

> Here we have presented, in the most sublime artistic symbolism, that Apollinian world of beauty and its substratum, the terrible wisdom of Silenus; and intuitively we comprehend their necessary interdependence. Apollo, however, again appears to us as the apotheosis of the *principium individuationis,* in which alone is consummated the perpetually attained goal of the primal unity, its redemption through mere appearance. With his sublime gestures he shows us how necessary is the entire world of suffering, that by means of it the individual may be impelled to realize the redeeming vision, and then, sunk in contemplation of it, sit quietly in his tossing bark, amid the waves. (*BT* sec. 4)

Thus, even though Apollo is the principle of harmony and beauty, Nietzsche clearly insists that neither Apollo nor Dionysus represents the highest moment of art. In fact, Dionysus and Apollo implicate each other; for just as Dionysus is the precondition for Apollo, without whom the Apollinian realm would not be necessary, so Apollo represents the necessary fulfillment and transfiguration of the Dionysian horror. Following the details of Nietzsche's own history, Apollo and Dionysus continually supersede each other until Greek tragedy finally emerges as the *unity* of the two. And *this* is the highest form of art, which also provides us with a model for understanding the highest form of the individual life.

The Birth of Tragedy thus elaborates a mythical genealogy that justifies Greek tragedy as the highest unity of Apollinian and Dionysian art impulses. According to Nietzsche, it is only in the dramas of Aeschylus or Sophocles that the orgiastic music of Dionysus achieves a stable relationship with the measured harmonies of Apollo. Tragedy is the greatest art because it presents the truth of Dionysus and all the suffering of the world within the Apollinian frame of the tragic drama. Through the destruction of the tragic hero the individual spectators can experience a brief moment of ecstasy in anticipation of their own destruction and return to the Dionysian order. In effect, they are allowed to participate in the sacred. But they are also saved from destruction by Apollo and the framework of the drama itself. And so they return to their own life, charged and enthused by what they have experienced.

To continue this story, Nietzsche argues that such an ideal synthesis was eventually shattered by the rationalist probings of thinkers like Euripides and Socrates, who appeared to believe that in order to be beautiful something had to be *intelligible*. He claims that they could not grasp the true meaning or the pathos of tragedy because they remained blind to everything that was not conceptually appropriable. Euripides placed a prologue at the start of his plays so that the audience could grasp the explicit reasons for the action and suffering of his characters. He was apparently disturbed by the unreasonable sufferings of the older dramas and felt that he had to explain and justify everything that he portrayed. Thus his own presentation of tragic wisdom took second place to the psychological realism of character and the details of the plot.

Socrates, however, is the real focus of Nietzsche's attack, and he quickly emerges as the paradigm figure of such a rationalist tendency. "Our whole modern world," Nietzsche writes, "is entangled in the net of Alexandrian culture. It proposes as its ideal the theoretical man equipped with the greatest forces of knowledge, and laboring in the service of science, whose archetype and progenitor is Socrates. All our educational methods originally have this idea in view: every other form of existence must struggle on laboriously beside it, as something tolerated but not intended" (*BT* sec. 18). Socrates stands condemned because he himself condemned tragic art and could not grasp the significance of the Dionysian wisdom, which runs deeper than any theoretical categories or the projections of the "subject." In fact, he revalued tragedy and condemned it as either dangerous or irrelevant.

> To Socrates it seemed that tragic art did not even "tell the truth"; moreover, it addressed itself to "those who are not very bright," not to the philosopher: a twofold reason for shunning it. Like Plato, he reckoned it among the flattering arts which portray only the agreeable, not the useful; and therefore he required of his disciples abstinence and strict separation from such unphilosophical attractions— with such success that the youthful tragic poet Plato first burned his poems that he might become a student of Socrates. (*BT* sec. 14).

Socrates is the one who condemned art as a deception and finally abandoned it. Because of his criticism, Nietzsche explains, art, even the tragic art, is now regarded as little more than a "tinkling of bells" or a holiday from life. Socrates is thus the villain in this story, for even if he was able to save our intellectual culture, he also sacrificed the power of art and the tragic experience of life to the shallow optimism of reason.[4] But the latter is not just another way of dealing with the Dionysian flux. Unlike Apollo, "Socrates" does not look into the horror and seek to transfigure it. In fact, he is bound to deny that there is a sacred dimension of experience that goes beyond the everyday; and he ignores all the depth of the world in his attempt to achieve a rational appropriation of it.

The critical debates over Nietzsche's readings of Sophocles, Aeschylus, Socrates, and Euripides will doubtless continue, but it is the broader perspective that concerns us here. "Socrates," who condemns what he could not understand, is the symbolic representative of our own scientific culture. From his perspective, the triumph of Dionysus is just an illicit release of emotions that must be ignored, or condemned as a mendacious fantasy. Following this, all poetry is just an "imitation of an imitation" and hence twice removed from reality itself. In our own culture this same Socratic spirit has inspired a philosophy of mastery and technique that *still* leads us to believe that reason can order everything in terms of its own reflective categories; or to think that one day we may build a machine that can fully reproduce the functioning of the human mind. In effect, we also possess "the unshakeable faith that thought, using the thread of causality, can penetrate the deepest abysses of being" (*BT* sec. 15); so that in this respect, Nietzsche's critique still concerns us.

In fact, the situation of our own time closely resembles what Nietzsche perceived in 1872. After two world wars, the Holocaust, and many other horrors, our absolute faith in an instrumental or "pure" reason can no longer be maintained. And along with the triumph of our rational scientific culture we have also experienced the loss of the sacred and the complete commodification of every aspect of life. "Let us think of a culture that has no fixed and sacred primordial site," Nietzsche writes, "but is doomed to exhaust all possibilities and to nourish itself wretchedly on all other cultures—there we have the present age, the result of that Socratism which is bent on the destruction of myth. And now the mythless man stands eternally hungry, surrounded by all past ages, and digs and grubs for roots, even if he has to dig for them among the remotest antiquities" (*BT* sec. 23). In *The Birth of Tragedy,* Nietzsche's task is certainly not to provide us with a ready-made mythology but to force us to recognize the limitations of our rationalist perspective and the need for alternative ways of thinking. We must have art, he says, lest we perish of "the truth." And even if we have now become more aware of the failure of instrumental reason, "Socrates" is still the paradigm of *our* scientific ideal, and he is also the guiding spirit of our decline, with respect to the most complete oblivion of all tragic wisdom. Nietzsche believed that he was living at a decisive turning point in world history, and in *The Birth of Tragedy* he engages himself in the struggle by depicting the imminent collapse of the Socratic world view. But this is meant to direct our attention toward whatever could take its place.

In the later sections of *The Birth of Tragedy,* Nietzsche claims that the optimistic rationalism of science and philosophy has already been called into question by the critical labors of thinkers like Schopenhauer and Kant. He argues that as scientists and scholars begin to recognize the subjective limitations of all their knowledge, the Socratic objective of a total explanation—and hence a justification of the world—will become increasingly problematic. Along with this theoretical culmination, however, Nietzsche also claims that a similar revolution is threatening society at large. The optimistic ideals of "Socratic Christianity"—equal rights for all, the dignity of labor, and so on—are now filtering down to direct the social and political demands of the lower classes. The "slaves," whose labor has supported the leisure of scholars and their whole Alexandrian culture will soon demand that their miserable existence be put right. And so, he claims we must be drifting toward a "dreadful destruction," for "there is nothing more terrible than a class of barbaric slaves who have learned to regard their own existence as an injustice, and now prepare to avenge, not only themselves but all generations" (*BT* sec. 18).

Thus, Nietzsche seeks to persuade us that Socratic optimism has already sown the seeds of its own destruction, and he argues that such an ending must be devastating since it leaves us without any ruling value or myth that might *encourage* the striving of the individual life in the absence of the Socratic framework. For as scientific rationality, this framework has always affirmed itself as *the* truth of Western culture, and it has marginalized or rejected everything that was "other" to it.

Finally, at the end of *The Birth of Tragedy* Nietzsche directs our attention toward Wagner, for he claims that Wagner's music achieves the same celebration of existence that recollects the spirit of tragedy. "Yes, my friends, believe with me in Dionysian life and the rebirth of tragedy. The age of the Socratic man is over; put on wreaths of ivy, put the thyrsus into your hand, and do not be surprised when tigers and panthers lie down, fawning at your feet. Only dare to be tragic men for you are to be redeemed. You shall accompany the Dionysian pageant from India to Greece. Prepare yourselves for hard strife, but believe in the miracles of your god" (*BT* sec. 20). And so he finishes with high rhetoric and the language of redemption that he was later to disavow.

So much, then, for Nietzsche's explicit argument and rhetorical strategy in *The Birth of Tragedy.* Sometimes, in fact, the tension between his argument and his rhetorical presentation serves to call into question the absolute status of his own specific claims. Nietzsche valorizes tragedy as the highest form of art, and yet, it has been argued that *The Birth of Tragedy,* with all its diversions and rhetorical interludes, is actually much closer in form to the Florentine opera that he condemns.[5] It is also important to remember that Nietzsche soon rejected his more excessive claims, condemning the teleological movement of Apollo and Dionysus as "offensively Hegelian," while denying the possibility of Wagnerian redemption as so much romantic nonsense.[6] But even if Nietzsche's historical and scholarly assertions in *The Birth of Tragedy* can now be discounted, in line with his own rhetorical strategy it would still be true to say that in the very progress of this history, and especially in the discussion of tragedy itself, there remains a particular vision of individual existence that he valued and that he hoped would be stimulated by the resurgence of German music. I have already suggested that such an ideal remains compelling, whatever we may think of Nietzsche as a cultural historian or as a "prophet" of the modern age. And I shall therefore move to Nietzsche's account of the individual against the background of his "artist's metaphysics," first by showing his movement beyond Schopenhauer, and then by attending to the details of tragic empowerment itself.

∾

In his later "Attempt at a Self-Criticism," Nietzsche condemns the Kantian and Schopenhauerian formulations in which his early ideas had been expressed: "How I regret now that in those days I still lacked the courage (or immodesty?) to permit myself in every way an individual language of my own for such individual views and hazards" (*BT* "Attempt at a Self-Criticism" sec. 6). Later though, in his final comments on *The Birth of Tragedy* in *Ecce Homo,* he claims that "the cadaverous perfume of Schopenhauer sticks only to a few formulas." At first glance, this seems to be a deliberate underestimation of Schopenhauer's influence. For quite apart from Nietzsche's language and philosophical formulas, the contrast between the primordial heart of being and the illusory realm of individuation appears crucial to each of these thinkers. Both are in essential agreement that life is birth, suffering, and death, and that ultimately there is nothing outside of this life, no final hereafter that could redeem this life or make it comprehensible. Nietzsche speaks darkly of "the veil of *māyā*" and he seems to rely especially on Schopenhauer's theory of music as the direct representation of the one primordial will. In his virulent contempt for the individual, Schopenhauer had written that "Every individual, every human apparition and its course of life, is only one more short dream of the endless spirit of nature, of the persistent will-to-live, is only one more fleeting form, playfully sketched by it on its infinite page, space and time; it is allowed to exist for a short while that is infinitesimal compared with these, and is then effaced, to make new room" (*WWR* 1:322). It is difficult to believe that such passages do not inform Nietzsche's discussion, for sometimes the very words he uses echo Schopenhauerian formulations. Thus, "We may assume that we are merely images and artistic projections for the true author," Nietzsche writes, "while of course our consciousness of our own significance hardly differs from that which the soldiers painted on canvas have of the battle represented on it" (*BT* sec. 5).[7] From this it could be argued that Nietzsche's later rejection of Schopenhauer derives from an anxiety of influence and his desire to distinguish himself from the one whose thought was closest to him. But I think this is wrong, and we can learn a lot by clarifying the real distance that separates their thinking.

In his later preface to *The Birth of Tragedy,* Nietzsche insists upon the absolute difference between the pessimism of the strong and the pessimism of the weak. "You will guess where the big question mark concerning the value of existence had thus been raised," he writes. "Is pessimism *necessarily* a sign of decline, decay, degeneration, weary and weak instincts . . . ? Is there a pessimism of *strength?* An intellectual predilection for the hard, gruesome, evil, problematic aspect of existence, prompted by well-being, by overflowing health, by the *fullness* of existence?" (*BT* "Attempt at a Self-Criticism" sec. 1). He argues that both kinds of pessimism agree as to the basic "facts" of human existence, but he also claims that the former, which is essentially modern and Schopenhauerian leads only to a desire for oblivion and individual self-denial; while in Greek tragedy the pessimism of the strong inspires the transfiguration of existence and the celebration of individual life. We can now see how this illuminates the difference between Schopenhauer and Nietzsche.

For Schopenhauer, as we have seen, the basic reality of the world is the one primordial "will," which objectifies itself in the individual forms of existence, though it remains doomed to continual dissatisfaction since its striving is forever blind and without any final issue. Through acting and willing we may experience the reality of this primordial will; while the misery and dissatisfaction of human existence follows necessarily from the will's unquenchable thirst. Like Schopenhauer, Nietzsche is also a "pessimist" insofar as he refuses to consider "otherworldly hopes," and condemns the modern optimism of science that treats suffering, both spiritual and physical, as if it were an objection to existence and something that must simply be removed. At the same time, however, Nietzsche's pessimism in *The Birth of Tragedy* is also heuristic. Let us assume the very worst, he is saying, that life in its most basic aspect is terrible and without any purpose or goal—even then, as the Greeks discovered, it may be transfigured through the power of art, or the basic energies of nature itself, so as to be absolutely valuable and worth living. Later, Nietzsche was to comment that judgments on the value of life, whether for it or against it, can never be true, for since we are all interested parties, such judgments can only tell us something about the one who makes them. In this context, then, it is not the theoretical *interpretation* of life that distinguishes Schopenhauer from the Greeks, for in this they are agreed; of much more significance is their final *evaluation* of life, which is symptomatic of their underlying spiritual health.

In most of his later writings, Nietzsche argues that the history of Western metaphysics, beginning with Plato, represents a devaluation of *this* world in favor of a higher realm of Being. For Nietzsche, the final effect of this devaluation is, however, to condemn this life and all our worldly purposes as nugatory by comparison. And this leads him to use the name of "Schopenhauer" for the whole tendency of *nihilism* and *will-lessness* that is inherent in Western thinking. As he comments in the following fragment, which is included in *The Will to Power:* "*Schopenhauer's* basic misunderstanding of the *will* . . . is typical: lowering the value of the will to the point of making a real mistake. Also hatred against willing; attempt to see something higher, indeed that which is higher and valuable, in willing no more, in 'being a subject *without* aim and purpose' (in the 'pure subject free of will')" (*WTP* sec. 84). The valorization of such complete will-lessness represents the total suppression of the individual as such; and it is precisely this general perspective on life that Nietzsche's account of the individual and sovereignty attempts to overcome.

It is important to remember, then, that Nietzsche incorporates Schopenhauer's pessimistic outlook on the value of human existence within *The Birth of Tragedy*. For the teaching of Schopenhauer is actually equivalent to the Dionysian wisdom of Silenus, which is the earliest "folk wisdom" recounted in the text. "There is an ancient story," he writes

> that King Midas hunted in the forest a long time for the wise Silenus, the companion of Dionysus, without capturing him. When Silenus at last fell into his hands, the king asked what was the best and most desirable of all things for man. Fixed and immovable, the demigod said not a word, till at last, urged by the king, he gave a shrill laugh and broke out into these words: "Oh, wretched ephemeral race, children of chance and misery, why do you compel me to tell you what it would be most expedient for you not to hear? What is best of all is utterly beyond your reach: not to be born, not to *be*, to be *nothing*. But the second best for you is—to die soon." (*BT* sec. 3)

Such a position invites an obvious comparison with Schopenhauer, who says that "the shortness of life, so often lamented, may perhaps be the very best thing about it" (*WWR* 1:325). But it is also clear that in *The Birth of Tragedy* this same position is quickly transcended. Nietzsche argues that an Apollinian culture emerges as the counter-thrust to the word of Silenus; and with the creation of the Homeric heroes and the artist's glorification of the eternal Olympians, life itself is transfigured. In this way, the wisdom of Silenus is superseded by the affirmation of Apollo, who uses the radiance of beautiful forms in order to seduce us into existence. "So that now," Nietzsche concludes, "reversing the wisdom of Silenus, we might say of the Greeks that to die soon is worst of all for them, the next worst to die at all." Exactly parallel to this, in writing *The Birth of Tragedy,* Nietzsche seeks to reverse Schopenhauer's perspective through the performance of his own text. For insofar as it is a celebration of the individual and sovereignty, *The Birth of Tragedy* actively engages and dissolves the lived experience of this "gloomy" pessimism and denial of life.

Nietzsche must separate Schopenhauer from the Dionysian wisdom that he recalls. For the latter is not a fixed theoretical perspective, but a profound experience of continuity and participation that cannot simply be described. In Schopenhauer, the basic categories of existence are immutable and suppression of the will is the only way of accommodation. But Nietzsche's thought attends to the movement of these categories—the Dionysian evokes the Apollinian and the two powers confront and augment each other at various levels. In this way, something new is continually created, which forces us to revalue the "original" Dionysian given. Indeed, as this "life" continually enhances itself it provides us with a model of sovereignty for the individual self.

Since Nietzsche describes Apollo as the very "apotheosis" of individuation, we might now expect that Nietzsche's vision of the individual life, its authentic nature and highest truth, would in some way follow from the portrait of the god that he provides us with. We are told, for example, that Apollo is the god of measured harmony, beauty, and form, and since his products are said to have the power of redeeming or transfiguring life, we might want to reason by analogy that the individual who lives a "beautiful" existence also justifies life by the perfect harmony of their every action, decision, and goal. Thus it might seem to follow that we are called upon to live our life as if it were a work of art, and while this may seem difficult in the extreme, it is apparently what Nietzsche has in mind when he writes that "it is only as an *aesthetic phenomenon* that existence and the world are eternally *justified*" (*BT* sec. 5). In the face of such a comparison, however, some very difficult questions arise—for exactly what *kind* of art work is the individual life, and how are we to evaluate it or determine its basic nature? And is it really the case that Nietzsche's celebration of art is finally just a form of aestheticism that calls for self-refinement and taste?[8]

Perhaps another perspective will help us. In his later essay on "Schopenhauer as Educator," Nietzsche argues that it is the supreme task of every culture to create the conditions that would be most favorable for the existence of "redemptive individuals." He says, "It is the fundamental idea of *culture*, insofar as it sets for each one of us but one task: *to promote the production of the philosopher, the artist and the saint within us and without us and thereby to work at the perfecting of nature*" (*UM* III sec. 5). And if we now take this as our guiding clue, we would of course expect that the highest form of individual existence must be associated with the highest form of culture. This means that the wisdom of Apollo, the summons to a beautiful existence, will continue to remain valid, but the most perspicuous vision of the individual must *now* be related to the tragic culture of fifth-century Greece. For it appears that such a culture goes beyond the purely Apollinian by yoking together the truth and the power of both Apollo and Dionysus. In short, we may now turn to Nietzsche's discussion of Greek tragedy as the apex of Greek culture, in order to illuminate the nature of the individual existence that is supposed to be empowered by it. His account of Greek tragedy, whether it is historically correct or not, allows us to approach his own emerging meditation on sovereignty; and it suggests the outline of that "ideal" that he had hoped for in Wagner, and that leads him later to the concept of the overman or the thought of eternal recurrence.

❧

In the central sections of *The Birth of Tragedy*, Nietzsche emphasizes that according to all historical research, the chorus is the original element of Greek tragedy from which everything else is derived. So that, far from being an authorial device—as the representation of the ideal spectator or the boundary of an ideal realm—the tragic chorus is actually the heart of Greek tragedy, which means that any discussion of the latter must accordingly start with it. According to Nietzsche, the prototype of the tragic chorus was the chorus of satyrs, "a chorus of natural beings who live ineradicably, as it were, behind all civilization and remain eternally the same, despite the changes of generations and of the history of nations" (*BT* sec. 7). Thus in the early festivals of Dionysus, the original "chorus" was composed of the frenzied votaries of the god, who had for the moment lost all sense of individual identity, rank, or distinction, and who felt themselves to be empowered by the instinctual forces of nature. Nietzsche now argues, however, that in tragedy the Dionysian excitement of the chorus gets communicated to all the spectators through the power of dithyrambic music. This intensifies the experience of the spectator and finally transforms the latter into one of the actual celebrants. "In the dithyramb," he writes, "we confront a community of unconscious actors who consider themselves and one another transformed. . . . In this magic transformation the Dionysian reveler sees himself as a satyr, *and as a satyr, in turn, he sees the god,* which means that in his metamorphosis he beholds another vision outside himself, as the Apollinian complement of his own state. With this new vision the drama is complete" (*BT* sec. 8). Because there was no distinction in the Greek theater between the place of the chorus and that of the audience, the ordinary spectator would come to share in this Dionysian transformation. And so he or she would experience the same rapturous vision of nature that underlies the pain of individuation.

It must be remembered, though, that Attic tragedy, at least according to Nietzsche, was not simply a more controlled enactment of the Dionysian festival. In the passage quoted above, Nietzsche emphasizes that tragedy is only completed through the mediation of myth, as the representation of Dionysian truth in the forms of Apollo. "The *tragic myth,*" he says later, "is to be understood only as a symbolization of Dionysian wisdom through Apollinian artifices" (*BT* sec. 22). This means that in tragedy life is not avoided but seen for what it is; though at the same time, it is also transfigured through the lens of the tragic hero. In effect, the tragic hero demonstrates the possibility of overcoming life's nausea and consecrates himself as a triumphant expression of nature. Yes, the hero must still suffer—for this is the truth of Dionysus that is now represented within the dramatic form—but the image of the hero, rather than acting as a remote but beautiful appearance, now charges our own life by showing us the essential truth about it: "it presents images of life to us, and incites us to comprehend in thought the core of life they contain" (*BT* sec. 21).

We have said that the Dionysian element of tragedy is that which questions and dissolves the fixed boundaries between individuals and between the individual and nature. In this way it achieves an intensification of existence, as the individual now feels reunited with the primitive energies of nature and experiences a participation in the sacred. In the tragic drama itself, this Dionysian wisdom is then reflected in the fate of the tragic hero, who as Oedipus or Prometheus or Hercules, is always a Dionysian figure who has transgressed the proper forms and limits that have been set by Apollo. He must be punished, and Nietzsche argues that in his fall the spectator of tragedy experiences a strange ecstasy, since the destruction of the hero suggests the final redemption of *all* individuality in "an augury of restored oneness." Without the restraining hand of Apollo, the release of such energies would probably lead to complete chaos and the utter breakdown of individual life, as in Nietzsche's account of the barbarian Saceae, or the folk epidemics of the Middle Ages, when people danced themselves into total self-abandon. But in the special case of tragedy Apollo preserves the individual spectator *as* an individual while allowing the latter to participate in the Dionysian ecstasy that accompanies the hero's destruction. "With the immense impact of the image, the concept, the ethical teaching, and the sympathetic emotion," Nietzsche comments,

> the Apollinian tears man from his orgiastic self-annihilation and blinds him to the universality of the Dionysian process, deluding him into the belief that he is seeing a single image of the world . . . and that, *through music,* he is merely supposed to see it still better and more profoundly. What can the healing magic of Apollo not accomplish when it can even create the illusion that the Dionysian is really in the service of the Apollinian and capable of enhancing its effects—as if music were essentially the art of presenting an Apollinian content? (*BT* sec. 21)

In this way, individuals are empowered: for while they are saved from dissolution by Apollo, they are able to share in the energies of Dionysus without experiencing the constraint of ordinary conventions and forms. This is the only proper relationship between Apollo and Dionysus, in which both powers elicit and oppose each other. It frames the individual life between the two axes of self-abandonment and self-appropriation and suggests an ideal of sovereignty in the very power that maintains the tension between them.

Through the spectacle of destruction and death, tragedy undermines the stability of the subject and challenges the fixity of every selfish determination. But by granting the individual access to the underlying Dionysian impulse, tragedy also promotes a fundamental attunement with nature and the sacred region of experience that is usually hidden. Using the terms of Nietzsche's later discussion, this encounter allows the individual to take charge of existence and to become what he or she is. Viewed in this way, tragedy is a mechanism that effects the continual enhancement of the individual will. In fact, it provokes a "will to will"; for in this movement of self-dispossession, openness, and self-appropriation, the will achieves its own sovereignty. Thus, "sovereignty" describes the empowerment of the individual self. While in later writings, the same movement also serves as the basis for Nietzsche's account of the "will to power" as the principle of all life.

This discussion remains fragmentary, but at least we can now specify the essential moments of sovereignty in terms of Apollo and Dionysus and the creative tension between them. Likewise, we can also illuminate this general schema by considering two possibilities that would have to be excluded. First, even though Nietzsche describes Apollo as the apotheosis of individuation, it follows that any *purely* Apollinian individuals would be completely fixed subjects who maintain and preserve their identity through the strictest self-discipline. Given the Apollinian demand for self-definition and self-knowledge, such individuals could only understand themselves as the product of various codifications—of class, race, gender, nation, and so on—and they would regard these determinations as absolutely valid and as the constituents of their own proper selfhood.[9] Such Apollinian individuals would be "subjects" in the fullest sense, for while they sustained a political tradition and a culture, their individual nature would be completely fixed by the tradition that supported them. In *Ecce Homo,* Nietzsche describes this imperative of self-definition as "a recipe for ruin"; and it is a paradoxical model, since it suggests that what is most essential to the individual are precisely those determinations that he or she shares with all the others. But sovereignty begins at the moment when these determinations are challenged; and "sovereign individuals" only exist insofar as they elude the system of codifications that order us in advance.

By the same token, the purely Dionysian individual would also fall short of Nietzsche's ideal; although it is not even clear that such an individual, who is totally removed from all codes and boundaries, could really be a distinct "person" at all. Nietzsche argues this point in all of his early writings, when one of his deepest concerns is to delineate the relationship between individuals and their culture. In the second "Untimely Meditation," for example, the question is not *whether,* but *how much* of a historical tradition do we need in order to enhance the individual life. "And this is a universal law," he writes, "a living thing can be healthy, strong and fruitful only when bounded by a horizon; if it is incapable of drawing a horizon around itself, and at the same time too self-centered to enclose its own view within that of another, it will pine away slowly or hasten to its timely end" (*UM* II sec. 1). It is absurd, then, to suppose that Nietzsche believed in the sudden explosion of "genius" as a totally spontaneous phenomenon and in defiance of every tradition. Such Dionysian individuality would simply be chaotic and self-destructive. In *The Birth of Tragedy* Nietzsche comments specifically on the exhaustion that a culture suffers if the Dionysian element is unconstrained. He also argues that if the Apollinian form of Socratic rationalism had *not* triumphed in Greece, then this whole civilization would probably have destroyed itself in anarchy and chaos. Now that Socratic rationalism is breaking down, Nietzsche fights for a culture that might inspire the return of the "tragic individual," who holds together the power of Dionysus *with* the power of Apollo.

Here we can suggest some conclusions. In *The Birth of Tragedy* the artistic impulse transfigures life; and as the highest form of art, tragedy achieves the highest transfiguration of all. The spectator of tragedy participates in the power of tragedy, and as such this "tragic individual" may serve as the type for an individual ideal. The analysis of the tragic individual suggests the outline of Nietzschean "sovereignty," according to which the highest version of individual existence expresses the continual movement of self-appropriation and empowerment that mirrors the tension between Apollo and Dionysus. Such sovereignty implies the constant overcoming of our own selfish nature, although it cannot be circumscribed as "the fulfillment of our rational part" or as anything else. For Nietzsche, sovereignty is something we can only achieve in going beyond ourselves, precisely in the going-beyond.

The tragic individual must therefore be distinguished from both the Apollinian and Dionysian types. On the one hand, Nietzsche is not advocating a Prussian doctrine of self-control or self-mastery that would fix individuals with certain determinate forms. Such individuals would be closed to new horizons and would seek to preserve themselves exactly as they were, so that their life would actually be a declining type. On the other hand, Nietzsche is not proposing a philosophy of "orgiastics." Tragic individuals must remain open to the world, but if the cultivation of experience became an end in itself they would be nothing more than the sum of these experiences. In this case, there could be no possibility of self-appropriation or sovereignty, since such individuals would be essentially passive.[10]

Except by way of negative comparison, however, it remains difficult to talk of this sovereign ideal, for even by definition such individuality continually escapes the fixity of all determinations. In the second "Untimely Meditation," Nietzsche relates the same problem when he argues that "youth," or all that is vital and living in the individual, can never be described, since its very nature is to transcend the established norms of the given:

> Its mission is to undermine the concepts this present has of "health" and "culture" and to excite mockery and hatred against these hybrid monsters of concepts; and the sign that guarantees the superior robustness of its own health shall be that this youth can itself discover no concept or slogan in the contemporary currency of words and concepts to describe its own nature, but is only aware of the existence within it of an active power that fights, excludes, and divides, and of an ever more intense feeling of life. (*UM* II sec. 10)

I suggest that in Nietzsche's later work it is the very awareness of this difficulty in communication that leads him to a deeply ironic position with respect to his own doctrines, with the overman and the eternal recurrence in some respects parodies of themselves as straightforward philosophical claims. After the *Birth of Tragedy*, Nietzsche's philosophy becomes more and more rhetorically complex. At the same time, the question of individual sovereignty remains one of his chief concerns—for both the Dionysian moment of openness to the world as well as the Apollinian moment of self-recollection are preserved as the essential moments of eternal recurrence, while they are also present in his final description of "How one becomes what one is."

In the history of modern ideas, Nietzsche has often been characterized as a rampant individualist in the very worst sense of the word.[11] So far I have suggested that Nietzsche's treatment of the individual is actually more subtle and thoughtful than such critics would allow; and in *The Birth of Tragedy* he articulates the outline of an empowering ideal that directs us toward the highest possibility of nature and art.

❧

To conclude this discussion we may finally turn to Nietzsche's *Untimely Meditations,* which were written in the years immediately following *The Birth of Tragedy.* There is no need to examine these works in great detail, for a brief account will show the continuation of Nietzsche's insistence upon the task of cultural renewal, as well as the reciprocal problem of individual sovereignty and how this is to be expressed and maintained.

Taken altogether, Nietzsche's earliest writings are devoted to a strange variety of themes: the origin of Greek tragedy is the given subject of *The Birth of Tragedy,* but then in the *Untimely Meditations* he goes on to consider the (ir)relevance of David Strauss, the relationship between history and life, Schopenhauer and the problem of education, and the cultural significance of Wagner. Despite this apparent diversity, however, it is also clear that behind these various inquiries there lies a single intense preoccupation with the "problem" of individual existence—its nature, its value, and the possibility of its justification. And while it is true that the problem of the individual is always subsumed within the broader problems of higher culture, there is also a real sense in which the individual gradually emerges over the course of these essays as a primary focus, and perhaps as the goal of culture itself.

At the beginning of "Schopenhauer as Educator," Nietzsche writes that, "In his heart every man knows quite well that, being unique, he will be in the world only once and that no imaginable chance will for a second time gather together into a unity so strangely variegated an assortment as he is." He knows it, Nietzsche comments, but he hides it out of fear of his neighbor and the desire to think and act like a member of the herd. The individual is charged with the task of sovereignty, but modern culture threatens this task and lures the individual into self-abandonment. In fact, Nietzsche claims that "the objective of all human arrangements is through distracting one's thoughts to cease *to be aware* of life" (*UM* III sec. 4). This suggests that even within the *Untimely Meditations* the problem of the individual is completely bound up with the issue of cultural renewal, as Nietzsche recognizes that the one is the key to the other.

Following *The Birth of Tragedy*, Nietzsche argues that the exceptional individual achieves the only redemption or transfiguration of nature; only now his real despair over the state of contemporary culture leads him to view the relationship between individuals and their culture as oppositional rather than reciprocal in form. The normative task of culture is to promote the production of "true human beings," but as he argues in "Schopenhauer as Educator," the *"misemployed and appropriated* culture" that prevails today has other ends and only educates everyone "in such a way that they can employ the degree of knowledge and learning of which they are capable for the accumulation of the greatest possible amount of happiness and profit" (*UM* III sec. 6). As a sign of this, Nietzsche argues that any philosophy worth its name should continually call the individual to task and challenge the validity of everything that exists. In our age, however, philosophy disturbs no one, for it has been appropriated by the state and its supporting "culture." "Our academic thinkers are not dangerous," Nietzsche writes, "for their thoughts grow as peacefully out of tradition as any tree ever bore its apples: they cause no alarm, they remove nothing from its hinges; and of all their art and aims there could be said what Diogenes said when someone praised a philosopher in his presence: 'How can he be considered great, since he has been a philosopher for so long and has never yet *disturbed* anybody?' " (*UM* III sec. 8).

At this point, then, it is not very difficult to apprehend the basic continuity in Nietzsche's earliest writings. After *The Birth of Tragedy*, and its celebration of Attic culture for its empowerment of the individual life, the critique of David Strauss is really a critique of modern culture, which does nothing to enhance the "spirit" of human existence. Specifically, Nietzsche argues that contemporary Germany has brought about the triumph of the "cultural philistine." As a result, the same cultural life that should promote individual striving has become nothing more than entertainment and a relief from the more "serious" business of life, such as family, profession, and civic responsibility.

The essay on history also describes the suppression of the individual that has been perpetrated in the name of its modern counterpart. For Nietzsche claims that the emergence of a responsible and free subject has actually achieved the most complete disindividuation of "man." "While the 'free personality' has never before been commended so volubly," he comments, "there are no personalities to be seen, let alone free personalities—nothing but anxiously muffled up identical people. Individuality has withdrawn within: from without it has become invisible; a fact which leads one to ask whether indeed there could be causes without effects" (*UM* II sec. 5). In this essay Nietzsche suggests a way of dealing with history in order to go beyond it; to destroy the domination of the past by forgetting it, incorporating it, and redeeming it within the horizon of the individual life. He argues that for the sake of the individual, the task of the true thinker is thus to articulate the most trenchant critique of modern education and culture. "He who wants . . . to shatter this education," he writes, "has to help youth to speak out, he has to light the path their unconscious resistance has hitherto taken with the radiance of concepts and transform it to a conscious and loudly vocal awareness" (*UM* II sec. 10). Here, however, he is obviously writing about himself and the meaning of his own philosophical mission.

I have argued how it is significant that the summons to individual existence is most forcefully expressed in "Schopenhauer as Educator," which Nietzsche later described as his most personal work. We are alive, and we find ourselves commanded to take command, to seize hold of our existence and to redeem it from the mindless accident of chance. Later he adds, "There exists in the world a single path along which no one can go except you: Whither does it lead? Do not ask, go along it" (*UM* III sec. 1). For Nietzsche, the self can only justify itself by refusing all ease and contentment and willing its own higher law. Following Kant, this suggests an ideal of sovereignty that is absolutely prior to all particular moral valuations: "the free man can be good or evil but the unfree man is a disgrace to nature and is excluded from both heavenly and earthly solace" (*UM* IV sec. 11). The problem, as Nietzsche saw it in the *Untimely Meditations,* was that such a freedom must presuppose a tremendous effort of individual will, since all of our social arrangements— culture, public opinion, the educational system, even the study of history and philosophy—are directed toward the suppression of the individual and the creation of the "subject" as the efficient tool of the state. The urgency of this situation now leads Nietzsche to condemn all of the present arrangements of society, including contemporary moral ideals. For regardless of their particular "justice," these are precisely the forms in which individuals must lose themselves as individuals and allow the opinions and even the worthiest goals of the herd to deflect them from their own proper task. And so, for the sake of the individual, living within a moribund culture, the "authentic" philosopher must now become the most malicious critic of everything previously considered "decent." He or she will necessarily be "untimely," for the task of philosophy is to educate us against our age.

Throughout "Schopenhauer as Educator" Nietzsche links the singular existence of the individual to the project of sovereignty. He argues that sovereignty is not a final achievement or goal, but, exactly as in *The Birth of Tragedy*, a continual movement of self-overcoming that has to be demonstrated over and over again. "It is only an illusion that a spirit can be free and independent," he writes, "if this achieved sovereignty—which is at bottom creative sovereignty over oneself—is not demonstrated anew from morn till night through every glance and every gesture" (*UM* III sec. 3). From such a perspective, Kant's submissiveness, and his cautious attitude toward the state and authority in general, offers a striking contrast to Schopenhauer, whose own life is presented here as the very expression of his antagonistic philosophy. "Kant clung to his university," Nietzsche writes, "submitted himself to its regulations, retained the appearance of religious beliefs, endured to live among colleagues and students: so it is natural that his example has produced above all university professors and professorial philosophy." Schopenhauer, on the other hand, "had little patience with the scholarly castes, separated himself from them, strove to be independent of state and society—this is his example, the model he provides—to begin with the most superficial things" (*UM* III sec. 3). We should beware of taking such comments at face value. But what is important here is that through his discussion of his own relation to Schopenhauer, and the "true" philosopher's oppositional relation to society, Nietzsche is able to offer us a strategy for self-recollection that may be more generally valid.

Finally, even though the last meditation is basically a panegyric on Wagner, it is clear that for Nietzsche "Wagner" is the epitome of the higher individual whose existence is supposed to transfigure the world. By relating Wagner's personal history, Nietzsche demonstrates how one becomes what one is, how the discovery and devotion to the "inner law" of one's being achieves a higher form of "naiveté," which is in total opposition to the distraction and dispersion of the modern personality. As Nietzsche comments, "No one is any longer capable of revealing himself, of speaking naively, and few are capable of preserving their individuality at all" (*UM* IV sec. 5). In this essay he therefore upholds Wagner as the symbolic possibility of individual renewal.

In *The Birth of Tragedy*, Apollo and Dionysus serve as the two great axes that allow us to understand what it means to be an individual. In this context, the "tragic individual"—or the individual empowered by tragedy—emerges as a sovereign ideal. Nietzsche, however, does not prescribe any particular content: the tragic individual is not an ideal model that is to be slavishly followed; it merely describes the general framework of the soul that corresponds to the greatness of Athenian culture. In the *Untimely Medita-tions* Nietzsche also proposes several ideal "types" that help to orient our understanding of the individual ideal, most notably through the discussion of philosopher, artist, and saint in "Schopenhauer as Educator," or the cele-bration of "Wagner" in the final essay. "Who are they who lift us?" Nietzsche asks, which is as much as to ask, Who are the ones who provoke us into sov-ereignty? He answers, "They are those true *men, those who are no longer an-imal*, the philosophers, artists, and saints." "It is the fundamental idea of *cul-ture*," he adds, "*to promote the production of the philosopher, the artist, and the saint within us and without us and thereby to work at the perfecting of nature*" (*UM* III sec. 5).[12] It is important to notice, however, that in the *Untimely Meditations* these ideal types are only very broadly sketched. This is because the individual as such is precisely that which cannot be prescribed or legis-lated in advance.

By definition, the individual is that which cannot be repeated or recon-stituted within thought. The individual as an individual necessarily escapes all conceptual appropriation. Thus the provocation of individual sovereignty, the very task that Nietzsche sets for himself as an educator, must refuse ev-ery explicit model that would only constrain and confine the individual life. In this respect, Nietzsche's use of "masks"—Dionysus, "Wagner," "the phi-losopher," "artist," and "saint"—is significant, insofar as it suggests his own increasing awareness of the problematic nature of his task. For the mask is a *type* of existence: it expressly conceals the individual by dwelling on those features that can be shared in common. Thus, we may add, it serves as a "neg-ative indication" that recalls us *to* the individual precisely insofar as it points us away.[13] In Nietzsche, nothing is ever easy or straightforward, and such levels of rhetorical and philosophical complexity will only increase as we turn to his later writings.

4 ❧

Against Idealism

In *The Birth of Tragedy*, Nietzsche suggests an account of individual sovereignty and empowerment that can be abstracted from the immediate context of tragedy and Athenian culture in general. But there is still a strong sense in which the "tragic individual" that he describes can only achieve a proper fulfillment within the structure of community itself. In the first part of Nietzsche's book, the Athenian citizen experiences Apollo and Dionysus through the *public* spectacle of the drama; while in the second part, our own culture, inspired and directed by the music of Wagner, now promises a spiritual renewal as the condition for individual sovereignty. All of which suggests that in *The Birth of Tragedy*, individuals are nothing apart from the culture in which they are embedded.

In Nietzsche's later writings, there is thus a considerable shift in emphasis, as he begins to envision the individual in strict opposition to the community itself. Zarathustra, for example, is deeply suspicious of every kind of community and condemns the state, neighbor-love, and "others" in general as the greatest possible threat. In order to preserve the goal of sovereignty, individuals must withdraw into their "loneliest loneliness" and question everything that attaches them to "the herd." Throughout his work, Nietzsche condemns all mass movements as forms of stupidity and self-abandon. But the deeper question is whether this *also* entails a final verdict against any form of human solidarity, where association with the other is always seen as contaminating and detrimental to the individual task.[1]

The apparent change in Nietzsche's position may simply relate to his own growing despair about contemporary society. For once he had abandoned his "faith" in Wagner, he soon realized that the contemporary forms of "nihilism" were nothing but the final consequence of the Christian-moral value standard that had ruled for the past two thousand years. And so he had nothing to expect from his own culture, except the final apocalypse that might overwhelm it and force this nihilism beyond itself. In effect, if the goal of sovereignty was to succeed, it would have to succeed *in spite of* the age.

This suggests, however, that there may be some more strategic reasons for Nietzsche's disavowal of community. In the *Untimely Meditations*, Nietzsche proclaims the need to disengage individuals from every institution or social form that could possibly ensnare them and take them from themselves. As we have seen, his criticisms of contemporary values are suspicious and even malicious, for in this way he makes the confrontation the most profound and unavoidable. In the so-called scientific works that now follow, *Human, All Too Human* and its sequels, *Daybreak* and *The Gay Science,* Nietzsche follows through on this project by launching an attack against all the prejudices of art and religion, morality and philosophy. In these works he also challenges every received idea and every romantic notion about the self, including the dogmas of free will and personal responsibility. In the end, however, this movement takes him *beyond* all negation and critique. For after the destruction or the deconstruction of freedom, the self, truth, art, religion, and metaphysics, the "free spirit" remains as a final goal and as an "end-in-itself." In effect, the ideal of sovereignty survives the malicious, scientific critique, and so comes to dominate the later phase of Nietzsche's writing.

Nietzsche is never in any doubt that sovereignty is an achievement of society itself. It is not an innate possibility that suddenly emerges without any history, but the outcome of a millennia of social training, and a historically determined result. In the scientific writings he insists that the free spirit is a pure "surplus," or a supplement that can only appear once the "common" forms of knowledge and morality, and even language, have been surpassed. On the other hand, Nietzsche also recognizes that *contemporary* society is sick and can no longer be relied upon to provide a framework for individual fulfillment. Thus in *Human, All Too Human,* he argues that the educational system is typical of the forms of modern life insofar as it transforms the individual into a docile and obedient "subject" who will then be useful to its class. "The environment in which he is educated seeks to make every man unfree, inasmuch as it presents to him the smallest range of possibilities," he argues. "The individual is treated by his educators as though, granted he is something new, what he ought to become is a *repetition* . . . by placing itself on the side of the fettered spirits the child first proclaims its awakening sense of community; it is on the basis of this sense of community, however, that it will later be useful to its state or its class" (*HH* I sec. 228). Similarly, it is this perspective that allows Nietzsche to distinguish between different levels of activity and to condemn the laziness of those who are usually considered the most "active." "Active men are generally wanting in the higher activity"; and he explains, "I mean that of the individual. They are active as officials, businessmen, scholars, that is to say as generic creatures, but not as distinct individual and unique human beings; in this regard they are lazy" (*HH* I sec. 283).

Nietzsche's persistent defense of "egoism" in both *Daybreak* and *The Gay Science* now becomes coherent and even necessary once we recall that there is a tremendous difference between the generic individual of modern society—who is determined as a subject and cleaves to the distinctions of country, class, race, and gender—and the sovereign individual or the "tragic individual" that we described above. The sovereign individual remains open for continual empowerment; and the willing of such an individual is not limited to the attempt to preserve and control, either self or others. We might say that egoism in the first sense involves an abandonment to ordinary visions and goals; whereas egoism in the latter sense remains the most difficult thing of all. "Whatever they may think and say about their 'egoism,'" he argues in *Daybreak,*

> the great majority nonetheless do nothing for their ego their whole life long: what they do is done for the phantom of their ego which has formed itself into the heads of those around them and has been communicated to them;—as a consequence they all of them dwell in a fog of impersonal, semi-personal opinions, and arbitrary, as it were poetical evaluations, the one for ever in the head of someone else, and the head of this someone else again in the heads of others: a strange world of phantasms—which at the same time knows how to put on so sober an appearance! . . . all these people, unknown to themselves, believe in the bloodless abstraction "man," that is to say in a fiction. . . . No individual . . . is capable of setting up a real ego, accessible to him and fathomed by him, in opposition to the general pale fiction and thereby annihilating it. (*D* sec. 105)

Thus, even if in one sense sovereignty *is* a social achievement, insofar as it presupposes the existence of a community, the project of sovereignty is in no way dependent upon "others," or the ordinary determinations and goals of the subject. The will must learn to will itself again and this means that it must be provoked and forced to will itself in defiance of everything that could lure it into self-denial. This means that Nietzsche's project is neither "social" nor "antisocial" but actually "Socratic" in nature; for it interpellates the individual within the existing cultural context, although it is not empowered by the vision of a new community, or by nostalgia for a "true" self that present society has somehow repressed. Following this reading, his critique of society is primarily strategic. The project of sovereignty is driven by an astonishment with the individual existence, which exists both as a given and as a goal that must be continually achieved. Nietzsche's task is to force this singularity to manifest and appropriate itself.

In his "scientific works," Nietzsche condemns every idealism of thought, including the doctrine of free will that seems to subtend the traditional ideal of autonomy. On the other hand, he consistently maintains his ideal of the free spirit as one who is both independent and sovereign. In this chapter, I want to question whether such a paradox can ever be resolved. I will also trace the transformation of Nietzsche's avowal of science into "gay science," and the emergence of the death of God as the new focus of his thinking.

⚓

In the very first aphorism of *Human, All Too Human*, Nietzsche announces a new "chemistry" of concepts and sentiments, which he will use to demystify all of our moral, religious, and aesthetic experience in the suspicion of the scientific gaze. "All we require," he writes, "and what can be given us only now the individual sciences have attained their present level, is a *chemistry* of the moral, religious and aesthetic conceptions and sensations, likewise of all the agitations we experience within ourselves in cultural and social intercourse, and indeed even when we are alone" (*HH* I sec. 1). Here Nietzsche's perspective is one of rigorous materialism, as he seeks to uncover the physiological or psychological basis of our most exalted beliefs. Thus he argues that every vision and rapture of the saint derives from a familiar form of illness, and he suggests that even Socrates' *daimonion* may have been nothing but a disease of the ear; he claims that art relies upon feelings and moods that originate from religion, and he speculates that the decline of religion must also involve the end of art.[2] Even logic is not exempt from Nietzsche's critique, as he suggests that all of our thinking follows from the original error of confusing similar things and experiences as identical, and that what we now call the world is only "the outcome of a host of errors and fantasies which have gradually arisen and grown entwined with one another in the course of the overall evolution of the organic being, and are now inherited by us as the accumulated treasure of the entire past" (*HH* I sec. 16).

Such arguments and speculations are quite interesting, but it would be foolish to suggest that they are in every case decisive. The point, however, is that Nietzsche does not *have* to provide a single alternative explanation for the illusions of morality, religion, and art. His task is simply to undermine the "faith" of the reader, and he achieves this goal of disengagement just as soon as he unsettles the ruling beliefs by whatever means he can. Thus in *Human, All Too Human*, Nietzsche condemns metaphysics as something invented to satisfy a human need, and he looks forward to a truly liberating "philosophical science," which instead of satisfying this need would expose it for what it is. In the same text, however, he also speculates that the metaphysical world has its origin in the second world of dreams, for without the latter there would never have been any impetus to divide the world in the way that we do.[3] The two suggestions are not wholly consistent with each other; but Nietzsche's goal is simply to overwhelm belief through the accumulation of hypotheses like these. In a later aphorism, he makes this strategy explicit: "A *multiplicity* of hypotheses, for example as to the origin of the bad conscience, suffices still in our time to lift from the soul the shadow that so easily arises from a laborious pondering over a single hypothesis which, being the only one visible, is a hundredfold overrated" (*HH* III sec. 7). This is the principle of Nietzsche's philosophical critique and it helps us to understand all of the writings that follow.

In the "scientific works," the most frequent target of Nietzsche's attack is the concept of free will. According to Nietzsche, this concept is the most fundamental error that denies the rule of nature and allows us to project ourselves as the "solution to the cosmic riddle." Once again, he uses several different lines of argument, but in the end these may be reduced to two. First, he argues that free will is an imaginary cause that follows from an erroneous way of thinking; and second, he argues that free will is a political construction, which is either a projection of the strength of the powerful or a form of domination and control that justifies punishment and maintains the accountability of all who are subject to order.

In the first part of *Human, All Too Human*, for example, Nietzsche comments extensively on the logic of dreams and how a real event, such as a noise from outside, can be incorporated into a dream as something that is apparently conditioned and even anticipated by the events of that dream: "that is to say, [the dreamer] accounts for the sound in terms of the dream, so that he *believes* he experiences the cause of the sound first, then the sound itself" (*HH* I sec. 13). He then claims, quite cogently, that in all likelihood this logic of dreaming more closely resembles the thinking of our earliest ancestors than modern conceptual thought; so that later, he can argue that "free will" is also derived from our primitive (and suspect) need to assign an imaginary cause for whatever has happened to us. In aphorism eighteen, for instance, Nietzsche speculates that the error of free will arises from the upsurge of particular desires and needs. But since the latter can only appear as separate and isolated events, we have invented a "will" that is responsible for them, so that we can then maintain the fiction of a continuous and conscious self. What we fail to grasp is that these desires and needs are simply the deeper goals of the body itself. "We are hungry," Nietzsche writes, "but originally we do not think that the organism wants to sustain itself."

In later passages, Nietzsche considers the legitimacy of punishment, and he reminds us that we hold people responsible because we think that they could have done otherwise. But if someone does something that is morally senseless and unreasonable, are we then to admit that they are responsible for their own lack of good sense and reason? Or if we say that they acted out of their own free will, wouldn't this signify that they acted without reason, for the *free* will is by definition unconstrained by anything in advance? Accordingly, such "free" actions cannot even be understood, and their justification or punishment is entirely inappropriate. "The offender certainly preferred the worse reasons to the better," Nietzsche writes, "but *without* reason or intention: he certainly failed to employ his intelligence, but not *for the purpose* of not employing it. The presupposition that for an offense to be punishable its perpetrator must have intentionally acted contrary to his intelligence—it is precisely this presupposition which is annulled by the assumption of 'free will.' You adherents of the theory of free will have no right to punish, your own principles deny you that right!" (*HH* III sec. 23). Through points like these, Nietzsche attempts a complete *reductio ad absurdum* of the concept of free will; and such arguments and suggestions must be answered by anyone who continues to believe in a faculty of freedom.

And yet, Nietzsche was quite aware that in spite of his critique the idea of free will would remain our deepest illusion and the hardest thing to overcome within ourselves. In the following passage, for instance, he condemns the doctrine of individual responsibility as a "myth," and he argues that it has to be rejected if we are ever to move beyond ourselves, to a new innocence and a new wisdom on life.

> *Unaccountability and innocence.*—The complete unaccountability of man for his actions and his nature is the bitterest draught the man of knowledge has to swallow if he has been accustomed to seeing in accountability and duty the patent of his humanity. All his evaluations, all his feelings of respect and antipathy have thereby become disvalued and false: his profoundest sentiment, which he accorded to the sufferer, the hero, rested upon an error; he may no longer praise, no longer censure, for it is absurd to praise and censure nature and necessity. . . . the chemical process and the strife of the elements, the torment of the sick man who yearns for an end to his sickness, are as little merits as are those states of distress and psychic convulsions which arise when we are torn back and forth by conflicting motives until we finally choose the most powerful of them—as we put it (in truth, however, until the most powerful motive chooses us). But all these motives, whatever exalted names we may give them, have grown up out of the same roots as those we believe evilly poisoned; between good and evil actions there is no difference in kind, but at the most one of degree. (*HH* I sec. 107)

But what exactly does Nietzsche intend by such an assault? Is there any further purpose to his critique of established ideas, or does all of this destruction simply exist for the sake of destruction itself? If we take this passage seriously, then skepticism concerning free will apparently implies that we can no longer praise or blame anything; for if everything is determined, then nothing merits a higher value than anything else. This suggests a complete relativism and an active denial of the significance of individual sovereignty. Nietzsche concludes this passage, however, by suggesting that even if the progress we make by overthrowing traditional ideas like freedom is very painful, this is only a "birth pang" through which we may finally emerge from our cocoons to be "blinded and confused by the unfamiliar light" that is nothing other than "the realm of *freedom* itself." With a similar intention, Nietzsche subtitles *Human, All Too Human* as "A Book for Free Spirits"; for by means of this work and its successors, he seeks to carry us beyond every romantic illusion and conventional idea to a position of absolute transcendence and freedom—in the sense of freedom from established values and thus freedom from "freedom" itself. It remains to be seen whether this entails a contradiction.

In a later preface to *Human, All Too Human,* Nietzsche considers the destructive arrows of his own free spirit as the necessary first stage of self-overcoming and renewal. In this regard, he says that all these critical interventions manifest the will to *free* will, for they are attempts to disengage the self from all of the common ideas and prejudices that normally weigh it down, so as to provoke the birth of something greater. In looking back, this free spirit now recognizes the goal of self-appropriation as the single guiding project of life—although the individual can still only describe it with the language of personal destiny. "'What has happened to me,' he says to himself, 'must happen to everyone in whom a *task* wants to become incarnate and "come into the world."' The secret force and necessity of this task will rule among and in the individual facets of his destiny like an unconscious pregnancy—long before he has caught sight of this task itself or knows its name. Our vocation commands and disposes of us even when we do not yet know it; it is the future that regulates our today" (*HH* I Preface sec. 7). In this passage the project of individual sovereignty is not described in the traditional terms of subjective decision and will. It is not a willful self-assertion on Nietzsche's part or a subjective achievement of self-mastery, but an outcome, and a result that he is bound to accomplish. The image of pregnancy, we might say, is an attempt to express the continuity of active and passive elements in the experience of sovereignty. "I" am not in control, in the sense that something is happening and growing inside me; but at the same time, I am not just an indifferent recipient of "destiny." By remaining open and ready for this experience, and by appropriating it as my own, I experience a reciprocal encounter with "life" that enhances my own existence. The whole of this process reflects the movement of sovereignty, for I will my own will; not in self-assertion, but insofar as I accept and appropriate what is given to me.

In one of the final sections of *Daybreak* this compelling image of a spiritual pregnancy reappears; and once again it is worth quoting this passage at length. "Everything is veiled," Nietzsche writes, and

> ominous, we know nothing of what is taking place, we wait and try to be *ready*. At the same time, a pure and purifying feeling of profound irresponsibility reigns in us almost like that of the auditor before the curtain has gone up—*it* is growing, *it* is coming to light: *we* have no right to determine either its value or the hour of its coming. All the influence we can assert lies in keeping it safe. "What is growing here is something greater than we are" is our most secret hope: we prepare everything for it so that it may come happily into the world: not only everything that may prove useful to it but also the joyfulness and laurel wreaths of our soul. It is in this *state of consecration* that one should live! It is a state one can live in! And if what is expected is an idea, a deed—towards every bringing forth we have essentially no other relationship than that of pregnancy and ought to blow to the winds all presumptuous talk of "willing" and "creating." This is *ideal selfishness:* continually to watch over and care for and to keep our soul still, so that our fruitfulness shall *come to a happy fulfillment!* Thus, as intermediaries, we watch over and care for to the *benefit of all.* (*D* sec. 552)

Here we have another denial of willing and creating, while at the same time the possibility of an "ideal selfishness" is accorded the highest esteem. Once again, this is a paradoxical suggestion, for the denial of willing devalues the individual as the self-determining origin of value, while the affirmation of "selfishness" seems to reinstate the priority of the individual in a higher form. But if Nietzsche rejects the doctrine of free will, then how can he celebrate the sovereign individual, or "the free spirit," as the highest goal, when, at least in its traditional sense, autonomy is nothing other than the fulfillment of freedom?

In the free spirit trilogy of *Human, All Too Human, Daybreak,* and *The Gay Science* that we are presently concerned with, the freedom of the free spirit is apparently affirmed at the same time as the faculty of free will is consistently denied. Certainly, some of the paradox is dispelled once we remember that for Nietzsche, the so-called free will is an erroneous implication of the powerful will, which experiences its own superiority; and it may be that Nietzsche intends the free will in this "erroneous" sense. But there is still a real tension here, for the powerful or strong will is a will capable of commanding itself, giving style to itself, and achieving sovereignty. Having freed itself from religion, art, morality, and philosophy, the free spirit is now ready to create itself without reference to any ordinary ideals. But *if* such a task is possible, it seems to entail the final reinscription of an authentic freedom, and self-determination, at the heart of nature itself. Can there be any reconciliation between these two sides?

In fact, the image of pregnancy, or being pregnant with one's own task and destiny is a preliminary attempt to think beyond this dichotomy, for it announces that while selfhood is given to one it must be cultivated and nourished by the one who receives it as a gift. The self, it appears, is not a personal achievement, for that would make it an impossible *causa sui*. But this does not mean that there is nothing to be done, or that every outcome is settled in advance; and in the free spirit trilogy of works, Nietzsche apparently views his task as one of spiritual midwifery, forcing the free spirit to become what it is and allowing individuals to follow their own rule.

At this point, then, there are perhaps three possible ways of understanding Nietzsche's basic response to the problem of sovereignty and freedom. First, we could insist that since everything is circumscribed by nature and necessity, the sovereign individual is not *really* free in any strong and original sense. Sovereignty is a product and an outcome of history; and while it may still be possible, and important, to celebrate the sovereign individual from an aesthetic perspective—as the highest (art) work of nature— such self-legislation is *finally* determined by something else. To admit any kind of freedom, even of a very limited kind, would be to go beyond nature and destroy the rule of necessity that Nietzsche seems to accept. Second, though, we could argue that since the sovereign individual does seem to be a genuine ideal in Nietzsche, the former *is,* in effect, the point at which nature opens and overcomes itself. Thus freedom is the product of necessity, and following the lead of Schopenhauer's philosophy, we would have to assert that the sovereign individual represents the transfiguration and salvation of nature from itself. For why would Nietzsche celebrate sovereignty if he thought that we simply have no choice? In the end, the imperative of sovereignty implies its possibility.[4]

There is evidence for both of these positions, which seem to be mutually exclusive. What I want to suggest, however, is that Nietzsche adopts a third *strategic* possibility that accepts at least the provisional validity of both the "cosmic" and the "human" viewpoints. The first perspective says that "everything is necessary," while the second says that the freedom of the free spirit is something that *can* be achieved. Like Apollo and Dionysus, these two perspectives continually challenge each other at different levels within Nietzsche's writing. This provides a major axis for understanding the "issue" of sovereignty; and through this conflict we are forced to experience the problem of sovereignty within ourselves. Thus sovereignty must remain problematic from a theoretical point of view; though from another, *performative* perspective, Nietzsche's encounter with sovereignty is intended to *provoke* the *very ideal* that he describes.

In *Human, All Too Human,* Nietzsche says that freedom is the goal of the free spirit; and he writes in a later preface that the "will to self-determination this will to *free* will" represents the initial victory of the free spirit over itself. "'You shall become master over yourself,'" he writes, "'master also over your virtues. Formerly *they* were your masters; but they must be only your instruments beside other instruments. You shall get control over your For and Against and learn how to display first one and then the other in accordance with your higher goal'" (*HH* I Preface sec. 6). Such "freedom" seems to exceed the established boundaries of "free will" versus "determinism," since it is both the expression of complete necessity as well as the genuine achievement of sovereign self-creation, and as such it must be celebrated. And yet, this is not simply to return to one of those romantic ideals that had previously been suspended—for the figure of the free spirit only emerges, like the certainty of the cogito, as the *result* of such a critique. In *The Gay Science,* Nietzsche adds, "One could conceive of such a pleasure and power of self-determination, such a *freedom* of the will that the spirit would take leave of all faith and every wish for certainty, being practiced in maintaining himself on insubstantial ropes and possibilities and dancing even near abysses. Such a spirit would be the *free spirit* par excellence" (*GS* sec. 347). But once again, the achievement of this free spirit is not a given, since it *presupposes* the attack on established ideals that the free spirit trilogy completes.

We should keep in mind, however, that at this point Nietzsche's free spirit is still incomplete. And it is significant that he can only describe this ideal in negative terms. The free spirit is liberated from ruling ideas and freed from all metaphysics and religion, but lacks any positive determination. In fact, all we know of the free spirit is that such an individual is of necessity isolated and remote from every community. As Nietzsche describes it, the free spirit hovers above existence, remote and unconcerned. "One lives no longer in the fetters of love and hatred," he comments,

> without yes, without no, near or far as one wishes, preferably slipping away, evading, fluttering off, gone again, again flying aloft; one is spoiled, as everyone is who has at some time seen a tremendous number of things *beneath* him—and one becomes the opposite of those who concern themselves with things which have nothing to do with them. Indeed, the free spirit henceforth has to do only with things—and how many things!—with which he is no longer *concerned.* (*HH* I Preface sec. 4)

In all these respects, then, the free spirit recalls the purely Apollinian impulse, which inhabits the serene world of the dream and remains oblivious to the everyday striving of existence. Apollo is also the apotheosis of the *principi-*

um individuationis; but as we saw in *The Birth of Tragedy,* such a principle still requires a necessary supplement in order to achieve the highest fulfillment of selfhood. Similarly, in the works we have discussed in this section, the free spirit is not a final goal but a provisional ideal; its gloomy, negative, and self-regarding aspect must be conjoined with a Dionysian philosophy of laughter—and it is this that now emerges in *The Gay Science.*

◦

The Gay Science can be read as the conclusion to a certain phase of Nietzsche's writing, for it announces itself as the last in a series "whose common goal is to erect a new image and ideal of the free spirit." In this work, the ideal of the free spirit is transformed and completed, so that what began in *Human, All Too Human* with a critique of all received ideas and values now emerges as a joyful wisdom and an affirmative celebration of laughter. In this respect, *The Gay Science* is equally important as a new beginning. All of the major themes of Nietzsche's later work are presented here, and although his explicit discussion of the death of God, the eternal recurrence, and the over-man may be brief and enigmatic, the overall context of his discussion allows us to grasp the essential continuity of these themes with the deeper avowal of sovereignty. Underlying all of these conceptual beginnings, however, is Nietzsche's commandment of strategy and style. *The Gay Science* is not just a collection of aphorisms on various topics; it is a book that operates with an intentionality all of its own, where themes build upon themes, and where the overall goal is not so much to enlighten or inform the reader, but to overwhelm and transform the reader through the provocation of the text.[5] In *The Gay Science,* the critique by science is continued and fulfilled by the critique of science, and the final result is not despair but the return of Dionysus in the total celebration of life.

In the very first aphorism of *The Gay Science,* Nietzsche declares his strategy and announces the beginning of a new philosophy of laughter. So far, he comments, the teachers of existence, the promoters of morality and religion, have always controlled our laughter, by decreeing that "There is something at which it is absolutely forbidden to laugh." And while he admits that such higher teachings may have served the ultimate preservation of the species, he suggests that in the end they will always be overwhelmed by waves of laughter, as the tragic sense of existence *must* give way to its deeper underlying comedy. Here he announces that the time has once again come to bury all these serious ideals in laughter:

> To laugh at oneself as one would have to laugh in order to laugh *out of the whole truth*—to do that even the best so far lacked sufficient sense for the truth, and the

most gifted had too little genius for that. Even laughter may yet have a future. I mean, when the proposition "the species is everything, one is always none" has become part of humanity, and this ultimate liberation and irresponsibility has become accessible to all at all times. Perhaps laughter will then have formed an alliance with wisdom, perhaps only "gay science" will then be left. (*GS* sec. 1)

Thus Nietzsche announces and justifies his own performative strategy. Reason and considered arguments will always leave the object of criticism basically unscathed, since the accepted ideal or the teaching that is in question has already helped to determine the nature and the limits of the subject who endorses it. The responsible and self-contained subject is just the counterpart of traditional values and ideals. Thus the *criticism* of these ideals must be allied to a deeper critique of the self—not a "formal" critique, which would tend, once again, to affirm what it is supposed to challenge, but a performative critique, a criticism through comedy and parody, which would overwhelm the ideal or the object at a deeper level than reason and also disperse the *subject* in the self-abandonment of laughter. This is not to suggest that *The Gay Science* is a book without arguments. As in the previous works, Nietzsche's arguments are always very present and compelling; but taken as a whole, this book proceeds along the performative register, where the overcoming of traditional ideals is actually inseparable from the disruption and the provocation of the reader.[6]

To understand Nietzsche's text it is therefore necessary to understand the significance of laughter and the meaning of Nietzsche's title, *The Gay Science,* or "The Joyful Wisdom." In the longer passage quoted above, Nietzsche speculates on an alliance between laughter and wisdom that would sanctify "gay science" as the only acceptable form of inquiry. In *The Gay Science* itself, he is still very much concerned with "scientific" questions of truth and validity. He continues his critique of morality, he offers an interesting account of willing and "cause and effect," and he provides sustained discussions of art, history, consciousness, and women. Despite this variety, however, two distinct yet related areas of concern tend to dominate the text. The first is Nietzsche's philosophical anthropology and his attempt to say something about the real nature of human beings without the distortions of the traditional "theological" perspective. The second is Nietzsche's radical questioning of the validity of science and even truth itself, which goes beyond anything in his earlier works. I will begin with the latter, since it will help us to understand what "gay science" means.

In fact, it is difficult to summarize Nietzsche's argument, for as a series of assaults and sallies it apparently operates on several different levels at once. In aphorism 110, for example, Nietzsche says that truth is a useful error that helped to preserve the species. In the same aphorism, however, he also claims that new thinkers have emerged who are driven by the will to truth to challenge all of the original certainties. Perhaps this means that the higher impulse for truth has itself become a life-preserving mechanism; or perhaps, as he suggests elsewhere, the will to truth is bound to call its own foundation into question and so reveals itself as an expression of the will to death. Again, in section 112, Nietzsche attacks all of our most basic concepts, such as "lines, planes, bodies, atoms, divisible time spans [and] indivisible spaces" as anthropomorphic projections. Since there is only one continuum, he insists, any attempt at knowledge becomes an arbitrary way of organizing the world by isolating aspects of existence that cannot justifiably be separated from the whole. In these passages, and in many others like them, Nietzsche is inspired by the same will to truth that directed his critique of art, metaphysics, and religion in the earlier works. Now, however, the will to truth goes even further by challenging itself; and this makes the final possibility of any *privileged* viewpoint deeply problematic.

In the final (and later) book of *The Gay Science,* such concerns come to the fore as Nietzsche argues that faith in science and the will to truth in general is actually inspired by the same *metaphysical* faith that should have been abandoned. "Even we seekers after knowledge today," he writes, "we godless anti-metaphysicians still take our fire, too, from the flame lit by a faith that is thousands of years old, that Christian faith that was also the faith of Plato, that God is the truth, that truth is divine" (*GS* sec. 344). But the critique that turns upon itself in this way cannot remain serious and out of play. It cannot retain the neutrality of method, for it must continually risk itself in order to recover itself over and over again.

This means that the science that challenges science cannot be science in any ordinary respect. Since it must contain an ironic commentary upon itself it must be a parodic science, or a gay science, which refuses all the encumbrances of "method" and every fixed presupposition. Indeed, in this respect *The Gay Science* is a work of philosophy that continually calls philosophy itself into question; although, as Nietzsche comments, the fact that it cannot take itself seriously is perhaps the mask of its own "deeper" seriousness.

In Nietzsche's later writings, his insistence upon comedy and the parodic dimension of the will to truth becomes more pronounced. Already in *The Gay Science,* however, there are many sections that explode a weighty philosophical theme in the sudden joy of laughter. This is still "science," since it is inspired by a will to truth, but it is *gay* science that declines the seriousness of any fixed perspective. One obvious example is the section on "Pessimists as victims," where Nietzsche writes about the relationship between thinking and diet:

> Wherever a deep discontent with existence becomes prevalent, it is the aftereffects of some great dietary mistake made by a whole people over a long period of time that are coming to light. Thus the *spread* of Buddhism (*not* its *origin*) depended heavily on the excessive and almost exclusive reliance of the Indians on rice which led to a general loss of vigor. Perhaps the modern European discontent is due to the fact that our forefathers were given to drinking through the entire Middle Ages, thanks to the effects on Europe of the Teutonic taste. The Middle Ages meant the alcohol poisoning of Europe.—The German discontent with life is essentially a winter sickness that is worsened by the effects of stuffy cellar air and the poison of stove fumes in German living rooms. (*GS* sec. 134)

Here Nietzsche attacks the great enemy, idealism, which ignores the most obvious physiological realities and translates a basic dissatisfaction or depression into a religious or philosophical framework. Christianity, Buddhism, or German philosophy in general may tell us that pessimism is justified since life is inherently unsatisfactory; and they will construct an entire intellectual edifice to prove their point. But all such attempts are based upon a deliberate or unconscious deception, which has to see everything in spiritual terms. Nietzsche therefore redresses the balance when he offers the materialist counterpart of such an explanation. And yet his own account is so deliberately excessive and absurd that it forces us to challenge the established opposition between these two extremes. Does one have to be either a materialist or an idealist? Or if we admit to the death of God and the complete de-deification of nature, is it not the case that all of these traditional categories must be abandoned, since they derive, either positively or negatively, from an impoverished theological view? In this passage, Nietzsche's criticism by laughter allows us to experience a perspective we might otherwise ignore.

Thus we return to the other major theme of *The Gay Science*—although I think it is clear that both the critique of truth and the project of an authentic philosophical anthropology are related consequences of a single event that is the death of God. At the beginning of the third book of *The Gay Science*, immediately after his discussion of the dead Buddha whose shadow lingered for centuries, Nietzsche asks, "When will all these shadows of God cease to darken our minds? When will we complete our de-deification of nature?" (*GS* sec. 109). Many of the sections that follow deal with the nature of humankind and are observations made in the best aphoristic tradition. The de-deification of nature involves an attempt to rethink the nature of existence without relying upon any disguised theological concepts—to think of the past, for example, without the imposition of "destiny," or any sense of purposiveness as some guiding power that goes beyond the events themselves. Likewise, the divinity of "man" must be challenged, for individual human beings do not represent the goal of nature or the final fulfillment of history. In short, the de-deification of nature requires an active forgetting of all of those concepts that formerly organized our experience in the image of God. Every concept of purpose and destiny must be rooted out and overwhelmed by laughter; while the hidden traces of God, in the concept of free will, for example, in the necessity of Christian values, and even in the sanctity of the will to truth, must be challenged and condemned. Though perhaps most important of all, the de-deification of nature also involves the end of the traditional concept of the self as a fixed and substantial unity.

We may now recall the original proclamation of the death of God, which seems to organize every other aspect of *The Gay Science:*

> *The madman.*—Have you not heard of that madman who lit a lantern in the bright morning hours, ran to the market place, and cried incessantly: "I seek God! I seek God!"—As many of those who did not believe in God were standing around just then, he provoked much laughter. Has he got lost? asked one. Did he lose his way like a child? asked another. Or is he hiding? Is he afraid of us? Has he gone on a voyage? emigrated?—Thus they yelled and laughed.
>
> The madman jumped into their midst and pierced them with his eyes. "Whither is God?" he cried; "I will tell you. *We have killed him*—you and I. All of us are his murderers. But how did we do this? How could we drink up the sea? Who gave us the sponge to wipe away the entire horizon? What were we doing when we unchained this earth from its sun? Whither is it moving now? Whither are we moving? Away from all suns? Are we not plunging continually? Backward, sideward, forward in all directions? Is there still any up or down? Are we not straying as through an infinite nothing? Do we not feel the breath of empty space? Has it not become colder? Is not night continually closing in on us? Do we not need to light lanterns in the morning? Do we hear nothing as yet of the noise of the gravediggers who are burying God? Do we smell nothing as yet of the divine decomposition? Gods, too, decompose. God is dead. God remains dead. And we have killed him.
>
> "How shall we comfort ourselves, the murderers of all murderers? What was holiest and mightiest of all that the world has yet owned has bled to death under our knives: who will wipe this blood off us? What water is there for us to clean ourselves? What festivals of atonement, what sacred games shall we have to invent? Is not the greatness of this deed too great for us? Must we ourselves not become gods simply to appear worthy of it? There has never been a greater deed; and whoever is born after us—for the sake of this deed he will belong to a higher history than all history hitherto."
>
> Here the madman fell silent and looked again at his listeners; and they, too, were silent and stared at him in astonishment. At last he threw his lantern on the ground, and it broke into pieces and went out. "I have come too early," he said then; "my time is not yet. This tremendous event is still on its way, still wander-

ing; it has not yet reached the ears of men. Lightning and thunder require time; the light of the stars requires time; deeds, though done, still require time to be seen and heard. This deed is still more distant from them than the most distant stars—*and yet they have done it themselves.*" (*GS* sec. 125)

There is a fairly standard interpretation of this passage that I will briefly repeat. The death of God, it is said, is a "cultural event." At one time in our history, God was indeed the absolute focus of all social and personal life; he was the central "sun" who served as the absolute foundation for all of our knowledge and morality. More recently, however, religious belief has declined, and even those who still accept the existence of God in a propositional sense are scarcely distinguishable from the others in terms of their actions or behavior. "God is dead" means that "God" is no longer relevant, for he no longer makes a difference; and our task is to think through all of the implications of this. The madman is not telling anyone anything new when he announces that "God is dead." Indeed, the townspeople laugh at him—"Did he get lost?; Did he lose his way like a child?"—for as atheists themselves, they think he is only repeating the obvious.

What the madman insists upon, however, are the incredible consequences of all of this. The death of God is the most momentous event in our history, because now every first principle and every foundation must be challenged and abandoned. God is himself the central sun, but in his image we have created the self, the subject, the enduring object, substance, cause, and atom as so many other substantial unities. All of these must now be called into question; and we must remain suspicious of any attempt to reinstall "God" under a different name—as humanity, for example, or the greatest happiness of the greatest number, or even as "the truth" itself—for such strategies presuppose the theological framework they are supposed to have surpassed.

Likewise, any attempt to cling to the precepts of Christian morality while abandoning belief in the Christian God becomes deeply problematic once we realize, as Nietzsche comments later in *Twilight of the Idols,* that "when one gives up the Christian faith, one pulls the right to Christian morality out from under one's feet" (*TI* "Skirmishes" sec. 5). Such a prospect finally allows us to experience what it means to stray "as through an infinite nothing." And it explains why the madman would be so obsessed with seeking God, or any secure point of reference, when thinking is no longer allowed an established point of departure. In short, the death of God requires the most complete reorientation of all our thinking. But we live in an intermediate age. The deed has been done, but the full consequences of the death of

God are yet to make themselves known: and this is why the people in the marketplace remain unconcerned.

This reading of the death of God is "correct," but it remains incomplete since it fails to emphasize the performative dimension of Nietzsche's parable, which makes it a paradigm for all of his writing. The fact is, God is dead, and *we have killed him!* And Nietzsche's parable, if not all of his work, is really an attempt to repeat this most shocking and scandalous event— which means, to empower the individual by releasing all of the energies of transgression. The important thing, then, is not to emphasize the despair that we must experience once we recognize the absence of all foundations. This is perhaps the first moment of the death of God; but even in the parable itself, Nietzsche's madman goes on to say that, "There has never been a greater deed; and whoever is born after us—for the sake of this deed he will belong to a higher history than all history hitherto"; and so despair gives place to exultation.

A little later in *The Gay Science,* Nietzsche argues for the superiority of polytheism over monotheism and suggests that the invention of gods, heroes, overmen of all kinds, undermen, dwarves, and so on, was the preliminary exercise for the justification of the egoism and sovereignty of the individual.[7] In this context, he calls monotheism "the greatest danger," for since it confines and depresses the spirit within a single narrow perspective it sanctions belief in a single normal type and so prevents the possibility of new perspectives and new creation in general. Thus the important point is that by killing God we restore the sovereignty of the individual and the sacred powers of existence that had previously been denied. In this respect, the death of God is not to be construed as a single event, whether "cultural" or otherwise. God must be killed over and over again; and we are meant to relish Nietzsche's blasphemous account of "divine decomposition" and every scandalous attack that he launches against art, religion, and morality. For these are not merely "stylistic" choices on his part, to underline or exaggerate, but attempts to repeat the death of God before our very eyes, so that we can experience the death of God and *incorporate* it—which is more than just to think about it or to have it in front of us as an interesting philosophical theme.[8]

When Nietzsche writes of the meaning of our cheerfulness, at the very beginning of book five, he actively celebrates the death of God, and he concludes that with the clearing of the horizon "all the daring of the lover of knowledge is permitted again" (*GS* sec. 343). The death of God opens up the possibility of new ways of thinking and new perspectives upon the world that were formerly impossible. It is important to emphasize, however, that if this were all, then the death of God would only be a cognitive event. And this means that we could understand it in "Apollinian" terms, as a victory for the free spirit who must now begin the task of creation and authentic understanding.

On the other hand, this would be to miss the essentially Dionysian encounter that the death of God reveals. For more than anything else, I would say that Nietzsche's parable of the death of God attempts to destroy the *traditional* domain of the sacred—the sacred as a beyond—in order to restore the sacred character of this life. Clearly, this represents a break with his earlier work. I have argued that in *Human, All Too Human* and in *Daybreak,* his stance is that of the free spirit who is solitary and "remote" from any human context of involvement. Likewise, in these earlier writings, Nietzsche uses rationalism as his philosophical compass, and following the privileged perspective of "science" he attempts a rigorous demystification of religion and life in general. With *The Gay Science,* however, the absolute privilege of science is abandoned, and in aphorisms like "The madman," and later "The greatest weight," the Dionysian element makes its reappearance as the complete celebration of life and the affirmation of its sacred character. In his next book, *Thus Spoke Zarathustra,* this return of Dionysus is even more obvious in Zarathustra's insistence upon the "deep eternity" of the world and of every moment in it. Quite apart from all the outstanding problems of knowledge, the figure of Dionysus (or Zarathustra) expresses the very intensification of existence that Nietzsche intends his writing to achieve.

All of this now brings us back to the issue of the individual self that I raised at the beginning of this section. I have argued that in serious philosophy the individual subject, or the reader, is always self-contained and out of play. The subject is thus an accomplice to the object and every other substantial unity that it apprehends. As long as the subject imagines itself as something fixed and enduring it also endorses the absolute separation of things and the stable identity of the world as a necessary reflection of its own image.

Once again, however, laughter is the key, because in laughter there is a real sense in which the self is "opened up," no longer separate and out of play, but absolutely continuous with the rest of life and with a whole community of others. Thus we say that someone "cracked up" or that they "fell apart laughing," which means that through laughter the self experiences the loss of its own self-containment and its illusory independence from everything that is. And in the context of this laughter it follows that the deepest and most urgent meaning of the death of God is the death of the self, or the end of any substantial and solitary account of the individual that traditional philosophy and "commonsense" has always presupposed. In Nietzsche's work, this opening and dispersion of the self is an enactment of the Dionysian moment that calls for our own recuperative response.

In fact, when we turn to Nietzsche's original presentation of eternal recurrence in the aphorism on "The greatest weight," we will find that a similar dialectic of selfhood prevails. "What, if some day or night," Nietzsche asks, "a demon were to steal after you into your loneliest loneliness and say to you: 'This life as you now live it and have lived it, you will have to live once more and innumerable times more; and there will be nothing new in it, but every pain and every joy and every thought and every sigh and everything unutterably small or great in your life, will have to return to you all in the same succession and sequence'" (GS sec. 341). Once again, the first response is one of complete despair; but Nietzsche adds that if this thought ever gained possession of you it would completely transform you so that your final response would be "*to crave nothing more fervently* than this eternal confirmation and seal." The intensification of the individual life is thereby transformed into the total celebration of existence for itself.

In the next chapter I will offer a sustained reading of the eternal recurrence, which is developed more completely in *Thus Spoke Zarathustra*. But for now, it can be pointed out that whenever Zarathustra encounters the thought of the eternal return, it is always accompanied by the wild laughter that shatters all things. Laughter dissolves the absolute separation between the self and the world, so that finally we are made to realize that the intensification of individual existence that the eternal recurrence seems to portend is actually inseparable from the destruction of all boundaries between self and non-self and the acceptance of oneself as a necessary piece of "fate." In this way, as I will argue later, the thought of eternal recurrence is absolutely crucial insofar as it embodies the tension between Apollo and Dionysus, and through it Nietzsche is able to reflect the most profound image of sovereignty that animates all his work.

৵

Throughout *The Gay Science*, Nietzsche writes of the "unique" and incomparable aspects of the individual self. He contrasts ordinary selfishness with a "noble" selfishness that follows the self's own law. Especially in his criticisms of Kantian autonomy, he places the highest value on self-creation and the cultivation of those virtues that would somehow express the complete singularity of the individual self. "We, however, *want to become those we are*—human beings who are new, unique, incomparable, who give themselves laws, who create themselves" (GS sec. 335). Clearly, in spite of his sustained critique of every form of idealism, Nietzsche still promotes the value of sovereignty as the highest fulfillment of the individual life. In this respect, despite all their obvious differences in style and tone, there is a profound continuity between *The Birth of Tragedy* and his other early essays and the free spirit trilogy, which culminates with *The Gay Science*.

But what exactly does it mean to be an individual? And what on earth can be said about the singular and unique? Nietzsche uses these concepts frequently enough, and the difference between the "common" and "exceptional" frames many of his discussions in *The Gay Science*. Likewise, the imperative, to become what you are, reverberates throughout this and his other early writings. But Nietzsche remains silent on what the individual is, and he refuses to legislate any specific formula that would allow us to configure the individual. Must we now conclude that "the individual" is simply an empty idea and a vapid fiction, or could there be some good reason for Nietzsche's refusal to speak?

Perhaps one thing that *has* emerged so far is that for Nietzsche, individuality is always something excessive. The individual as such is an absolute surplus, because it is that which remains after every conceptual appropriation. It is that which cannot be repeated or divided, because in every act of repetition or division the concept dissolves particularity by subsuming it under a general term. We can go even further and say that the individual is quite useless, indeed the individual is literally good for nothing, for individuality is an absolute end that cannot be justified outside itself since it exists quite apart from every calculation of utility. Philosophy, or even language in general, may never grasp the individual because the former is only concerned with whatever can be understood and held "in common" by everyone.

In section 354, in the final book of *The Gay Science*, Nietzsche argues, ahead of his time, that consciousness arises with the need for communication. Likewise, he suggests that the development of language, as a social necessity, determines the development of individual self-reflection: "It was only as a social animal that man acquired self-consciousness—which he is still in the process of doing, more and more." This means that self-consciousness is not an original and private given, the privileged origin of thought, but a relatively recent formation that is completely dependent upon the development of our social existence. Nietzsche explains:

> My idea is, as you see, that consciousness does not really belong to man's individual existence but rather to his social or herd nature; that, as follows from this, it has developed subtlety only insofar as this is required by social or herd utility. Consequently, given the best will in the world to understand ourselves as individually as possible, "to know ourselves," each of us will always succeed in becoming conscious only of what is not individual but "average." . . . whatever becomes

conscious *becomes* by the same token shallow, thin, relatively stupid, general, sign, herd signal; all becoming conscious involves a great and thorough corruption, falsification, reduction to superficialities, and generalization. (*GS* sec. 354)

Language is a falsification; whatever can be conceptually appropriated is necessarily "common" for it is what we have *in* common with everyone else. And this means that whatever is exceptional and individual must forever remain unsaid.

At this point, then, we may return to the problem raised at the beginning of this chapter, to reflect on Nietzsche's real distance from any kind of community. For if his analysis is correct, then the way to the individual can only be through the deliberate and violent rejection of everything that is grasped in common—not in order to return to a simple individualism, but in order to evoke the possibility of the individual in the moment of opposition to that which continually overwhelms it. Perhaps it follows that we cannot in principle say anything "about" the individual, even though all of Nietzsche's writing is itself an attempt to provoke it. But Nietzsche himself understood this; and in his account of the free spirit he nevertheless continues a thoughtful and sustained meditation upon the meaning of individual sovereignty, and it is to this that we must now return.

We have certainly come a long way from Kant's account of autonomy as rational self-mastery. Kant stands at the beginning of the modern age and his ideal of autonomy as self-legislation is nothing other than the defining feature of modernity itself. Now Nietzsche comes on the scene and appropriates Kant's guiding question, though out of concern for the individual as such, he shows that sovereignty must resist all conceptual appropriation. Perhaps this makes Nietzsche a more consistent thinker of autonomy than Kant, for it may be argued that if any standard is given, even if it is the standard of our own reason, then autonomy is denied as the will is forced to go outside itself in order to discover the rules for its heteronomous legislation. In Nietzsche, the goal of sovereignty implies self-appropriation, but as we have seen, it also suggests a non-appropriative mastery, and a continual self-achievement, which is linked, necessarily, to the continual rupturing of selfhood and the refusal to constrain the individual with any preestablished rule.

But what does all of this mean? Can we say anything determinate about Nietzsche's version of sovereignty, beyond the negative account of the free spirit or any other oblique promotion? Perhaps, we might reflect, the problem is not with Kant, but with the very ideal of autonomy itself, and the variations of "sovereignty" and "individuality" might be just as open to the fundamental criticism that challenges autonomy as an impossible concept or denies it as a valid philosophical ideal. Perhaps the reason why Nietzsche cannot express sovereignty is simply that there is nothing there to express!⁹

It can be argued, for example, that every attempt to isolate and define sovereignty must involve separating it from every other content, so that finally, sovereignty must be distinguished from reason, desire, tradition, the body, society, and everything else in the world. But would this not effectively destroy sovereignty as a determinate possibility? For either sovereignty is something particular, and something that actually makes a difference in the world, or else it is nugatory, the final remnant of an imperious self-legislation that no longer makes any sense. Likewise, it may be held that any ideal of autonomy rests upon an absolute distinction between the inner and the outer, for to be autonomous requires that there is something unique to one's own will that would provide the condition for an authentic self-determination, in opposition to an external or heteronomous rule.¹⁰ Is this the place for the concept of the individual? Or does this reflection upon the very problematic of sovereignty force us to abandon "the individual" as an obscure and impossible ideal?

In fact, insofar as Nietzsche has anticipated much of this, his thought already belongs to the contemporary age, which grasps autonomy as a problem. This is revealed in various contexts by his attention to style, his sense of philosophical strategy, and above all by his attempt to think by dancing, leaping over and beyond the traditional pitfalls of every discussion about the self. Likewise, Nietzsche's account of autonomy does *not* focus on the content but upon the movement that constitutes sovereignty itself. In the following chapter, we will see how his attempt to place the individual within the cosmos finally leads him to *challenge* the absolute separation between the inner and the outer. Even if for Nietzsche the opposition between freedom and necessity is necessarily "undecidable," his goal remains one of fulfilling, rather than destroying, the project of sovereignty. For whatever its ultimate origin or status, whether this is life working *through* us or the commandment of the individual will, the imperative of sovereignty remains unavoidable once it has been experienced as given. What is *not* unavoidable are the interpretations of sovereignty that have traditionally prevailed.

In the work that follows, Nietzsche reflects, through Zarathustra, on how it could ever be possible to *teach* the sovereign ideal. Thus he resumes the examination of sovereignty, whose final issue can be nothing other than the experience of sovereignty itself.

5 ❧

Zarathustra and the Teaching of Sovereignty

Nietzsche always regarded *Thus Spoke Zarathustra* as his greatest accomplishment and gift to mankind. Later, in *Ecce Homo*, he says that it is the *"deepest"* book, which was "born out of the innermost wealth of truth, an inexhaustible well to which no pail descends without coming up again filled with gold and goodness" (*EH* Preface sec. 4). *Thus Spoke Zarathustra* is also a very difficult book, however, since it operates on so many different levels at once. It is a work of philosophical poetry and a parody of religion; but it is also a transformative text, for in following Zarathustra's own philosophical progress we are likely to undergo a similar progress within ourselves.[1]

At the beginning of *Thus Spoke Zarathustra*, the true meaning of Zarathustra's mission is apparently obvious. For Zarathustra proclaims himself as the teacher of the overman, and in his very first speeches he harangues the assembled multitude with the smallness of "man" and the need to go beyond him. Now that "God is dead," and there is nothing before which we could all be equal, Zarathustra announces the overman as our new ideal. "*I teach you the overman*," he says. "Man is something that shall be overcome. . . . The overman is the meaning of the earth. Let your will say: the overman *shall be* the meaning of the earth!" (*TSZ* Prologue sec. 3). It is clear that Zarathustra never abandons this great longing. But as the story of his wanderings continues, his teaching of the overman becomes more equivocal and less direct. He soon realizes that this is not a doctrine that can be taught like any other, and he despairs that even the highest men will never grasp his proper meaning. After part one of *Zarathustra*, moreover, the exhortation to prepare a place for the overman grows less frequent, as Zarathustra becomes obsessed with another thought—the eternal recurrence—which slowly absorbs and torments him, even in his dreams. The thought of eternal recurrence dominates the rest of Zarathustra, and it is only at the very end that Zarathustra seems capable of bearing it.

Perhaps it follows that if we want to understand *Thus Spoke Zarathustra* as a unitary work, and if we want to grasp the logic that underlies Nietzsche's strange phantasmatology—of visions and riddles, dreams, songs, and festivals—we must now try to understand the fundamental connection between these leading ideas. Such a reading may appear to be an act of hermeneutic faith. For one of the main reasons why *Zarathustra* is so difficult to grasp is because there is such an obvious tension between these concepts. The teaching of the overman looks forward to the final emergence of something beyond man, it encourages us to participate in this final goal by practicing self-overcoming within ourselves and abandoning all of our restricted notions of selfhood. But the teaching of the eternal recurrence announces the continual return of the same, where what is most unbearable is the eternal recurrence of "everything small," including the "maggot man," which the coming of the overman was supposed to consign to oblivion. Must we then conclude that any higher truth in *Zarathustra* is destroyed in the mutual cancellation of Zarathustra's own incompatible doctrines? Or can we show that these thoughts are finally not incompatible with each other and that in some way they actually perform a mutual illumination?

In his discussion of Nietzsche, Heidegger argues that as the teacher of the overman, Zarathustra must also be the teacher of eternal recurrence, since it is only through the acceptance of eternal recurrence that the overman goes over man, by releasing himself from the domination of time, and its "It was."[2] Focusing his discussion upon the section, "On Redemption," Heidegger argues that Nietzsche understood the history of the human spirit as the history of a "revenge" against time, for the suffering and transience of human life has always sought to revenge itself by rejecting this existence in favor of some timeless religious or metaphysical Absolute. Thus it follows that Heidegger's final verdict on Zarathustra is a negative one; for while he praises Nietzsche's understanding of the "metaphysical problem," he argues that the eternal recurrence is actually the most spiritualized form of this revenge. By affirming the eternal recurrence, the overman effectively achieves the most complete domination of time, and the retrieval of the "It was." "What else remains for us to say," Heidegger continues, "but that Zarathustra's doctrine does not bring deliverance from revenge?"[3]

In the end, Heidegger's discussion is therefore typical, for like other early commentators, he finally views the overman and eternal recurrence as contradictory principles.[4] The overman is initially put forward as the one who will deliver us from the spirit of revenge; but then the eternal recurrence is grasped as the final revenge against time, and hence the finale of all metaphysical thinking. I have suggested that the whole drama of Zarathustra is propelled by the thought of the overman and the thought of eternal recurrence, and the apparent antagonism between them. After preaching the possibility of a new dawn and the arrival of a being who will surpass man as he has been hitherto, how could Zarathustra not be horrified by the thought that everything small must return, or the verdict of the soothsayer that "All is empty, all is the same, all has been!" (*TSZ* II "The Soothsayer"). Clearly, it *is* the confrontation between these two thoughts that accounts for the frequent changes in Zarathustra's resolution and the emergence of a noon wisdom of the sun, in opposition to a midnight wisdom of the moonlight. In the end, however, Zarathustra comes to realize that both of these visions are equivalent: "Midnight too is noon . . . night too is a sun" (*TSZ* IV "The Drunken Song" sec. 10). In this respect, the final part of *Zarathustra* achieves both a dramatic and a philosophical resolution, by showing that the sovereign will, which the overman was meant to provoke, is actually strongest of all in the thought of eternal recurrence.

In part one, the overman is distinguished only by the absence of any precise determinations. "I teach you the overman," Zarathustra proclaims, "Man is something that shall be overcome"; and he says that the overman is the "lightning" and "frenzy" that should lick us with his tongue. In this respect, the overman embodies a very general ideal of autonomy or individual sovereignty that is reflected upon and transformed once we approach the thought of eternal recurrence. As readers, we are meant to accompany Zarathustra in this philosophical journey, and this means that we must begin by endorsing the overman as an immediately attractive sovereign figure, but then we must think through the complete nature of this sovereignty in the overall context of "life." Thus, the thought of eternal recurrence does not submerge the overman, but forces us to abandon the individualistic reading of the overman as one who is both separate and self-contained. Zarathustra's progress, from insight to despair and back again, allows us to apprehend the full extent of the problem of sovereignty, and shows us that the latter is only fully understood once it is grasped as a moment in eternity. This is not to render sovereignty absurd and meaningless, but to underline the value of sovereignty as the final celebration of life itself.

In this chapter I will focus upon Zarathustra's discussion of the overman as a provisional ideal; then I will suggest how this goal of individual sovereignty is directed and subsumed by the thought of eternal recurrence. Finally, I will look at the resolution of Zarathustra's teaching with the appearance of his followers in part four. There is no question, however, of offering an exhaustive analysis of all of the figures and ideas that *Zarathustra* contains. For *Thus Spoke Zarathustra* is not a philosophical treatise in any straightforward sense, and its parabolic wisdom will resist every attempt at a final appropriation or closure.

In the very first section of the prologue to *Zarathustra*, Nietzsche clearly intends an ironic contrast between Zarathustra and the avatars of the Christian-metaphysical ideal. Thus, at the beginning, "when Zarathustra was thirty years old," he does not begin a Christ-like ministry among men, but actually withdraws into the solitude of the mountains. Here he lives for several years in his cave, but instead of following the philosopher's movement from the cave into the sunlight, he begins his going under by reminding the sun that its happiness consists in bringing light to the cave. "You great star," he asks, "what would your happiness be had you not those for whom you shine? For ten years you have climbed to my cave: you would have tired of your light and of the journey had it not been for me and my eagle and my serpent" (*TSZ* Prologue sec. 1). Such a pointed use of symbols associates Zarathustra with the very reversal of the Christian-metaphysical ideal; and this is only confirmed in the next section, when Nietzsche distinguishes Zarathustra from the religious hermit "who loves only God." The hermit avoids mankind because it is too imperfect for him. Zarathustra, however, does not live alone just to escape from something else. And while he will later suffer the great nausea over the smallness of man, his "going under" and his mission as a teacher is explicitly directed toward others. "I bring men a gift," he says, and he can scarcely believe that the old hermit would waste his celebration upon a God who no longer exists. "Could it be possible?" he asks himself, "This old saint in the forest has not yet heard anything of this, that *God is dead!*" (*TSZ* Prologue sec. 2).

In the previous chapter I sought to elaborate the full significance of the death of God in Nietzsche's original parable of the madman. In the rest of the prologue to *Zarathustra*, the real meaning of the death of God is brought to light by Zarathustra's speeches on the overman. Once again, however, his wisdom is intended to inspire and provoke. He does not offer a straightforward account of the necessary and sufficient conditions for being an overman, for at this point his goal is simply to evoke an ideal—of the one who somehow transcends humanity as it has been hitherto—in order to begin a meditation on the general theme of sovereignty. "Behold, I teach you the overman," he proclaims,

> "The overman is the meaning of the earth. Let your will say: the overman *shall be* the meaning of the earth! I beseech you, my brothers, *remain faithful to the earth*, and do not believe those who speak to you of otherworldly hopes! Poison-mixers are they, whether they know it or not. Despisers of life are they, decaying and poisoned themselves, of whom the earth is weary: so let them go.

"Once the sin against God was the greatest sin; but God died, and these sinners died with him. To sin against the earth is now the most dreadful thing, and to esteem the entrails of the unknowable higher than the meaning of the earth. . . .

"Not your sin but your thrift cries to heaven; your meanness even in your sin cries to heaven.

"Where is the lightning to lick you with its tongue? Where is the frenzy with which you should be inoculated?

"Behold, I teach you the overman: he is this lightning, he is this frenzy." (*TSZ* Prologue sec. 3)

Such passages involve the general recognition that transcendent and "otherworldly" ideals have always imprisoned humankind within the shadow of a higher realm. As values they can hardly inspire us to go beyond ourselves, since their very existence is an accusation against us and the implication of our own inherent guilt. In this context, to proclaim the death of God is to accept the failure of all transcendent ideals and to seek for a new mode of valuation that would lead us back to the earth and finally inspire the movement of self-overcoming.

It is precisely in this respect that Zarathustra teaches the necessity of a new kind of willing. He praises the great reason of the body over the soul; he condemns the timidity and contentment of modern man, and he focuses all of this longing onto the figure of the overman, who now emerges as the embodiment of his alternative ideal:

"I love those who do not first seek behind the stars for a reason to go under and be a sacrifice, but who sacrifice themselves for the earth, that the earth may someday become the overman's.

"I love him who lives to know, and who wants to know so that the overman may live some day. And thus he wants to go under. . . .

"I love him whose soul squanders itself, who wants no thanks and returns none: for he always gives away and does not want to preserve himself." (*TSZ* Prologue sec. 4)

In these lines, and in others like them, the idea of the overman functions as a general prescription that outlines a particular attitude toward existence. This involves a sovereign indifference to every selfish project, insofar as the self is open at every moment to the sacred order of "life." After the death of God, the figure of the overman must represent the complete de-deification of nature; and it also entails the overcoming of every traditional notion of the self, morality, mind and body, which asserts the absolute distinction of the subject and the world.

This means, then, that even though the overman is supposed to go "over" and beyond man, he cannot be understood as a new transcendent ideal, since this would only repeat the original mistake of metaphysics in the most facile way. Zarathustra's overman is not a super human being, or even the particular vision of a new humanity: for if his nature were that fixed he could only function prescriptively, as the embodiment of a new system of values, which would tyrannize us in exactly the same way as the previous otherworldly ideals.[5] Zarathustra realizes this when at the end of the prologue he decides that it was a mistake to preach the ideal of the overman to the assembled crowds: "No shepherd shall I be, nor gravedigger. Never again shall I speak to the people: for the last time have I spoken to the dead" (*TSZ* Prologue sec. 9). And from this point on his teaching becomes less direct, but much more "strategically" aware.

Instead of understanding the overman as a positive idol, it would therefore be more consistent to think of the overman as a "negative ideal," which draws its meaning from that which it is supposed to repudiate. Thus it is important that in part one, what sickens Zarathustra, and what he actively seeks to destroy is the self-satisfaction and "wretched contentment" of modern man. In pointed contrast to the overman, this vision of the *last* man depicts one who is so comfortable with himself and with all present arrangements, that he has finally ceased to will beyond himself for anything: "'What is love? What is creation? What is longing? What is a star?' thus asks the last man, and he blinks. The earth has become small, and on it hops the last man, who makes everything small. His race is as ineradicable as the flea-beetle; the last man lives longest. 'We have invented happiness,' say the last men, and they blink" (*TSZ* Prologue sec. 5). Using the broadest terms possible, we might say that in the first part of *Zarathustra* the sickness of modern life may be characterized as a sickness of the will. After two thousand years of herd Christianity and metaphysics "man" has lost the power of "willing," and so he must surrender himself to something else—to his religion, or his work, to his duty or his country. Likewise, if the modern age that Zarathustra describes is actually an age of "nihilism," then the most essential feature of that nihilism must be will-lessness itself.

The proclamation of the death of God and the critique of modern life, together with the alternative possibility of the overman, are all initial attempts to confront us with the reality of our spiritual situation. In his speeches in part one, Zarathustra seeks to uncover every subtle strategy that allows us to justify our weakness to ourselves. Later, the theory of eternal recurrence becomes the ultimate test that forces us to experience our own will-lessness as an affliction from which it is impossible to escape.

In view of all of this, it is hardly surprising that Zarathustra should refer to himself as the teacher of a new will, which celebrates this earth instead of denying or condemning it. "Willing liberates," he says, "that is the true teaching of will and liberty—thus Zarathustra teaches it" (*TSZ* II "Upon the Blessed Isles"). And elsewhere, he affirms the value of sovereignty and self-legislation as an ultimate goal. "Can you give yourself your own evil and your own good," he asks, "and hang your own will over yourself as a law? Can you be your own judge and avenger of your own law? Terrible it is to be alone with the judge and avenger of one's own law. Thus is a star thrown out into the void and into the icy breath of solitude" (*TSZ* I "On the Way of the Creator"). In other passages, of course, Nietzsche seems to condemn the very notion of the will as a unitary or separate phenomenon. But in the present context, the idea of the powerful will has a definite strategic importance, in pointed opposition to the lack of will or denial of life that is grasped as a feature of modern society. Similarly, it is significant that in Zarathustra's speeches the overman is not portrayed as a great-souled individual, but as lightning and frenzy and the meaning of the earth.[6] Such epithets are meant to recall the Dionysian aspects of the self that the Christian-metaphysical ideal has always denied.

All of this suggests a *via negativa* that leads us toward an understanding of the overman by rejecting every traditional conception of value. It remains unclear whether a more determinate account of the overman can ever be forthcoming, though, since Zarathustra himself warns his followers against apprehending his teachings in any precise or straightforward sense. Echoing an argument from *The Gay Science,* for example, Zarathustra suggests that the sovereignty of the individual must remain inexpressible, for as soon as it is given a name it enters into the common order of discourse that corrupts and consumes it. "May your virtue be too exalted for the familiarity of names," he says, "and if you must speak of her, then do not be ashamed to stammer of her" (*TSZ* I "On Enjoying and Suffering the Passions").

Elsewhere, however, Zarathustra insists that the highest wisdom can only speak in parables. In the final section of part one he offers us a parable of sovereignty itself in his account of the gift-giving virtue. "Tell me," he asks,

> How did gold attain the highest value? Because it is uncommon and useless and gleaming and gentle in its splendor; it always gives itself. Only as the image of the highest virtue did gold attain the highest value. Goldlike gleam the eyes of the giver. Golden splendor makes peace between moon and sun. Uncommon is the highest virtue and useless; it is gleaming and gentle in its splendor: a gift-giving virtue is the highest virtue. (*TSZ* I "On the Gift-Giving Virtue" sec. 1)

Gold is the image of sovereignty, and it corresponds to the highest virtue, because it is practically useless: whatever is useful has a natural equivalence or an exchange value and may be held in common by many. But the sovereignty of the individual has no equivalent and so far transcends all equivalences that there is nothing to compare it with. Or perhaps we should say that sovereignty, like gold, underlies all equivalences since it is that which first allows us to esteem or value anything.

Earlier, Zarathustra had proclaimed that "to esteem is to create. . . . Through esteeming alone is there value: and without esteeming, the nut of existence would be hollow" (*TSZ* I "On the Thousand and One Goals"). The gift-giving virtue is this original virtue of estimation, which serves as the condition of possibility for all other values, and which first transfigures the world by making it a valuable place. In this sense, however, it is both original and excessive, for insofar as it transcends all considerations of use and exchange it restores us to the sacred character of existence that our ordinary calculations cannot apprehend.

Once again, Zarathustra speaks to his disciples:

> Verily, I have found you out, my disciples: you strive, as I do, for the gift-giving virtue. . . . This is your thirst: to become sacrifices and gifts yourselves; and that is why you thirst to pile up all the riches in your soul. Insatiably your soul strives for treasures and gems, because your virtue is insatiable in wanting to give. You force all things to and into yourself that they may flow back out of your well as the gifts of your love. Verily, such a gift-giving love must approach all values as a robber; but whole and holy I call this selfishness. (*TSZ* I "On the Gift-Giving Virtue" sec. 1)

This passage underlines the transformative and transfiguring aspect of the gift-giving virtue, which apprehends all things in order to ordain them as sacred. It also suggests that the gift-giving virtue is not one virtue among many and is not simply equivalent to a superior magnanimity or largeness of soul. Here, the gift-giving virtue is the originary virtue of the individual, insofar as the latter achieves self-appropriation in the movement of sovereignty. Let us notice, however, that such an individual is not self-enclosed or simply self-contained; for in gift-giving the individual is open to others and the world. The gift-giving virtue is the parabolic key to the overman; it elaborates the original possibility of value that gives us access to the sacred, and it explains the meaning of sovereignty as an aspect of the sacred itself.[7]

Thus, I think we must conclude that the overman is not an independent ideal, but another element in Nietzsche's rhetorical strategy and philosophy of will. The overman is not a prescription, but another parable, which is meant to attune us to a new perspective upon the earth and so inspire us to reach beyond our selves. Such a reading is later confirmed by Zarathustra's own strategic explanation in part three, where he comments, "Must there not be that over which one dances and dances away?" And he answers, "There it was too that I picked up the word 'overman'. . . and that man is something that must be overcome" (*TSZ* III "On the Old and New Tablets" sec. 3). In this respect, we are not to reverence the overman by "praise," but by "going under," or dying to ourselves as we have been hitherto, because this is the condition for "going over," which creates the possibility of self-overcoming in general. Likewise, it is entirely appropriate that at the end of part one Zarathustra sends away his followers, so that they may begin to follow themselves. For this is exactly Zarathustra's own teaching of the creative will: that there is no single way, only my way and your way, since *the* way does not exist; indeed, it cannot exist, for it would only imprison the autonomous and creative will, which Zarathustra reveres as the most important goal. "You had not yet sought yourselves: and you found me. Thus do all believers; therefore all faith amounts to so little. Now I bid you lose me and find yourselves; and only when you have all denied me will I return to you" (*TSZ* I "On the Gift-Giving Virtue" sec. 3). In fact, Zarathustra's children can only return to him after he has worked through the thought of eternal recurrence in the rest of the book.

~&

The second and third parts of *Thus Spoke Zarathustra* record Zarathustra's spiritual progress, from his initial avoidance and refusal of his own "deepest thought" to his final acceptance and longing for it. Hence the drama of parts two and three is directed by the thought of eternal recurrence, for this is Zarathustra's worst nightmare, as well as his final redemptive joy. In the movement between these two poles, Zarathustra achieves a profound self-understanding. As the teacher of the overman, he initially deplores that which "brings back" the smallest man, but his eventual acceptance of eternal recurrence entails a necessary re-vision of the overman and a more complete understanding of what it means to be "the meaning of the earth."

In support of this reading, part two actually begins with a crucial misunderstanding, which only later becomes apparent. After he has returned to his cave and his solitude, Zarathustra dreams of the child with the mirror: "'O Zarathustra,' the child said to me, 'look at yourself in the mirror.' But when I looked into the mirror I cried out, and my heart was shaken: for it was not myself I saw, but a devil's grimace and scornful laughter" (*TSZ* II "The Child with the Mirror"). Zarathustra immediately interprets this dream as a warning that his own teaching is in danger because his enemies have succeeded in distorting it. He fears for his friends and followers and determines to go back down to refresh them with his wisdom.

Zarathustra's concern for his teaching and for his followers is surprising, for it seems to conflict with his earlier renunciation of the role of shepherd and his complete disavowal of the overman as a herd doctrine. These suspicions are only confirmed when a similar image reappears in another dream, toward the end of part two, but in a context that calls for an entirely *different* interpretation. Zarathustra recounts his second dream in the section on "The Soothsayer." He dreamt he was "a night watchman and a guardian of tombs upon the lonely mountain castle of death," who is summoned by a furious knocking at the gate:

> "Alpa," I cried, "who is carrying his ashes up the mountain?" . . . And I pressed the key and tried to lift the gate and exerted myself; but still it did not give an inch. Then a roaring wind tore its wings apart; whistling, shrilling, and piercing, it cast up a black coffin before me.
>
> "And amid the roaring and whistling and shrilling the coffin burst and spewed out a thousandfold laughter. And from a thousand grimaces of children, angels, owls, fools and butterflies as big as children, it laughed and mocked and roared at me." (*TSZ* II "The Soothsayer")

One of Zarathustra's disciples interprets this dream by identifying Zarathustra with the mocking wind and laughter. As with "The Child with the Mirror," he also relates the dream to Zarathustra's struggle with his enemies: "'Verily, *this is what you dreamed of:* your enemies. That was your hardest dream. But as you woke from them and came to your senses, thus they shall awaken from themselves—and come to you.'" But this time the section ends with Zarathustra looking into the face of his disciple and simply shaking his head.[8]

Zarathustra realizes that his disciple's interpretation is unsatisfactory. Perhaps he is now reminded that any concern for followers is completely antithetical to his own project—certainly in the sense of having individuals "awaken from themselves" in order to follow him. But what is most problematic in the disciple's interpretation is that Zarathustra actually dreamed of *himself* as the guardian of the tombs and as the one who was frightened by the rushing wind and laughter. In this respect, Zarathustra must reject the interpretation because he knows that he is not yet equal to the task that has been imposed upon him. Earlier he had praised his own creative will as a "liberator" and as "the *shatterer* of all tombs" (*TSZ* II "The Tomb Song"). But now, his midnight nightmare reveals that he is still in the service of the past and its inherited burden of values. Likewise, with the earlier dream, the image of the devil in the mirror is explained by his own later pronouncement, that the overman must always appear that way to those who are not yet ready for him. "You highest men whom my eyes have seen," he comments, "this is my doubt concerning you and my secret laughter: I guess that you would call my overman—devil" (*TSZ* II "On Human Prudence"). It seems that Zarathustra is still far from what he must become. The section that follows Zarathustra's dream in "The Soothsayer" makes it clear what he still has to do.

In this section, called "On Redemption," Zarathustra argues that in revenge for its own sufferings and impotence in the face of the irredeemably transient character of things, the will has created a second "metaphysical" world of Permanence and Unity. This is then used to justify the will's suffering as the suffering of that which does not deserve to be:

> *The spirit of revenge,* my friends, has so far been the subject of man's best reflection; and where there was suffering, one always wanted punishment too. . . . Because there is suffering in those who will, inasmuch as they cannot will backwards, willing itself and all life were supposed to be—a punishment. And now cloud upon cloud rolled over the spirit, until eventually madness preached, "Everything passes away; therefore everything deserves to pass away." (*TSZ* II "On Redemption")

From the outset, the will knows that it is forever limited for it can never change what has happened or alter the fundamental character of human life. The ordinary dream of individual mastery is thus frustrated, and this leads to despair. Such a will seeks to destroy itself, for its pain can only be stilled where it no longer has to will: and it follows that whatever is created in this "spirit of revenge" can never testify to the productivity of life, but only to its ultimate betrayal.

At this point, however, it is clear that Zarathustra stands condemned by his own teaching, for he has shown that his own ideal of the overman is inspired by a hatred of the present and the past and by the desire to "redeem" both of these with an alternative future. And this implies that the overman was created in the spirit of revenge. As he exclaims, "The now and the past on earth—alas, my friends, that is what *I* find most unendurable; and I should not know how to live if I were not also a seer of that which must come" (*TSZ* II "On Redemption"). This passage recalls all of those earlier occasions where Zarathustra fulminates against the smallness of man. His hatred is obsessive; the sight of humanity, even its highest exemplars, "nauseates" him; and it is the Soothsayer's prediction that all of this must return that brings on the nightmare of the tombs.

Thus by the end of part two Zarathustra is still imprisoned by the same humanity that he sought to overcome. Using the later language of *On the Genealogy of Morals,* his "action" is only a "reaction"; and it is precisely this nausea and disgust with modern man that does not allow him to speak the eternal recurrence as his own creative word:

"You know it, Zarathustra, but you do not say it!" And at last I answered defiant-
ly: "Yes, I know it, but I do not want to say it!". . . Then it spoke to me again without voice: . . . "You are one who has forgotten how to obey: now you shall command. Do you not know who is most needed by all? He that commands great
things. To do great things is difficult; but to command great things is more
difficult. This is what is most unforgivable in you: you have the power, and you
do not want to rule." (*TSZ* II "The Stillest Hour")

Here, Zarathustra is commanded to command. The imperative of sovereignty
is placed upon him as the imperative of life, which demands that he should
will his own will instead of willfully denying it. And yet, even though this is
Zarathustra's philosophy of will—where "life" reveals "I am that which must
always overcome itself" (*TSZ* II "On Self-Overcoming")—at the end of part
two he finds that he is still unequal to the task.

At this point in *Thus Spoke Zarathustra,* the eternal recurrence has therefore emerged as the great Unsaid, which exists as a kind of dreadful summons
before it is ever actually spoken. "I know it," Zarathustra says, "but I dare not
say it" (*TSZ* II "The Stillest Hour"). We must emphasize, however, that for
Zarathustra, the task is not simply to enunciate the thought of eternal recurrence—for even his animals and the spirit of gravity are capable of doing that.
For Zarathustra, the hardest task is to confront and so experience the thought
of eternal recurrence by incorporating it into the deepest level of his own
existence, not as a thought experiment, but as a fundamental possibility and
imperative of existence itself.[9]

I have suggested that the eternal recurrence is Zarathustra's own deepest
abyss, because it appears to represent the most extreme counter-thought to
that of the overman and the possibility of a final redemption. Long anticipated and dreaded by Zarathustra, the eternal recurrence is a silent mockery of all final ends and redemptive moments. By announcing the inevitable
collapse and reappearance of every possible purpose or value, as well as the
return of the last man, the eternal recurrence seems to express the most complete version of meaninglessness that could ever be imagined—a world without ends, from which it is impossible to escape. In a related note, collected
in *The Will to Power,* Nietzsche writes, "Let us think this thought in its most
terrible form: existence as it is, without meaning or aim, yet recurring inevitably without any finale of nothingness" (*WTP* sec. 55). In this respect, the
eternal recurrence is the thought of the purest nihilism, and apparently the
worst of all possible worlds for the purposeful creature, man.

On the other hand, if Zarathustra could really endure such a thought, or
even had the strength to will it, then he might experience the most comprehensive state of soul and the maximal feeling of existence that comes from
affirming and celebrating this life in spite of its greatest objection. From *this*

perspective there would be no final contradiction between the overman and the eternal recurrence, for the strength of soul that is required to affirm the eternal recurrence and every aspect of this existence is precisely the same as that which earlier placed us in relation to the overman himself. In this respect, Zarathustra says, "peak and abyss . . . are joined together," for the first terrible aspect of eternal recurrence is a necessary condition for its other transfiguring moment. And for this reason, the "great noon" that is so longingly awaited must also be prepared for by a midnight vision and riddle, in which the abysmal thought of eternal recurrence is first spoken. Zarathustra the godless will only *become* Zarathustra the godless once he experiences and incorporates the most godless thought imaginable.

The section on "The Vision and the Riddle" now offers an oblique presentation of eternal recurrence as Zarathustra's own vision of the loneliest. In the first part of this story, he is climbing a mountain path, though burdened and tormented by "his devil and archenemy," the spirit of gravity. As Zarathustra ascends, the spirit of gravity continues to mock him and predicts his fall, until finally, Zarathustra summons the courage to proclaim the eternal recurrence in order to destroy him. Elsewhere in Zarathustra, the spirit of gravity is described as the representative of all "constraint, statute, necessity, and consequence and purpose and good and evil" (*TSZ* III "On the Old and New Tablets" sec. 2). It is not surprising, then that this spirit should weigh Zarathustra down, for these are precisely the chains that bind the individual to the herd and so prevent the achievement of sovereignty.

Zarathustra speaks of eternal recurrence and the two long lanes of eternity, past and future, which meet at the gateway called moment. "Must not whatever *can* walk have walked on this lane before? Must not whatever *can* happen have happened, have been done, have been passed by before? And if everything has been there before—what do you think, dwarf, of this moment?" When he finishes, the dwarf has disappeared. Perhaps we can assume that the revelation has destroyed him, for by announcing the impossibility of any justification or "end" to suffering, the eternal recurrence forces the dwarf to come to terms with his own most basic dissatisfaction with life—which he can neither affirm nor avoid. In effect, the eternal recurrence cuts through every layer of self-deception; and in this way, the spirit of gravity goes under.

The second part of Zarathustra's story begins with the terrifying image of the shepherd, writhing and gagging with "a heavy black snake hung out of his mouth." But when the shepherd bites the head off the snake he becomes totally transformed, so that by the end of "The Vision and the Riddle," the thought of eternal recurrence inspires the most complete celebration of life:

The shepherd . . . bit as my cry counseled him; he bit with a good bite. Far away he spewed the head of the snake—and he jumped up. No longer shepherd, no longer human—one charged, radiant, *laughing!* Never yet on earth has a human being laughed as he laughed! O my brothers, I heard a laughter that was no human laughter; and now a thirst gnaws at me, a longing that never grows still. My longing for this laughter gnaws at me; oh, how do I bear to go on living! And how could I bear to die now! (*TSZ* III "On the Vision and the Riddle" sec. 2)

Of course, we remember this wild laughter! But until this point, Zarathustra had always feared it as the scornful, mocking laughter that appeared to call him into question and ridiculed all of his teachings. Here, he apprehends it as a joyful laughter, which accompanies the self-overcoming of life. And since he has now experienced the truth of eternal recurrence, he yearns for this elevated laughter, which mocks the spirit of gravity and expresses the final opening-up of the individual subject to that deep eternity of life that forever surrounds us.[10]

It is not clear what we should make of all this, however, since the philosophical status of eternal recurrence remains in doubt. In spite of Nietzsche's occasional sketches for a scientific proof, the eternal recurrence is not a philosophical or scientific theory in any ordinary sense, since it is completely overdetermined by the conditions of its emergence—as a counter to the overman, for example, as a figure within the logic of nihilism, or as a response to the traditional conception of eternity. Likewise, it is important to remember that in *Thus Spoke Zarathustra* the eternal recurrence is not presented as a philosophical idea by Nietzsche himself, but as the leading thought of his character Zarathustra, and even Zarathustra is very wary of expressing it. In part three, for example, he is silent about eternal recurrence, apart from what he says to the dwarf. And when his animals try to express his teaching—"Everything goes, everything comes back; eternally rolls the wheel of being" (*TSZ* III "The Convalescent" sec. 2)—he berates them and lets them know that they have not really understood; for what this idea attempts to articulate is apparently unsayable.

Perhaps we are on firmer ground if we say that instead of being a literal truth about the world, the eternal recurrence functions as a transformative idea, which can orient the listener toward a new perspective upon existence. It thus joins the Apollinian and Dionysian, the idea of "gay science," and the overman as strategic ideas and figures that are meant to illuminate the nature of the individual and the world in order to transfigure existence for the future. Here, however, there is a paradox: for the eternal recurrence seems to separate and distinguish the individual, while at the same time it also disperses the individual within the immensity of eternity. If eternal recurrence is a provocation, we might ask, then what is the relation that it establishes between the individual and the world? Does it suggest a resolution of individual sovereignty, or does it simply dissolve it?[11]

In *The Gay Science,* the original presentation of eternal recurrence made it abundantly clear that it is a device that intensifies individual existence by forcing us to confront ourselves within the perspective of eternity. The demon creeps into our loneliest loneliness, just as Zarathustra can only encounter the idea when his loneliest loneliness has begun. If we are doomed to live this life over and over, innumerable times more, then every moment of it becomes absolutely valuable in itself. Given that the past will once again become future and the present moment will also return, we can no longer just muddle through, or engage in any kind of regretful thinking about the way things might have been. The eternal recurrence announces that we can no longer look forward to any kind of heaven or nothingness, a final state of rest or even an end of time that could release us from ourselves. Somehow—and this is to treat the eternal recurrence as an "existential imperative"—what we do now creates a pattern for the rest of eternity. If such a thought produces nausea, this is nothing other than the nausea of our own present existence when this is taken as the measure for eternity itself.

From this perspective, then, the eternal recurrence may act as a transformative thought. For if it is accepted on its own terms, then all the forms of nihilistic response, such as will-lessness, pessimism, fatalism, and ressentiment become too painful to bear, since future consolation is now impossible.[12] Once the last man, or the slave, incorporates the thought of eternal recurrence he will either try to destroy himself or die of despair, or else he will discover the strength to destroy himself as a slave by purging himself of all the forms of nihilism that had previously confined him. In this way, the eternal recurrence forces us out of our will-lessness and provokes us into willing again: for when we endorse the eternal recurrence we are actually affirming the return of our own will.

Earlier, in the section "On Redemption," Zarathustra offered the guiding clue that makes this self-affirmation possible. "This is all my creating and striving," he says, "that I create and carry together into One what is fragment and riddle and dreadful accident"; and, "To redeem those who lived in the past and to recreate all 'it was' into a 'thus I willed it'—that alone should I call redemption." It can be argued that in passages like these Zarathustra offers a very basic account of self-appropriation. We are called upon to examine ourselves and to create our life as a work of art by integrating every accidental or trivial aspect of our being as a necessary feature of the whole—to redeem the accident of birth, for example, by showing how such a particular origin was essential for becoming what I am now; or to redeem the accident of religion or a strictly moral upbringing, by showing that without it I would not have achieved what I have. In this way, we may gain complete possession of ourselves; and only such a unified and unitary existence will be capable of the resolute affirmation of its recurrence.[13]

Such an interpretation emphasizes the respect in which eternal recurrence promotes the most complete intensification of individual existence insofar as it isolates the individual from the herd and from everything else that is. It cannot be denied that numerous passages in *Zarathustra* support such a reading, especially those that emphasize the need for a *new* will or that condemn the halfhearted willing that eternal recurrence is meant to preclude. "Do whatever you will," Zarathustra comments, "but first be such as are *able to will*" (*TSZ* III "On Virtue That Makes Small" sec. 3); and "Those who have become weary are themselves merely being 'willed' and all the billows play with them" (*TSZ* III "On the Old and New Tablets" sec. 16). In this regard, Zarathustra is very careful to distinguish the true affirmation of eternal recurrence from the bogus acceptance of those he calls the "omnisatisfied." The latter accept everything without discrimination, and their thoughtless and easy claim that all is for the best is like the braying of an ass that never changes. But the authentic affirmation of eternal recurrence must singularize individuals by placing them face to face with themselves in eternity; and it would require a tremendous discrimination and a watchful eye in order to overcome every moment of nausea and despair that threatens this creative sovereignty over oneself.

Such an interpretation is very compelling, but it is, I think, only half of the story. For if we examine the thought of eternal recurrence more closely, it really seems to entail the complete dispersal of the individual within the immensity of eternity.[14] And this is not merely another philosophical paradox that the eternal recurrence can appear to generate, for it is recognized and strongly affirmed by Zarathustra. In his conversation with the spirit of gravity, for example, Zarathustra comments that "all things [are] knotted together so firmly that this moment draws after it *all* that is to come" (*TSZ* "On the Vision and the Riddle" sec. 2). Later, his animals repeat this point when they say that "the knot of causes in which I am entangled recurs and will create me again. I myself belong to the causes of the eternal recurrence. I come again, with this sun, with this earth, with this eagle, with this serpent" (*TSZ* "The Convalescent" sec. 2). The problem is simply that I cannot separate *myself* from the world. And since everything is knotted together so firmly, it is not just a question of affirming my own existence in the rest of eternity, but affirming the existence of everything—including the last man, the whole nightmare of the past, and whatever else is beyond my control, as equally important and necessary. Strictly speaking, as Zarathustra comments in part four, to completely will the return of one thing you are bound to will the return of everything:

> Have you ever said Yes to a single joy? O my friends, then you said Yes too to *all* woe. All things are entangled, ensnared, enamored; if ever you wanted one thing twice, if ever you said, "You please me, happiness! Abide moment!" then you wanted *all* back. All anew, all eternally, all entangled, ensnared, enamored—oh, then you *loved* the world. Eternal ones, love it eternally and evermore; and to woe too, you say: go, but return! *For all joy wants—eternity.* (*TSZ* IV "The Drunken Song" sec. 10)

Like the gift-giving virtue, the eternal recurrence blurs the boundaries between the individual and whatever lies "outside," so that after "The Vision and the Riddle," Zarathustra concludes that such a separation no longer makes any sense.

It is important to notice that this opening of the self to everything that is is experienced with joy, as a moment of empowerment and ecstatic abandon. Earlier, the thought of the eternal recurrence was threatening because it seemed to negate the overman and every achievement of self-overcoming. But by the end of part three, in "The Seven Seals," Zarathustra celebrates the nuptial ring of eternity, a symbol for his own reinscription and immersion into the cosmos, where such self-dispossession is not feared but actively longed for. Likewise, it is significant that the whole philosophical drama of Zarathustra reaches a provisional conclusion at last with this triumphant song that is repeated at the end of every section: "Never yet have I found the woman from whom I wanted children, unless it be this woman whom I love: for I love you, O eternity" (*TSZ* III "The Seven Seals"). This is Nietzsche's "theodicy" and final celebration of life. Not just the life of the overman or the life of the sovereign individual, but an affirmation of the sacred character of all things, which only a thought like the eternal recurrence can allow us to experience.[15]

The eternal recurrence is apparently a contradictory thought, which, from different perspectives may intensify or overwhelm the individual life. Perhaps in this respect it fails to resolve the question of sovereignty, or even leaves it deliberately ambivalent. The earlier model of *The Birth of Tragedy*, however, suggests that here we are again confronted by the Dionysian and Apollinian aspects of a single idea, and the final truth about the individual does not belong to either one of them, since the image of sovereignty is only expressed by the idea that can hold them both together. All existence, or at least all

human existence, is bounded by the two axes of self-mastery and self-abandonment. Our life is a continual movement of appropriation, dispossession,
and empowerment, and it is precisely this that the thought of eternal recurrence seems to embody with its different aspects. In this respect, it only
confirms and condenses what was earlier given in Nietzsche's discussion of
tragedy.

More significantly, however, the eternal recurrence also expresses the final
goal of sovereignty that the idea of the overman was originally intended to
provoke. The overman is an important but limited ideal that gives us an initial perspective upon the imperative of sovereignty. Perhaps it is a necessary
stage of thinking that helps us to overcome the present, but it cannot be the
final stage, for as Zarathustra realizes, in order to escape the spirit of revenge
one must overcome the very rejection that inspired the initial overcoming.
Only then can one affirm the eternal recurrence of all things, including that
which is most objectionable, for only then is one attuned to the innocence
of becoming. In "Before Sunrise," Zarathustra proclaims the ecstatic teaching: "I carry the blessings of my yes into all abysses. I have become one who
blesses and says Yes; and I fought long for that and was a fighter that I might
one day get my hands free to bless. But this is my blessing: to stand over every single thing as its own heaven, as its round roof, its azure bell, and eternal security; and blessed is he who blesses thus" (*TSZ* III "Before Sunrise").
What is significant here is that such a speech can only occur after Zarathustra's confrontation with the spirit of gravity and his final victory in "On the
Vision and the Riddle." This joyful acceptance of eternal recurrence does *not*
mean the abolition of sovereignty, or, *pace* Heidegger, a betrayal of the imperative to destroy the spirit of revenge.

The thought of the overman is thus incorporated into the eternal recurrence, so that what began as a straightforward call for self-overcoming and
individual greatness is finally reconstrued as an essential aspect of Zarathustra's own Dionysian theodicy. As we have seen, however, Zarathustra opposes everything that suppresses the individual will, and his teaching of the eternal recurrence continues to be associated with the affirmation of a creative
sovereignty. In this context, Zarathustra makes it clear that resignation, fatalism, or "omnisatisfaction" are incomplete responses to eternal recurrence,
for they continue to maintain the essential separation of the individual and
the cosmos. If I view the eternal recurrence as something that must happen
to me, for example, then I am bound to regard it as a threat that can only be
nullified by despair or another attitudinal response. The high point of Zarathustra's meditation, however, lies in the experience of his own existence as
something that is totally integrated into the absolute flux of becoming. From

this highest point, it is not a matter of the individual versus the world, since the individual *is* the "gift" of Dionysus and the highest expression of the continual generosity of life.

Thus, on the one hand, the creative will of sovereignty is decentered, for it is no longer to be understood as an individual achievement, but as an achievement of the cosmos itself. On the other hand, neither Zarathustra nor Nietzsche ever abandons the ideal of sovereignty, and the latter remains an individual goal and the original imperative that summons us to become who we are. There is obviously some tension, if not a contradiction, between these final positions. But it is the same tension and apparent contradiction that runs throughout Nietzsche's writings: when he condemns the myth of free will, for example, while he also celebrates the free spirit as one who has *become* free; or when he later reduces all human actions to the manifestation of a nonsubjective will to power, while he also charges the individual with the task of self-appropriation and "becoming what one is." This is the continual interplay between the human and the "cosmic" perspectives that I mentioned above.[16] In the affirmation of eternal recurrence, however, the awareness of absolute necessity, which recognizes that things must be as they are, is conjoined with the highest possible experience of freedom, which proclaims, "Thus I willed it!" Here, the absolute distinction between freedom and necessity is apparently overcome.

↝

Many commentators have argued that part four offers a ludicrous conclusion to the drama of Zarathustra.[17] For after the sustained intensity of part three, with the revelation of eternal recurrence, and the final consecration of eternity in "The Seven Seals," Nietzsche's sudden shift to comedy is philosophically and dramatically inappropriate. In part four Zarathustra goes fishing on the mountains; the comical higher men make their appearance one after the other; they prepare their own Last Supper, and they hold an "Ass Festival," which celebrates the braying of an ass. In part one Zarathustra had spoken of the great noon, when man stands "in the middle of his way between beast and overman and celebrates his way to the evening as his highest hope" (*TSZ* "On the Gift-Giving Virtue" sec. 3). Further, it is significant that whereas the overman was previously the focus of his discussion, in part four the text is crowded with animals—eagles, snakes, donkeys, fish, leeches, and lions—which suggests a movement away from the philosophical high ground. Likewise, part four is preoccupied with the themes of eating and drinking and sexual desire. Perhaps all of this represents a renewed attention to the body and a return to the earth, which Zarathustra had earlier called for. On the other hand, this strange comic reversal seems out of place and inconsistent with the rest of this work. Whatever else may be going on in *Zarathustra,* the accumulated "power" and the dramatic tension of part three is rapidly destroyed, leaving us with something that is closer to farce.

Clearly, though, there is some point to this parody of religious themes, this renewed attention to the body, and mockery of "virtuous European dignity." The fourth part of Zarathustra may not succeed as a solemn philosophical text, but this is not its basic intention. Perhaps Zarathustra's own comments may help here. "Has a man ever caught fish on high mountains?" he asks. "And even though what I want and do up here be folly, it is still better than if I became solemn down there from waiting, and green and yellow—a swaggering wrathsnorter from waiting, a holy, howling storm out of the mountains, an impatient one who shouts down into the valleys, 'Listen or I shall whip you with the scourge of God!'" (*TSZ* IV "The Honey Sacrifice"). Earlier, Zarathustra had taught in the marketplace, as a "swaggering wrathsnorter," ranting against the last man and his wretched contentment. He is still concerned with his followers, and in this respect the end of part three is full of lyrical descriptions of his "children" and how he will soon encounter them. What he has learned in the meantime, however, is that to make someone into one's follower is only to destroy their creative will; and if the sovereignty of the other is seen as the goal, then one must maintain the separation between self and other that ordinary tendencies, summarized by "pity," have tended to destroy. Thus in part four Nietzsche uses the devices of comedy to create an ironic distance between Zarathustra and the reader's own "highest longing." For even if he has charted the very peak and abyss of the human spirit, Zarathustra cannot be taken as a new redeemer. Part four performs a necessary revaluation of Zarathustra's place as both prophet and teacher, which tells us, like the higher men, that we should not seek Zarathustra but only ourselves. And in this final movement of parody, which we could also call the self-deconstruction of *Thus Spoke Zarathustra,* the priority of individual sovereignty is thus preserved and strengthened as the central concern of the drama as a whole.[18]

The parody begins with the successive entrances of the higher men: the soothsayer, the two kings, the conscientious scholar of the leech, the magician, the last pope, the ugliest man, the voluntary beggar, and the wanderer's shadow. They are a strange collection of misfits, and Zarathustra has a comic encounter with each of them. We soon learn that each of these characters is filled with disgust for the present state of man; they have obviously heard something of Zarathustra's teaching, and being inspired by one of his sayings or another, they now come to Zarathustra as the one who will *deliv-*

er them from their nausea. Zarathustra quickly realizes, however, that all of these "higher men" are failures; for though they are disgusted with their own life, they are still incapable of achieving sovereignty, and instead they revere Zarathustra as another transcendent ideal. "*Who* else matters to me any more in this life but this one man, Zarathustra," says the conscientious scholar (*TSZ* IV "The Leech"). Even after Zarathustra has rapped him on the head with his stick, the magician cries out, "Do you not know it, Zarathustra? *I seek Zarathustra*" (*TSZ* IV "The Magician" sec. 2).

It is clear that Zarathustra must now reject the higher men—they are not his children because they are still too "crooked" and determined by what they must overcome. "You are mere bridges," he tells them at the end of his welcome, "may men higher than you stride over you. You signify steps: therefore do not be angry with him who climbs over you to *his* height" (*TSZ* IV "The Welcome"). Such a welcome is in fact appropriate, because more than anything else, the higher men need to be disengaged from Zarathustra. His strategy, and Nietzsche's strategy in general, is therefore to evoke sovereignty at one level, but to exacerbate the individual at another level so that we do not simply become the followers of a new sovereign ideal.

Accordingly, after the parodic Last Supper, Zarathustra sees it as a real sign of "convalescence" when the higher men invent their own ass festival. Zarathustra is delighted because this shows the emergence of their own creative will and sacred affirmation, as distinct from their earlier obsequious homage. Indeed, the very fact that he initially misunderstands their parody now signifies the creation of a distance between them that opens up the space of sovereignty. "Amen," cries the ugliest man, who is kneeling in front of the ass with all of the others: "And praise and honor and wisdom and thanks and glory and strength be to our God, from everlasting to everlasting. But the Ass brayed: Yea-Yuh" (*TSZ* IV "The Awakening" sec. 2). Like the "Last Supper," this section is clearly a parody of traditional Christian themes and so it links up with the original lines of the prologue. The Christian method of comfort and redemption is basically wisdom for donkeys. But more than this, however, the ass festival is also a mockery of Zarathustra's own teaching. The sacred "yes" to life, which Zarathustra finally experiences after so much struggle at the end of part three, is here reduced to the "Yea-Yuh" of the ass, who is "beyond good and evil."

Thus, having reached a certain philosophical standpoint on life and sovereignty in general, in part four *Zarathustra* becomes ironic and parodies its own claims to ultimate authority. Likewise, all observances, religious and otherwise, are challenged by the ass festival, which uses the parodic forms of worship in order to repudiate worship itself. As the ugliest man explains to Zarathustra,

"It was from you yourself that I learned it once, O Zarathustra: whoever would kill most thoroughly, *laughs*.

"'Not by wrath does one kill, but by laughter'—thus you once spoke. O Zarathustra, you hidden one, you annihilator without wrath, you dangerous saint—you are a rogue!" (*TSZ* IV "The Ass Festival" sec. 1)

This section brings together two earlier themes—the death of God and the celebratory experience of laughter. In fact, the second death of God is accomplished through laughter, not merely reflected on as before but actually experienced in the laughter that tears everything substantial apart. At the end of this section, Zarathustra's words suggest that this experience is thoroughly conjoined to the final experience of sovereignty:

"Do not forget this night and this ass festival, you higher man. *This* you invented when you were with me and I take that for a good sign: such things are invented only by convalescents.

"And when you celebrate it again, this ass festival, do it for your own sakes, and also do it for my sake. And in remembrance of *me*." (*TSZ* IV "The Ass Festival" sec. 3)

Because it is the goal of his most fundamental teaching, to will one's own will is in fact the only praise of Zarathustra that is possible. To the very end Zarathustra stresses the absolute priority of sovereignty, not as a means—a "because" or "in order to"—but as the highest expression of life itself.

Zarathustra's teaching of sovereignty culminates in "The Drunken Song," which now follows as the penultimate section of part four and provides a dramatic climax to the whole book. Here the parody disappears and we are recalled to Zarathustra's midnight vision, as the howling dog and the spider in the moonlight announce the return of the most abysmal thought. Once again, midnight reveals the deepest suffering at the heart of the world, and pronounces its "woe" for everything that is an objection to life. But this time Zarathustra welcomes the revelation of midnight, since he now understands that the highest triumph of life, its fulfillment and goal, is necessarily conjoined to its deepest suffering, for only that which suffers has the longing to overcome itself.

Woe entreats: Go! Away, woe! But all that suffers wants to live, that it may become ripe and joyous and longing—longing for what is farther, higher, brighter. "I want heirs"—thus speaks all that suffers; "I want children, I do not want *myself*."

Joy, however, does not want heirs, or children—joy wants itself, wants eternity, wants recurrence, wants everything eternally the same. (*TSZ* "The Drunken Song" sec. 9)

Ever since he repudiated his need for mere followers in part one, Zarathustra has been looking for his children; and this quest has become a constant theme that raises the most general questions about what it means to teach another, especially where one cannot prescribe, or how a teacher like Zarathustra is finally related to those who are inspired by him. Part four does not provide an explicit solution to these questions, but in Zarathustra's own ironic relationship to the higher men he comes closer to his goal by simultaneously inspiring and repelling them. The passage above, however, appears to suggest that only that which is inherently dissatisfied will look for redemption in its "children"; while, whatever is strong enough to experience a deeper triumph of joy will actively crave its own recurrence for the rest of eternity—for this formula expresses the maximal feeling of existence and a complete attunement to the sovereign will.

We have seen how in the earlier parts Zarathustra was always concerned for his "children" and whether or not they were being misled by others. It seems that he has always been on the way to his children, although until this moment he has never yet been with them. Perhaps it is significant, then, that after the rapture of this "Drunken Song," and the joyful affirmation that does not want children "but only itself," Zarathustra claims that the sign has finally come and that his children are at hand. "About all this Zarathustra spoke but a single sentence: '*My children are near, my children.*' Then he became entirely silent. But his heart was loosed, and tears dropped from his eyes and fell on his hands" (*TSZ* IV "The Sign"). I would hesitate to suggest a single interpretation of this, but in continuity with the whole direction of our discussion we can now suggest that one's "children," one's true spiritual heirs, cannot exist for as long as one seeks them out or attempts to mold them by prescription or decree. In this respect, a following can never be more than a sum of zeros. At the end of part four, however, Zarathustra has overcome his pity and distracting concern for the higher men and is able to celebrate the eternal recurrence as his own "eternal confirmation and seal." Precisely now, and only now, will his children appear to him, not as servile followers but as those who are also engaged in the project of self-appropriation and who are inspired, we might say, by the brightness of this midnight sun. In short, given the priority of sovereignty, there is no final contradiction between the deepest concern for the Other, which Zarathustra shows by continual going under, and the noble "selfishness" of autonomy. In the case of Zarathustra, the latter is meant to provide the illumination of the first.

At the end, it is midnight that brings Zarathustra to his "great noon." As in the earlier "Vision," the terrors of midnight prepare the way for the rapture of noon, so that the two are finally indistinguishable. Suffering and joy succeed and inspire each other; curses and blessings call each other forth, and everything is entangled in everything else. All this is the basic character of existence that Zarathustra describes as the eternal recurrence of all things, where "Midnight too is noon; pain too is a joy; curses too are a blessing" (*TSZ* IV "The Drunken Song" sec. 10). To affirm such a vision is to affirm the image of life as a will that continually strives for its own empowerment, regardless of all the objections that the midnight has to offer. In this respect, life is most basically a "will to power," and its highest expression is the creative will of sovereignty. The poem *Thus Spoke Zarathustra* is a song to this creative will and a celebration of the individual as such. It is an evocation that calls upon the will to will itself.

6 ❧

The Return of the Master

In the second part of *Thus Spoke Zarathustra,* in the section "On Self-Overcoming," Nietzsche offers a very significant discussion of the will to power, which he describes as "the unexhausted procreative will of life." After beginning this section with an account of the will to truth and the process of valuation, he appears to project the will to power as the most basic principle of life and the underlying force that actively creates every ruling conception and every table of values. Of course, all of this is still expressed in the parabolic wisdom of Zarathustra, and it does not really constitute a straightforward philosophical claim. But given its central place within the text, and the breadth of its concerns, I think this section offers us a very powerful and condensed expression of Nietzsche's mature philosophical position. It is significant because it suggests a preliminary understanding of the will to power. Likewise, it shows us once again how the issue of sovereignty really brings us back to the core of Nietzsche's thinking. "I pursued the living," Zarathustra proclaims, and

> I walked the widest and the narrowest paths that I might know its nature. With a hundredfold mirror I still caught its glance when its mouth was closed, so that its eyes might speak to me. And its eyes spoke to me.
>
> But wherever I found the living, there I heard also the speech on obedience. Whatever lives, obeys.
>
> And this is the second point: he who cannot obey himself is commanded. That is the nature of the living.
>
> This, however, is the third point that I heard: that commanding is harder than obeying; and not only because he who commands must carry the burden of all who obey, and because this burden may easily crush him. An experiment and hazard appeared to me to be in all commanding; and whenever the living commands, it hazards itself. Indeed, even when it commands *itself,* it must still pay for its commanding. It must become the judge, the avenger, and the victim of its own law. How does this happen? I asked myself. What persuades the living to obey and command, and to practice obedience even when it commands?

> Hear, then, my word, you who are wisest. Test in all seriousness whether I have crawled into the very heart of life and into the very roots of its heart.
>
> Where I found the living, there I found will to power; and even in the will of those who serve I found the will to be master. (*TSZ* II "On Self-Overcoming")

A few lines later Zarathustra emphasizes the importance of this teaching when he refers to it as the secret of life. "Behold," life tells him, "I am *that which must always overcome itself*. Indeed, you call it a will to procreate or a drive to an end, to something higher, farther, more manifold: but all this is one, and one secret." Briefly, then, the essential points are these: whatever lives obeys; he who cannot obey himself is commanded; and commanding is harder than obeying. If we look at each of these points in turn, we will see how the focus of sovereignty can now help us to understand the structure of the will to power.

First, "whatever lives obeys" implies that whatever lives finds itself under an imperative that it is bound to follow. Of course, the section on self-overcoming refers explicitly to the nature of *all* life; but since this section is framed by a discussion of the will to truth and the nature of good and evil as an expression of the will to power, Zarathustra's claim is most directly a comment upon *human* life and individual willing. "Whatever lives obeys" means that whatever is capable of directing itself as a specific individual must always place itself under the constraint of values and ideals. For according to Zarathustra, this is how "life" itself progresses: it projects these goals and ideals beyond itself, and by inspiring the striving of the individual it thereby achieves its own self-overcoming. In *Beyond Good and Evil* there is a related passage on the distinction between "nature" and morality, where Nietzsche argues that even though every morality may appear to be a piece of "tyranny against nature," in the final analysis it is really the vehicle of life, for without the constraint of moral law there could be no determinate horizon for individual development and growth. "Consider any morality with this in mind," he concludes, "what there is in it of 'nature' teaches hatred of the *laisser aller*, of any all-too-great freedom, and implants the need for limited horizons and the nearest tasks—teaching the *narrowing of our perspective*, and thus in a certain sense stupidity, as a condition of life and growth" (*BGE* sec. 188). In this context, Nietzsche's basic objection to contemporary values is that they no longer inspire and enhance "life" in any significant respect. To say that "God is dead" means, in part, that our traditional Judeo-Christian ideals have lost their power as values, because they suppress and constrain the individual will instead of enhancing it.

The second point explains the nature of the highest value: "he who cannot obey himself is commanded"—which implies that whoever *can* obey himself is exempt from such a penalty and is the sovereign creator of his own law. Thus Zarathustra affirms the self-legislation of sovereignty as the highest expression of life, for those who are incapable of self-appropriation and inner constraint are forever dependent upon the commandments and values of others. "In other words," as Nietzsche comments elsewhere, "the less one knows how to command, the more urgently one covets someone who commands, who commands severely—a God, prince, class, physician, father confessor, dogma, or party conscience" (*GS* sec. 347). Life commands a continual self-overcoming, but only that which commands itself adequately responds to the commandment that is given.

The third point explains why this is so: "Commanding is harder than obeying." It is easy enough to order people about; but commanding in an authentic sense is not just a matter of communicating one's will, for in order to have a will, one must first be capable of commanding something within oneself that renders obedience.[1] This means that the power of commanding cannot be measured by the position one occupies within the social-political hierarchy, for such power is not a quality of the individual life, but only an effect of one's "role."[2] Nietzsche emphasizes, in fact, that the sovereign individual is the one who is capable of maintaining himself, like Zarathustra, at a complete distance from all of the established forms. And hence, even when he commands himself, such an individual must *pay* for his commanding, for he is bound to refuse every fixed and secure horizon. In opening himself to the "experiment" and "hazard" of sovereignty he must continually risk himself and his own destruction; and yet he must also discover the strength to be the judge, the victim, and the avenger of his own law. In *The Gay Science,* Nietzsche writes that "Will, as the affect of command is the decisive sign of sovereignty and strength" (*GS* sec. 347). In this respect, the commandment that is placed upon the will—the imperative of sovereignty—must also be reckoned as the "hardest" imperative of life.

Thus it appears that the real focus of interest in this passage from *Zarathustra* is the quality of the individual will. For while there is constant reference to "life" and the living as such, the important question is *not,* "What is life?" but more specifically, "How are all our values and commandments related to the determinations of the individual will?" Indeed, it is only in the context of the latter question that the difference between self-commandment and following the commands of others is in any way relevant at all. This helps us to situate Zarathustra's final comment, when he announces that the will to power is the basis of everything that is alive; for at this point in the discussion, we can only understand the will to power according to the model of individual willing. This suggests that the will to power is not intended as a metaphysical ultimate, but an anthropomorphic projection that recognizes itself to be such.

Nietzsche's later writings are increasingly dominated by the thought of the will to power. In *Beyond Good and Evil*, for example, there is no mention of the overman and only one oblique reference to eternal recurrence, but there are several discussions of the will to power, including Nietzsche's general claim that "a living thing seeks above all to *discharge* its strength," and "life itself is *will to power*" (*BGE* sec. 13). In section 23, for instance, he suggests the possibility of a new psychology that would avoid the pitfalls of moral prejudice by examining everything in terms of "morphology and the doctrine of development of the will to power." Clearly, in this context, he wants to sound out the true values of contemporary ideals and distinguish the various "types" of individuals, cultures, and morals in terms of the will to power as his ultimate principle of explanation. To say that "everything" is will to power is to say that everything is involved in a quest for empowerment. But to determine the specific nature of that quest—whether it is directed toward power over others or power over oneself, whether it is a power that enhances life or a power that confines it—one must also specify the different modalities of the will to power itself. This suggests a psychological reading of the will to power in terms of masters and slaves, or the active discharge of affect as opposed to *ressentiment*.

Later, in the same text, Nietzsche goes even further when he suggests that there might actually be an intellectual obligation to order the world according to the determinations of individual willing. For the economy of principles seems to justify the will to power as the most scientific hypothesis of all; and in this respect, the psychological reality of willing may be transformed into an ontological postulate. "Not to assume several kinds of causality until the experiment of making do with a single one has been pushed to its utmost limit (to the point of nonsense if I may say so)—that is a moral of method which one may not shirk today . . . one has to risk the hypothesis whether will does not affect will wherever 'effects' are recognized—and whether all mechanical occurrences are not, insofar as a force is active in them, will force, effects of will." And he continues,

> Suppose . . . we succeeded in explaining our entire instinctive life as the development and ramification of one basic form of the will—namely of the will to power, as *my* proposition has it; suppose all organic functions could be traced back to this will to power and one could also find in it the solution of the problem of procreation and nourishment—it is *one* problem—then one would have gained the right to determine all efficient force univocally as—*will to power*. The world viewed from the inside, the world defined and determined according to its "intelligible character"—it would be will to power and nothing else. (*BGE* sec. 36)

It is important to notice that here Nietzsche does not grasp the will to power in terms of a metaphysical or biological model, but only through the most complete examination of individual willing. This is crucial, for it suggests that the will to power is not simply intended as another cosmological principle, as many commentators would have us believe. Nietzsche calls himself a "godless antimetaphysician," and in all of his writings he undermines the traditional metaphysical ideas of God and the immortal soul, while he pursues all the correlates of such ideas that the prejudice of language still maintains. It would be strange to conclude that Nietzsche only repeated the mistakes of metaphysics by offering "the will to power" as his own name for the being of all beings, or that Nietzsche was himself a "metaphysical monist."[3]

In fact, at the same time that Nietzsche uses the will to power as a principle of explanation, he also develops the notion of perspectivism that challenges the received idea of "Truth" as a single and unitary ideal.[4] In earlier works, Nietzsche had argued that truth is a kind of error without which some species could not survive. In *Beyond Good and Evil,* he now repeats and develops such claims when he argues that the will to knowledge may itself be founded upon a will to ignorance; since in order to know anything, he asserts, we must be capable of ignoring the overwhelming manifold of experience that we are given, so as to focus upon those significant features that conform to our established perspectives.[5] Likewise, Nietzsche also argues that Plato's *denial* of perspective, and his dogmatic elevation of *the* good and *the* true, represents a disastrous constraining of life. He suggests that every great philosophy is nothing but "a personal confession of its author and a kind of involuntary and unconscious memoir" (*BGE* sec. 6), and this implies that the will to truth is always ordered by a particular ruling drive that seizes and organizes the manifold of experience in terms of its own perspective. In complete accordance with the death of God, perspectivism repudiates all monolithic metaphysical claims. And even if this does not imply the rejection of every kind of truth, the whole ideal of "truth" must now be placed within quotation marks. All of which would appear to undermine the status of the will to power as an ultimate metaphysical truth.

Thus we should say that the will to power is Nietzsche's most basic principle of interpretation, which is justified in terms of its explanatory value. It is not a metaphysical substratum, but the final instance of interpretation "beyond which we cannot go." We have already seen in the case of Nietzsche's other leading concepts—eternal recurrence, the overman, and the death of God—that his thinking is only falsified if these are treated as univocal philosophical claims. In his later writings, the will to power becomes Nietzsche's ultimate principle of interpretation, but it must still be remembered that it is a principle of interpretation that is significantly dependent on interpretation itself. This is not because the will to power is an inherently vague idea, but because it is completely overdetermined by psychological, metaphysical, and biological considerations. At the end of *Beyond Good and Evil*, for example, Nietzsche uses the idea of the will to power to determine the order of rank between master and slave moralities. But if, as we shall see, the master grasps value and power in one way, while the slave construes them quite differently, it becomes very difficult to grasp the will to power itself as a single and unitary phenomenon, or as an absolute truth that could exist outside of all perspectives. The "final meaning" of the will to power is forever dependent upon the one who interprets it; and the slave will always construe it differently than the master.

At the same time, however, if Nietzsche's philosophy expresses a radical disavowal of all substantial unities and organizing centers of thought, then the very idea of the will to power may *also* be the best expression for this absolute lack of foundation and the denial of a center of thinking. The will to power, we might say, is intrinsically plural. It is not some basic "stuff" that antedates things and supports them, since it is nothing but the manifestation of "force" in conflict with other forces, against which it is measured as active or reactive, ascending or declining. The will to power, it may be said, is an attempt to think the original difference of things in a nonreductive way. It is an appropriate image that attempts to capture the idea of absolute becoming and flux; and in this respect, it conforms to the same process that Nietzsche also describes in *Beyond Good and Evil*. "As soon as any philosophy begins to believe in itself, it always creates the world in its own image; it cannot do otherwise. Philosophy is this tyrannical drive itself," he writes, "the most spiritual will to power, to the 'creation of the world' to the *causa prima*" (*BGE* sec. 9).

Nietzsche self-consciously affirms the will to power as his own philosophical mythology; but while he bases the will to power on the immediate reality of "willing," it would not be correct to say that he simply follows Schopenhauer by making "willing" into the essential determination of reality itself. For one thing, Nietzsche condemns such metaphysical moves; and even though he seems to model the will to power on individual willing, he also calls the very reality of such willing into question—when he claims that the substantial ego, or the subject of the will, is really a fiction. From one perspective, the will to power may be an anthropomorphic projection that asserts that everything, including nature itself, must be comprehended within the human frame. But at the same time, the will to power is also used to dissolve the subject and every ideal unity, for Nietzsche recognized that the anthropological perspective must finally be reinscribed *within* nature as an "effect" of the cosmos itself. Once again, whatever "truth" there is can only emerge in the tension between these two perspectives; and we are bound to apprehend sovereignty *both* as a self-creation and as a result.

In order to understand the will to power we must now pay attention to what Nietzsche says about the nature of willing. In the remainder of this chapter I will focus on Nietzsche's discussion of selfhood and will, insofar as this is significantly developed in *Beyond Good and Evil*. In this work Nietzsche consistently attacks every traditional model and support of the fixed and unitary self, and his analysis of willing suggests an alternative account of the self as a multiplicity. It remains to be seen whether this radical dispersion of the self can be reconciled with the insistent imperative of sovereignty. Through a reading of *On the Genealogy of Morals*, however, I will show how the provocation of the *individual*, or the "return" of the master, remains one of Nietzsche's most important goals.

۰

In *Beyond Good and Evil*, Nietzsche conducts an extended meditation upon the nature of the self. At the same time as he shows the limitations of most conventional notions of ego and selfhood, he calls upon thinkers to offer "new versions and refinements of the soul hypothesis" such as "mortal soul," "soul as subjective multiplicity," or "soul as social structure of the drives and affects" (*BGE* sec. 12). The death of God means that all the daring of the lover of knowledge is once again permitted, and we must construct new models of subjectivity that avoid the traditional prejudices of thinking that Nietzsche illumines so well. In *Beyond Good and Evil*, Nietzsche explicitly challenges the prejudice of unity, the prejudice of independence, and the prejudice of freedom that we typically associate with the self. In his discussion of the soul, for example, he criticizes the Christian soul atomism, which takes the inner principle of selfhood as something indivisible and eternal. As we have seen, the death of God implies the end of all fixed centers and principles of organization, not simply because the world is a construction of the subject, but more radically, because the very idea of the self-sufficient and independent subject is itself a construction that reflects and resembles the discredited model of God. But Nietzsche does not simply argue that the self is a nugatory concept, or that a materialist reduction would effectively dissolve the problem. By unraveling ordinary conceptions of subjectivity, he poses the more difficult task of rethinking, as opposed to rejecting, the self. "Between ourselves," he comments, "it is not at all necessary to get rid of 'the soul' at the same time, and thus to renounce one of the most ancient and venerable hypotheses—as happens frequently to clumsy naturalists who can hardly touch on 'the soul' without immediately losing it" (*BGE* sec. 12).[6]

Much of Nietzsche's discussion is focused upon the will and his critique of free will as an error. In section 21, for example, he argues without qualification that the traditional postulate of free will "in the superlative metaphysical sense" is a logical contradiction of the most blatant sort, for it suggests that the individual is somehow capable of a magical self-creation, so that in spite of every familial or social determination, one is completely responsible for what one becomes. Insofar as it follows the model of divine self-creation, Nietzsche suggests that this *causa sui* "is the best self-contradiction that has been conceived so far." It is a "rape and perversion of logic," he adds, "but the extravagant pride of man has managed to entangle itself profoundly and frightfully with just this nonsense." Nietzsche makes a very strong point here, but it is significant that in the rest of this section he goes out of his way to condemn the complementary error of the "unfree" will. "In the in-itself," he writes, "there is nothing of 'causal connections,' of 'necessity,' or of 'psychological non-freedom'; there the effect does not follow the cause, there is no rule of 'law.' It is we alone who have devised cause, sequence, for-each-other, relativity, constraint, number, law, freedom, motive, and purpose" (*BGE* sec. 21).

On the one hand, the idea of the unfree will has to be rejected because, like its counterpart, it suggests the possibility of a will that is self-contained and somehow separate from the world that acts upon it. But at a deeper level, Nietzsche's rejection of both the free will and the unfree will is also an attempt to overcome the traditional dualities that have always constrained our thinking. There is a word, "will," and because it is a single word, we assume that it refers to a single enduring faculty, and the only question is whether this faculty is constrained or independent. By showing the problematic assumptions that have been made at every point, Nietzsche forces thinking beyond such limited possibilities.

In section 19 of *Beyond Good and Evil*, Nietzsche provides us with an extended phenomenological account of the process of willing. His basic conclusion, in opposition to the traditional view, is that willing is a very complicated phenomenon. In this section Nietzsche distinguishes three distinct moments involved in the act of willing. First, he argues that in all willing there is a plurality of sensations and a muscular tension "towards" something and "away" from something else that exists by force of habit, even before the body is set in motion. Next, in addition to these sensations, every act of willing is organized around a "ruling thought" that directs the willing in question. "Let us not imagine it is possible," he writes, "to sever this thought from the 'willing,' as if any will would then remain over!" Finally, he argues that the will is above all an affect, and more specifically, the affect of command: "That which is termed 'freedom of the will' is essentially the affect of superiority in relation to him who must obey." "But now," he continues,

> let us notice what is strangest about the will—this manifold thing for which the people have only one word: inasmuch as in the given circumstances we are at the same time the commanding *and* the obeying parties, and as the obeying party we know the sensations of constraint, impulsion, pressure, resistance, and motion, which usually begin immediately after the act of will; inasmuch as, on the other hand, we are accustomed to disregard this duality, and to deceive ourselves about it by means of the synthetic concept "I," a whole series of erroneous conclusions, and consequently of false evaluations of the will itself, has become attached to the act of willing—to such a degree that he who wills believes sincerely that willing suffices for action. . . .
>   "Freedom of the will"—that is the expression for the complex state of delight of the person exercising volition, who commands and at the same time identifies himself with the executor of the order—who, as such, enjoys also the triumph over obstacles, but thinks within himself that it was really his will itself that overcame them. In this way the person exercising volition adds the feelings of delight of his successful executive instruments, the useful "under-wills" or under-souls—indeed, our body is but a social structure composed of many souls—to his feelings of delight as commander. *L'effet c'est moi.* (*BGE* sec. 19)

To will is always to command, but every commandment implies the existence of one who is there to obey. And for every impulse to do something, there are a multitude of other impulses that must be overcome if this impulse is to achieve the commandment of sovereignty. Thus willing seems to imply the essential multiplicity of the individual, as a "community" of different souls and different impulses. The subject "I" is just an effect of the whole—a trick of grammar, perhaps—that is posited whenever we identify *ourselves* with the commanding impulse and its feeling of delight.

Nietzsche's analysis is quite compelling, and it lies behind much work in recent Continental philosophy, which emphasizes the decentering of the self and the overcoming of the enthroned subject of consciousness. His analysis emphasizes that there is no original and unitary self.[7] There is only a totality of impulses that compete for mastery—and as such, the idea of a singular *true* identity is really a fiction. For Nietzsche, as with St. Paul, the experience of subjectivity begins with the awareness of an essential division within the self that emerges in the very act of willing. This means that the self is inherently divided and multiple; and insofar as the subject wills something, even its own self, this is only a derivative result of a process that forever exceeds it.

This critique of substantial selfhood is in complete accordance with Nietzsche's own elevation of the will to power as the basic imperative of life. For if willing must continually seek its own empowerment and increase, then every attempt to reduce the individual to something fixed and determinate is necessarily a falsification. But if there is no single "true" self, then this also seems to threaten the possibility of sovereignty, in the sense of willing one's *own* will, that we have attributed to Nietzsche until now. The multiplicity and the impersonality of the individual agent does not obviously cohere with the goal of sovereignty, when this is understood in the minimal sense of commanding one's own law. Does Nietzsche's thought rest upon a contradiction, or would it be true to say that the multiplicity of the self is only a partial point of view?

In fact, we must not forget that there are two dominant registers at work in *Beyond Good and Evil.* In addition to the dispersion of the self, which is accomplished in passages like those discussed above, there is also an imperative summons to sovereignty and a recollection of the self, which is especially prominent in Nietzsche's later account of masters and slaves. In the concluding part of *Beyond Good and Evil,* called "What Is Noble," Nietzsche introduces his distinction between master and slave morality as a difference between two basic versions of valuation, and hence of the will to power. The master celebrates life as it shines forth in his own existence, as something utterly singular and differentiated from the rest of creation. "The noble type of man," Nietzsche writes, "experiences *itself* as determining values; it does not need approval; it judges, 'what is harmful to me is harmful in itself'; it knows itself to be that which first accords honor to things; it is *value-creating.* Everything it knows as part of itself it honors: such a morality is self-glorification" (*BGE* sec. 260). By contrast, the slave feels his own impotence in comparison with the master. Out of the spirit of revenge he denigrates the master and the master's values as "evil"; and to forget his own wretchedness he reduces everything to his own wretched level. The values of the slave are thus the values of utility—moral and social conformity, science and "progress"—that serve to normalize society by suppressing individual difference.

Nietzsche's distinction between masters and slaves is very significant because it suggests that the absolute dispersion of the self that he posits at the beginning of *Beyond Good and Evil* is not his final word on the individual. Presumably, if reduction to the will to power involved the complete death of the self, then there would be no evaluative difference between masters and slaves, since each would be an impersonal and unavoidable expression of the will to power. And there could be no imperative to sovereignty if sovereignty were *only* an effect. At the same time, however, Nietzsche *does* insist upon an order of rank between the different values and moralities that exist, and in this respect, the master and the slave embody the forms of ascending and declining life. It therefore makes sense to say that the sovereignty of the master is intended as a model and as a prescriptive ideal, and this means that a self-gathering, or an affirmative relation of the self to itself, must complement the radical self-dispersion.

Looking back at section 21, then, it is important to remember that after Nietzsche rejects the freedom of the will in the superlative metaphysical sense, along with the idea of the "unfree" will, he says that in real life it is always and only a matter of strong and weak wills. This comment should help us to understand his later claim, that the philosophers of the future will owe their spiritual independence and courageous will to truth "to an excess of free will" (*BGE* sec. 44). It also helps us to follow his diagnosis of the sickness and nihilism of modern life in terms of a general "paralysis of the will" (*BGE* sec. 208). Let us accept that the will, as the principle of individual command, is absolutely inseparable from nature. In this sense, Nietzsche argues that individual selfhood is an outcome. In *Thus Spoke Zarathustra,* for example, the soul is regarded as an effect of the body; while in *On the Genealogy of Morals,* Nietzsche describes "the responsible subject" as a convenient fiction, which is created by the need to punish or control. But once the self has been fabricated, and once a sense of individual responsibility has been produced, or even burned into the subject through a long and bloody process of moral training, the possibility of an individual strength of will is bound to grow accordingly. And this is the origin of sovereignty as a determinate possibility of life.

In *Beyond Good and Evil* and elsewhere, Nietzsche argues that the unconditional commandment of morality, the categorical imperative of whatever kind, has only depressed and diminished the human spirit. In the following passage, for example, he writes of our need for the unconditional, and he suggests that the art of obeying has only prospered at the expense of the art of commanding. "It may fairly be assumed," he writes,

> that the need for it is now innate in the average man, as a kind of *formal conscience* that commands: "thou shalt unconditionally do something, unconditionally not do something else," in short, "thou shalt." This need seeks to satisfy itself and to fill its form with some content. According to its strength, impatience, and tension, it seizes upon things as a rude appetite, rather indiscriminately, and accepts whatever is shouted into its ears by someone who issues commands—parents, teachers, laws, class prejudices, public opinions. (*BGE* sec. 199)

Such comments are typical of Nietzsche's general stance against the seductions of morality. What is not sufficiently recognized, however, is that in this passage and in others like it, Nietzsche suggests an alternative outcome to the whole of this moral process. Moral training, through the conditioning of the body that Nietzsche records in *On the Genealogy of Morals,* has actually created the responsible subject, the creature who has the right to make promises, with its self-discipline and power of disposal over itself. So that now, the force of such an existence, which had previously been constrained by ordinary moral categories, threatens to advance beyond the old morality and to command its existence in terms of its own self-given law. "It was this morality itself that damned up such enormous strength and bent the bow in such a threatening manner," he writes. "Now it is 'outlived,' the dangerous and uncanny point has been reached where the greater, more manifold, more comprehensive life transcends and *lives beyond* the old morality; the 'individual' appears, obliged to give himself laws and to develop his own arts and wiles for self-preservation, self-enhancement, self-redemption" (*BGE* sec. 262).

In Nietzsche's terms, such an individual would be "sovereign and free," for here as elsewhere, he stresses the opposition between individual sovereignty and morality. This is not to say that sovereignty involves moral abandonment, but only that the ideal of sovereignty can no longer be conflated with a strictly moral ideal. In opposition to Kant, the fulfillment of the individual is not equivalent to a moral fulfillment, and even if there is at least a historical link between morality and sovereignty, the latter cannot be viewed as an ordinary "moral" demand.

So while there is a real tension between Nietzsche's disarticulation of the self and his emphasis on sovereignty, it is not a conflict that must destroy either one of these two poles. In Nietzsche, the self, like Dionysus, is continually dismembered and regathered, and it is finally this very movement that reflects the movement of sovereignty itself. In one respect, the self or the ego is just an effect; but it is also an effect that is capable of subduing the manifold of its experience and appropriating itself. In the earlier passage on willing, for example, Nietzsche does not argue that selfhood is an illusion, but only that selfhood is a "result." We could say that when I identify myself with my "ruling thought" I am willing my own will; though even when I identify my ruling thought as an external command, I can say that "I" am following orders. The essential difference between master and slave is the difference between those who have this self-commandment to express a ruling thought and those who cannot or do not.

Later, Nietzsche claims that a spirit is distinguished by how much truth it is capable of bearing. In this respect, the very process of Nietzsche's thinking appears to mirror the absolute complexity of existence itself. Nietzsche tries to grasp the world from both the human and the cosmic perspectives. Thus he attempts to "translate man back into nature," which calls for a materialist critique, while at the same time he also tries to grasp the specific difference of human existence and the contributions of the self. As readers we are forced to encounter this contradiction so that we can finally *experience* the complex thought that holds both of these moments together.

In *On the Genealogy of Morals,* Nietzsche goes on to describe the original confrontation of the master and the slave, and he shows how the slave has triumphed. By recalling the forgotten position of the master, he seeks to restore the possibility of sovereignty that had previously been denied. Once again, however, the imperative of sovereignty is not a determinate ideal, but a possibility that must be *experienced* in terms of the original opposition between masters and slaves. The thinking that attends to Nietzsche's fantastic "history" of morals must now reflect and reconstrue this opposition in order to apprehend the image of sovereignty that it contains.

✧

Nietzsche has taught us to be wary of origins and to despise every account that recalls "the origin" as the ideal moment of some essential value or truth. In the very first aphorism of *Human, All Too Human,* for example, he exposes the glorification of the origin as a metaphysical subterfuge. He claims that one evades all the complex problems of historical emergence—"How did reason come from unreason, or altruism from egoism, or disinterested contemplation from out of covetous desire?"—when one assumes the conceptual and historical priority of the favored term as a privileged origin that precedes all dissociation.

In *On the Genealogy of Morals,* Nietzsche tells us a story of masters and slaves to describe the origin of our most basic moral values. But given his earlier strictures against "the origin," I think we have good reason to maintain an ironic distance from his account. Even though he seems to praise the master far more highly than the slave, we cannot read the *Genealogy* as if it were a straightforward historical narrative that laments a lost origin. Nietzsche certainly does use the conflict of master and slave as an analogue to specific historical situations—where, for example, the triumph of Christianity over the classical ideal is said to embody the triumph of the slave. But in a deeper sense the terms "master" and "slave" refer to basic modalities of individual existence, and in this respect they are types that still concern us all.

In fact, Nietzsche makes it clear from the very beginning of the *Genealogy* that in this inquiry the issue of the origin is entirely subordinate to the issue of value. He thus poses his guiding question as follows: "Under what conditions did man devise these value judgments good and evil? *and what value do they themselves possess?* Have they hitherto hindered or furthered human prosperity? Are they a sign of distress, of impoverishment, of the degeneration of life? Or is there revealed in them, on the contrary, the plenitude, force, and will of life, its courage, certainty, future?" (*GM* Preface sec. 3). Such fundamental questions require us to re-view the whole horizon of morality "as if with new eyes." Nietzsche must wrench us free from our established perspectives and confound all our moral prejudice. Precisely because of this, he returns to the origin of morality—not to legitimate contemporary values ("in the fashion of the English")—but, as he says, to pose them as a problem for the very first time.

In this respect, Nietzsche *uses* the story of the master and slave in order to suggest a *double* origin of value. The master is the one who celebrates life as it shines forth in his existence, by consecrating his instinctual power as something "good"; the slave is the one who suffers this discharge of strength, though he finally revenges himself in the revaluation of all active instincts as "evil," and his own passivity as "goodness." Following the guiding thread of his philology, Nietzsche suggests that there cannot be an "original" or "true" designation of value since the master and the slave must always evaluate the world in entirely different ways. Then, in the rest of the *Genealogy,* he goes on to detail the history of the West as the history of the slave's triumph, in which all the "active" forces of life have been negated or suppressed. As he comments, "the masters have been disposed of; the morality of the common man has won" (*GM* I sec. 10). Indeed, he argues that the master has not only been defeated—because he has lost his original voice the master has been condemned to silence, and this means that the very possibility of "mastery" has been forgotten. Thus, everything now hides the *exclusion* of the master: art, religion, morality, even science, which comprehends the world with entirely slavish categories like "reaction" and "adaptation," "struggle" and "universal law."[8]

By describing the victory of the slave, Nietzsche's strategy in *On the Genealogy of Morals* is to force us to undertake a *recollection* of the master. This is not to say that the *Genealogy* must be understood as a careful work of scholarship that simply aims to put the record straight. In the third essay Nietzsche rejects all scholarly pretensions when he suggests that interpretation is always a matter of violence, "forcing, adjusting, abbreviating, omitting, padding, inventing, falsifying, and whatever else" (*GM* III sec. 24). He also describes himself as "the comedian of the ideal," and though he uses the mask of the scholar it is only to explode the sober horizons of all traditional scholarship. Instead, I think it would be more helpful to understand the *Genealogy* as a type of *performative critique*, where in accordance with the second "Untimely Meditation," Nietzsche uses his reading of the past in order to direct us toward a particular vision of the future. He uses genealogy to recall the forgotten position of the master; he describes the logic of history that suggests the imminence of the slave's final victory; and he attempts to inspire us with an urgent longing for the master's return.

In the first essay of the *Genealogy*, Nietzsche clarifies his basic typology of masters and slaves within the context of a mythical prehistory. Here he describes the noble master as a man of "overflowing health," who celebrates all of the instinctual powers of life in the constant turmoil of "war, adventure, hunting, dancing, war games, and in general all that involves vigorous, free, joyful activity" (*GM* I sec. 7). Such an individual, living "in complete trust and openness with himself," does not seek to preserve or justify his life. Indeed, when he is free of the usual social constraints he abandons himself to the ferocious forces inside him and discharges all of his strength in "a disgusting procession of murder, arson, rape, and torture . . . as if it were no more than a student's prank" (*GM* I sec. 16). As the victim of these unconscious cruelties, the slave is one of the peace-loving herd who simply does not have the power to resist. Because he lacks every outlet, his suffering feeds upon itself as he is forced to experience his own weakness over and over again; until eventually, such *ressentiment* is established as memory, which allows him to calculate his own revenge.

Having established this distinction, Nietzsche then demonstrates how in a variety of different languages the words that are used to designate "good" and "bad" are all derived from words that express the self-affirmation of the master, or his indifferent contempt for the slave. The Latin *bonus*, for example, derives from *duonus*, which signifies a man of war, while *malus* stems from *melas*, which designates the common man as "the dark colored one." Likewise, the German *gut* means "godlike" or "the man of godlike race," which probably reflects the original significance of the Goths; while in Gaelic, the word *fin* came to mean "good" through its association with "the fair-haired," who were the Celtic conquerors of the native dark-haired population. By multiplying such examples, Nietzsche's ultimate aim is to show that value can have another meaning than one of simple utility. We may be accustomed to thinking of "the good" as equivalent to whatever is useful, or perhaps to what all people could affirm without contradiction. But if we accept Nietzsche's philology, it now appears that at the very start of history, or the origin of language itself, "good" is the name and celebration of life as it appears in its most powerful exemplars. Both here and elsewhere, Nietzsche insists that this proto-morality is not oriented toward the self-preservation of the individual, but the self-glorification of life.

But how are we to understand this parable of masters and slaves? If Nietzsche's philology is correct then it *is* the forgotten master who expresses the most primordial meaning of value: and in this way he *re-calls* us. And yet, while the noble master is an attractive and compelling figure in many respects, it also seems clear that Nietzsche deliberately *destroys* the possibility of our identification with him, by stressing his most horrible aspect as a murderous "beast of prey." Similarly, though the servility of the slave invites our contempt, Nietzsche also reminds us that without the slave, man would have remained an entirely stupid creature, and that all the achievements of our culture actually derive from the internalization of his suffering. In short, we must conclude that neither the master nor the slave are intended as simple ideals.

In a significant passage, Nietzsche suggests elsewhere that the democratization of Europe represents nothing other than the irreversible *mixing* of master and slave races. "In accordance with the slowly arising democratic order of things (and its cause, the intermarriage of masters and slaves), the originally noble and rare urge to ascribe value to oneself on one's own and to 'think well' of oneself will actually be encouraged"; and he concludes, "it is 'the slave' in the blood of the vain person, a residue of the slave's craftiness—and how much 'slave' is still residual in woman, for example!—that seeks to *seduce* him to good opinions about himself" (*BGE* sec. 261). In a similar sense he also declares that it would be "the surest sign of commonness" to be related to one's parents.[9] Clearly, in such passages Nietzsche is using the language of race and heredity in order to describe something that transcends the narrowly biological. I would suggest that the whole dialectic of master and slave must also proceed along the same "psychohistorical" or "psychodramatic" register. Of course, there are *no* pure masters and slaves, because the races have been mixed, and probably they *always were* mixed. Nevertheless, Nietzsche wants to isolate and typify these two principles, because the conflict between master and slave must always continue within the individual life as well as in history itself.

Thus in section 18 of the second essay, Nietzsche describes the creative imposition of form upon one's own animal nature as exactly similar to the master's own unconscious imposition upon the unfortunate slave:

> Fundamentally it is the same active force that is at work on a grander scale in those artists of violence and organizers who build states, and that here, internally, on a

smaller and pettier scale, directed backward, in the "labyrinth of the breast"
... creates for itself a bad conscience and builds negative ideals—namely the *in-stinct for freedom* (in my language: the will to power); only here the material upon
which the form-giving and ravishing nature of this force vents itself is man him-self, his whole ancient animal self—and *not,* as in that greater and more obvious
phenomenon, some *other* man, *other* men. This secret self-ravishment, this art-ists' cruelty, this delight in imposing a form upon oneself ... eventually ...
brought to light an abundance of strange new beauty and affirmation, and per-haps beauty itself. (*GM* II sec. 18)

Once we allow ourselves to go beyond the fable of a *literal* prehistory—
though as Nietzsche says, "this *is* present in *all* ages" (*GM* II sec. 9)—the
guiding question is no longer, "How can the individual abrogate his own
conscience and attachment to society in order to recover himself as a spon-taneous and instinctual being?" but "How can the individual reaffirm and
celebrate the original happiness of the master, given a society that has always
been the effective instrument of the slave's success?" Through attention to
etymology, Nietzsche has reawakened the essential possibility of the master—
and now we are called to confer a meaning upon the master's return, to
change the direction of history with the meaning of our slavish life.

In fact, if we read the story of the master and slave on this psychohistor-ical level it is relatively easy to comprehend them as the fragments of a sin-gle identity. In an obvious respect, for example, the master is simply the
embodiment of pure *activity.* As Nietzsche remarks, "[His] his work is an
instinctive creation and imposition of forms" (*GM* II sec. 17), while the slave
seems purely suffering and *passive.* But more crucially still, I think we can
also understand the master as the expression of an ideal and unmediated
autonomy. The master creates and affirms himself in everything he does, but
exactly like Kant's God, he is not commanded to good actions because ev-erything he does is *ipso facto* a creation of "the good."[10] In like manner, the
slave is supposed to be powerless and ruled by *ressentiment,* and this implies
that his actions are entirely determined by a principle of sensibility. His re-venge against the master, and his denial of the active powers of man, suggest
that he is the embodiment of heteronomy, insofar as his will is always deter-mined from outside itself.

If we follow this suggestion, then the question of the master's return be-comes equivalent to the question of sovereignty—not within its Kantian
context of reason and adherence to the categorical imperative, but in a broad-er Nietzschean context of "life." So that, given the victory of the slave, and
Nietzsche's diagnosis of "the degeneration and diminution of man into the
perfect herd animal" (*BGE* sec. 203), our guiding question becomes: "How

can the individual affirm himself as an *autonomous* individual, given a society that has steadily suppressed all active forces, and thus established willlessness, or *self*-denial, as the dominant moment of contemporary life?" In order to answer this, however, we must first rehearse the details of the slave's revenge, since this will illuminate Nietzsche's alternative ideal. More specifically, we must consider the tactics of the priest, who as the guardian and director of the slave establishes himself, within the *Genealogy*, as Nietzsche's own counter-principle and his most dangerous enemy.

In the second and third essays of *On the Genealogy of Morals*, Nietzsche seeks to show how the historical dominion of the slave has been strengthened and brought to its most incredible forms through the supreme artistry of the Judeo-Christian priest. As a necessary moment of his own "counter-artistry," Nietzsche exposes the various stratagems that the priest has used in order to maintain the most complete enslavement of man—characterizing Christianity in general as "a great treasure house of ingenious means of consolation . . . a collection of refreshments, palliatives, and narcotics" (*GM* III sec. 17). Nietzsche argues that while the priest has seduced the slave by providing some meaning for his suffering, all of his so-called remedies have only weakened the slave and ensured his continued enfeeblement.

To make us fully aware of the priest's own cunning and artistry in guilt, Nietzsche provides us from time to time with the elements of a "natural history of society," which functions within the *Genealogy* as a kind of ideal correlate.[11] In the first sections of the second essay, for example, he claims that the proper *result* of the long development he relates is the "sovereign individual" and that this "autonomous" individual is capable of commanding his own nature because he has learned how to promise himself, in sustaining his will over a period of time. Nietzsche argues, moreover, that such an individual can only emerge after a long process of social training in which the *slavish* qualities of memory and calculation are steadily branded into his soul. Similarly, he stresses that "the bad conscience" is the inevitable outcome of man's confinement within society and the consequent redirection of his cruelty against himself. Though as we have seen, he describes this happening as an *active* bad conscience and suggests that it is the origin of all beauty, and even justice, since it can lead to the overcoming of *ressentiment*. It is clear, then, that Nietzsche does not regard society itself as an original evil, for both here and in *Beyond Good and Evil* he valorizes the submission to law as "the categorical imperative of nature," and the only means by which individual sovereignty is achieved.

On the other hand, when Nietzsche considers the *priestly appropriation* of bad conscience—as a morbid consciousness of guilt before God and total self-disgust—he argues that it is precisely *this* that has produced "the most terrible sickness that has ever raged in man." According to Nietzsche, the priest turns the individual will against itself, not in order to bring about a sovereign self-control, but self-laceration and the mortification of the will through guilt. As he comments:

> This man of the bad conscience has seized upon the presupposition of religion so as to drive his self-torture to its most gruesome pitch of severity and rigor. Guilt before God: this thought becomes an instrument of torture to him. He apprehends in "God" the ultimate antithesis of his own ineluctable animal instincts; he rein-terprets these animal instincts themselves as a form of guilt before God (as hostility, rebellion, insurrection against the "Lord," the "father," the primal ancestor and origin of the world). (*GM* II sec. 22)

In this respect, the story of Christ the Redeemer must be considered as a real "stroke of genius." For if Christ's sacrifice is a debt that can *never* be repaid, then it must follow that we are all eternally guilty. Henceforth, we have to consider ourselves as the creatures of sin, and the only possible release from our suffering and guilty existence is through ascetic denial or the destruction of our individual will. In effect, the priest directs us to use our power to destroy our power; he explains the meaning of our unhappy suffering (when the latter is just the impotence of the slave and his basic physiological depression); and his "ministry" is to make us forget this pain by forgetting ourselves.

In the third essay, Nietzsche goes on to describe the whole variety of ascetic ideals and practices that the priest has promoted to preserve a declining life and to ensure its continued sickness. Thus he relates the "innocent" forms of the ascetic ideal that tend toward self-narcosis and allow the slave to avoid the reproach that his own existence offers him. In this category are the hermit's fasting and withdrawal from life; complete immersion in some form of mechanical activity like work; and "petty devotion to others"—an involvement in the communal life of the herd that allows individuals to forget themselves in the shadow of something grander. More dramatically, Nietzsche then reviews the "guilty" forms of asceticism: the penitent's scourge, the hair shirt and starving body, and the dancing epidemics of the Middle Ages. He claims that all of these remedies sought to deaden our secret suffering through the production of an orgy of feeling—although their final effect has only been to weaken us even further.

At the end of the *Genealogy* Nietzsche turns to the state of contemporary scholarship, to argue that in modern times yet another version of the ascetic ideal has become dominant: one that is manifest by the scholar's unselfish devotion to the truth, for which he is ready to sacrifice anything, including himself. Thus he talks of "the proficiency of our finest scholars, their heed-less industry, their heads smoking day and night, their very craftsmanship," and he comments, "How often the real meaning of all this lies in the desire to keep something hidden from oneself! Science as a means of self-narcosis: *do you have experience of that?*" (*GM* III sec. 23). We should notice, however, that the ascetic ideal of the scholar is definitely *not* a function of his religious belief. Indeed, in several passages Nietzsche emphasizes that such a total devotion to the truth eventually leads every good scholar *away* from the lie that supports belief in God; and in this respect, the will to truth brings about the complete self-overcoming of Christianity and Christian morality. Hence, in promoting *this* form of asceticism Nietzsche's priest must survive the aban-donment of explicitly religious forms. It follows that the latter is more than the representative of a particular religion, or even the avatar of religion as such. And, while Nietzsche uses the *Genealogy* to uncover various strategies and disguises that the priest has used in the past, we are made to realize that we cannot expect the latter to appear in the same (religious) masks he has always worn before. In this way, Nietzsche suggests the necessity for a con-tinual "revision" of the *Genealogy,* for the priest can always assume new masks, though the ultimate effect of his machinations will always be the same.

Finally, then, as the heirs to all of the priest's disastrous remedies, Nietz-sche gives us to understand that the overall tendency of the priestly ideal has actually been to diminish man completely and to turn him into a timid herd animal. He concludes that the continual suppression of the individual will has its issue in "will-lessness" as the basic characteristic of modern life:

> We can no longer conceal from ourselves *what* is expressed by all that willing which has taken its direction from the ascetic ideal: this hatred of the human, and even more of the animal, and more still of the material, this horror of the senses, of reason itself, this fear of happiness and beauty, this longing to get away from all appearance, change, becoming, death, wishing, from longing itself—all this means . . . —*a will to nothingness,* an aversion to life, a rebellion against the most fundamental presuppositions of life. (*GM* III sec. 28)

And again,

> the diminution and leveling of European man constitutes *our* greatest danger. . . . We can see nothing today that wants to grow greater, we suspect that things will continue to go down, down to become thinner, more good natured, more prudent, more comfortable, more mediocre, more indifferent, more Chi-nese, more Christian—there is no doubt that man is getting "better" all the time.
>
> Here precisely is what has become a fatality for Europe—together with the fear of man we have also lost our love of him, our reverence for him, our hopes for

him, even the will to him. The sight of man now makes us weary—what is nihilism today if it is not *that*?—We are weary *of man*. (*GM* I sec. 12)

The *Genealogy* has revealed that the progress of *nihilism,* or the will to nothingness, is the hidden direction of history that now becomes explicit. In other words, the meaning of nihilism is nothing other than the triumph of the slave and the continued destruction of the individual as such. And, as the artist of such a history, the priest is also revealed as the world-historical agent of nihilism itself.

It follows, then, that "the *return* of the master" corresponds to the overcoming of nihilism, with the destruction of the priest in history and the slave within ourselves. For in the celebration of an *active* will to self-empowerment, the master provides us with a new ideal that opposes the will to nothingness and may even reverse it. As this conflict continues—with Nietzsche against the priest, the master against the slave, and *Dionysus versus the Crucified*—we must now consider Nietzsche's attempt at a legislation of the future.

I have argued that for Nietzsche the essential meaning of nihilism is the destruction of the individual will as an active and distinctive power. In the final analysis, nihilism is to be identified with the will to nothingness—and this is a will not to have to will, which craves its release from willing. Hence, Nietzsche's ideal of autonomy, or sovereignty, may be understood as the most extreme counter-thought to nihilism, since the autonomous will, the will of the master, is precisely the one that celebrates and affirms itself in the joy of self-creation. Simply put, whereas nihilism is fundamentally the will *not* to will, sovereignty is at bottom the will to will.

Of course, Nietzsche was fully aware of the antipodal nature of these themes, primarily in the symbolic opposition of master and slave, but also in his continual exhortation of the individual will in the face of a growing will-lessness. In *Beyond Good and Evil,* for example, he diagnoses the sickness of modern Europe as a "paralysis of will," suggesting that as modern individuals grow ever "smaller" and more similar they will succumb to "a new European Buddhism." For Nietzsche, writing as a "philosopher of the future" and not merely as a cultural critic, the only possible remedy is to recreate those conditions that might produce a *sovereign* will. In this respect his analysis of history is itself an attempt to force the direction of the future.

Thus, as we have seen, in the *Genealogy* Nietzsche envisages the bearer of this sovereign will—or the sovereign individual—as the longed-for justification of history. Through the long and bloody training of culture, a will is created that must eventually appropriate its slavish presuppositions and achieve the total commandment of its own existence. Nietzsche argues that such a will finally secures the freedom of "autonomy":

> If we place ourselves at the end of this tremendous process, where the tree at last brings forth fruit, where society and the morality of custom at last reveal *what* they have simply been the means to: then we discover that the ripest fruit is the *sovereign individual*, like only to himself, liberated again from morality of custom, autonomous and supramoral (for "autonomous" and "moral" are mutually exclusive), in short, the man who has his own independent, protracted will and the *right to make promises*—and in him a proud consciousness, quivering in every muscle, of *what* has at length been achieved and become flesh in him, a consciousness of his own power and freedom, a sensation of mankind come to completion. (*GM* II sec. 2)

This sovereign individual is the one who orders and overcomes all of that brutal "accident" that constitutes his own prehistory or past. In this respect he is capable of pledging himself as the master of his own future; for as the one who possesses a *commanding* will he alone has acquired the right to "make promises."

We may accept that for obvious reasons, Nietzsche's only direct presentation of the master's return is through such fragments and moments of evocation as the passage quoted above. Indeed, it has been argued that any account of sovereignty is necessarily suggestive and incomplete, since the sovereignty of the individual must exceed all conceptual determinations. Even so, there is still another important objection, for at first glance it seems that Nietzsche's account of history gains its most compelling power through a dialectical sleight-of-hand. First, the powerful master tyrannizes the slave and makes him suffer; then the calculating slave subdues the master through the ploy of a revaluation of values; and finally, now that the slave's triumph is almost complete, we are made to anticipate the master's return as the final synthesis of two opposing moments—following exactly the same logic of *The Birth of Tragedy*, where the "music-practicing Socrates" is scheduled to appear only when spiritual conditions in Europe have reached their lowest ebb.

Such a reading, however, would only obliterate the very deep awareness that Nietzsche had of the complete chance and fortuity of human events and human history. As he says, the creation of the bad conscience was "a lucky dice throw," and the domination of the ascetic ideal an incredible "accident" that only occurred because no other ideals were proposed over the past two thousand years. In this sense, Nietzsche writes of history as "a game in which no hand, and not even a finger, of God took part as a player" (*BGE* sec. 211). Thus, if there is any kind of teleology in the *Genealogy*, I would say that it belongs to Nietzsche's counter-artistry, as a strategy to compel us toward the recollection of the master, but always within the deliberately *irreal* context of a mythological history.

On the other hand, it is also clear that there is no *final* teleology or destiny at work in this text. Just as Nietzsche gave us a double origin of good and evil at the beginning, so at the end he offers the possibility of two different conclusions to our history, which allow us to choose how the story will end. The first suggestion is that we must be headed for the final victory of the slave, as the triumph of the tame man, the "maggot man" who has destroyed every distinction of rank. Here, Nietzsche suggests that the spur of ideals will soon become unnecessary as everyone will be content with their lot, and the utter will-lessness of the last man will thus inspire only nausea and pity. "Suppose these two were one day to unite, they would inevitably beget one of the uncanniest monsters: the 'last will' of man, his will to nothingness, nihilism. And indeed a great deal points to this union" (*GM* III sec. 14).

In opposition to such a gloomy prediction, however, Nietzsche uses a figure like "the sovereign individual" in order to awaken us to the possibility of a different future. This is his evocation of the master's return: "This man of the future who will redeem us not only from the hitherto reigning ideal but also from that which was bound to grow out of it, the great nausea, the will to nothingness, nihilism; this bell-stroke of noon and of the great decision that liberates the will again and restores its goal to the earth and his hope to man; this Antichrist and antinihilist; this victor over God and nothingness—*he must come one day*." (*GM* II sec. 24). Nietzsche clearly believed that with the unraveling of the death of God, and the questioning of all ideals that have hitherto inspired us, mankind stood at a crossroads. The logic of history suggests his final decline, but *On the Genealogy of Morals* shows that another outcome is possible. Indeed, Nietzsche's text is itself an attempt to produce that different future: it is a *performative* critique insofar as it aims to inspire the individual with the promise of the master's return.

In this respect, Nietzsche's philosophical activity in the *Genealogy* corresponds exactly to the model of "the philosopher of the future," which he describes in *Beyond Good and Evil*: "*Genuine philosophers, however, are commanders and legislators:* they say, '*thus* it *shall* be!'. . . With a creative hand they reach for the future, and all that is and has been becomes a means for them, an instrument, a hammer. Their "knowing" is *creating*, their creating is a legislation, their will to truth is—*will to power*" (*BGE* sec. 211). Without any context, these descriptions would be difficult to grasp. But now that we have traced the scope of Nietzsche's artistry, and suggested the subtle mechanics of his performative critique, the essential activity of this philosopher of the future is much easier to understand. One final quotation may help to explain.

> Toward *new philosophers;* there is no choice; toward spirits strong and original enough to provide the stimuli for opposite valuations and to revalue and invert "eternal values"; toward forerunners, toward men of the future who in the present tie the knot and constraint that forces the will of millennia upon *new* tracks. To teach man the future of man as his *will,* as dependent upon a human will, and to prepare great ventures and over-all attempts at discipline and cultivation by way of putting an end to that gruesome dominion of nonsense and accident that has so far been called "history." (*BGE* sec. 203)

In the *Genealogy,* Nietzsche *revalues* and *inverts* the established values. His genealogy is an attempt *to force the will of millennia upon new tracks* by recollecting all that was *nonsense* and *accident* in our history and showing how it may be redeemed with the return of the master, or the sovereign individual, as the fulfillment of the individual life. In this way he suggests that the slave may free himself from the cancer of *ressentiment,* for the will loses "its ill-will against time," when, as a sovereign will, it finally becomes capable of embracing every stage of its accidental history as a necessary moment of its own self-appropriation. And hence, on both the individual and world-historical levels, Nietzsche's typology of masters and slaves is a performative critique, since it promotes the possibility of a *transformation* of types.[12]

◦

The idea of the "philosophy of the future" becomes crucial in Nietzsche's later writings, not as an explicit theme, but as a focal point of his own self-understanding. In *Beyond Good and Evil,* he condemns traditional philosophers as a timid and gullible lot who are basically content to rationalize or reconstruct the given truth of the age. He claims that Kant himself, "the great Chinese of Königsberg," was "merely a great critic" (*BGE* sec. 210), and he comments elsewhere that modern philosophy in general suffers from a fundamental hesitation and a refusal to acknowledge its own potential greatness. "Philosophy reduced to 'theory of knowledge,'" he argues, is "philosophy in its last throes, an end, an agony, something inspiring pity. How could such a philosophy—*dominate!*" (*BGE* sec. 204). In opposition to these philosophical laborers, Nietzsche therefore proposes the superior ideal of the philosopher of the future, as a thinker who has come to terms with the past, but who also creates new truths and values and who is capable of impressing his thought upon existence as a whole. As we have seen, the genuine philosophers of the future are both commanders and legislators: "Their knowing is *creating,* their creating is a legislation, their will to truth is—*will to power*" (*BGE* sec. 211). All of this is anticipated by Zarathustra's words to the wisest men in the section "On Self-Overcoming": "You still want to create the world before which you can kneel: that is your ultimate hope and intoxication."

In this chapter I have suggested that in *On the Genealogy of Morals* Nietzsche writes as a philosopher of the future who attempts to provoke a transformation of the self by reconstructing and revaluing the past and by impressing the value of sovereignty upon us. Even in *Beyond Good and Evil*, however, there is a certain "voice" and a tone of calculation that Nietzsche uses when he considers religion and other social forces as devices of this new philosophy. "The philosopher as we understand him," he writes, "as the man of the most comprehensive responsibility who has the conscience for the over-all development of man—this philosopher will make use of religions for his project of cultivation and education, just as he will make use of whatever political and economic states are at hand" (*BGE* sec. 61). In a later section, Nietzsche considers the spiritual condition of Europe and contemplates the vast "strength of will" stored up in Russia as the possible key to the spiritual transformation of the West. "I do not say this because I want it to happen," he comments. "The opposite would be rather more after my heart—I mean such an increase in the menace of Russia that Europe would have to resolve to become menacing too, namely, *to acquire one will* by means of a new caste that would rule Europe, a long, terrible will of its own that would be able to cast its goals millennia hence—so the long drawn-out comedy of its many splinter states as well as its dynastic and democratic splinter wills would come to an end" (*BGE* sec. 208).

In his later writings, and especially in his notes and plans for the unpublished *Will to Power*, Nietzsche often adopts this world-historical stance of the philosopher of the future, dealing with ideas and doctrines, not so much in terms of their truth value, but in terms of their final effect upon humankind. Following Plato's model of the noble lie, he proposes various experiments and new caste systems that would oppose and reverse the systematic taming of man with the conscious breeding of a superior type. Thus he writes of the eternal recurrence as a doctrine that will "sift humanity" by separating the strong from the weak, and he speculates on the transformative power of eternal recurrence if it were ever accepted as a religious truth. In other passages he seems to view the West as a vast laboratory for the creation of a higher type of man. From a great distance, he watches the growth and decline of certain values and ideals, and in each particular case he calculates exactly what strategy would most encourage the rise of the human spirit. Once again, he speaks cooly and remotely, as a philosopher of the future whose final end is the total destiny of humankind:

Good Europeans that we are—what distinguishes us above the men of father-lands?—First, we are atheists and immoralists, but for the present we support the religions and moralities of the herd instinct: for these prepare a type of man that must one day fall into our hands, that must *desire* our hands.

Beyond good and evil—but we demand that herd morality should be held sacred unconditionally.

We hold in reserve many types of philosophy which need to be taught: possibly, the pessimistic type, as a hammer; a European Buddhism might perhaps be indispensable.

We probably support the development and maturing of democratic institutions: they enhance weakness of the will: in socialism we see a thorn that protects against comfortableness.

Position towards peoples. Our preferences; we pay attention to the results of interbreeding . . .

Preparation for becoming the legislators of the future, the masters of the earth, at least our children. Basic concern with marriages. (*WTP* 132)

Speculative fragments like these can be found throughout *The Will to Power*. And while it must be remembered that Nietzsche did not want to publish everything that he wrote, there are enough comments in his later published writings, from *Beyond Good and Evil* onward, to suggest that he continued to view his task in terms of this new philosophical and experimental perspective. Thus, in his call for a revaluation of values, and in his sustained confrontation with nihilism, the performative aspect of his work, by which I mean the effort to provoke the individual reader, is finally taken up into the world-historical task of directing the future as a whole.

If we now turn to *Twilight of the Idols, The Antichrist,* and *Ecce Homo*, we will see how Nietzsche's philosophy of the future and his call for a large-scale politics can be understood as the necessary counterpart and the consequence of his concern for the individual life. It would be easy to interpret Nietzsche's final preoccupation with grand politics and the philosophy of the future as the expression of his own mania. In the next chapter, I will suggest that through the focus on the individual and the political he actually returns to the fundamental issue of community and the goal of a higher humanity, which had concerned him so much earlier in *The Birth of Tragedy*.

7 ❧

Ecce Homo, or the Revaluation of Values

Two very distinct themes seem to emerge in Nietzsche's final published writings. The first is the tremendous project of a revaluation of all values, which inspires the testing of eternal truths and ideals in *Twilight of the Idols,* while it also serves as the explicit warrant for Nietzsche's reconstruction of Christianity as nihilism in *The Antichrist.* The second theme becomes central with *Ecce Homo,* when Nietzsche answers the question of how one becomes what one is by using his own life as an example. It is this final preoccupation with the details of his own unique existence that explicitly returns him to the issue of the individual and the problematic of sovereignty.

In his preface to *Twilight of the Idols,* Nietzsche comments on his own subtitle, "How One Philosophizes with a Hammer," by explaining that he will use his philosophical hammer like a tuning fork to demonstrate the hollowness of established ideals. At the very end of the book, however, he returns to a section from *Zarathustra,* "The Hammer Speaks," which indicates that the task of revaluation is not such an innocent affair. "For all creators are hard," he writes, "and it must seem blessedness to you to impress your hand on millennia as on wax, blessedness to write on the will of millennia as on bronze—harder than bronze, nobler than bronze. Only the noblest is altogether hard. This new tablet, O my brothers, I place over you: become hard!" (*TI* "The Hammer Speaks"). In this respect, the revaluation of values is Nietzsche's world-historical project, for it suggests an attempt to direct humanity toward a higher future than it has known hitherto. As the intended first volume of "The Revaluation of All Values," for example, *The Antichrist* deepens Nietzsche's critique of Christianity by showing how Christian ideals are inspired by ressentiment and the hatred of life. He claims, in particular, that St. Paul was a genius in hatred who successfully revalued the higher culture of the ancient world as so much sinfulness and pride. Now, in explicit opposition to St. Paul, he himself attempts a *second* reversal and revaluation that would overwhelm the monotonous Christian-value standard and force us to recognize that in spite of its apparent success, its origin lies in sickness and a declining will to power.

Thus, in both *Twilight of the Idols* and *The Antichrist*, Nietzsche pays excessive attention to physiology: Christianity condemns the senses, philosophy has forgotten about the body, and both of them put their faith in a "true" world that somehow stands behind this one. As the deliberate and parodic remedy for such a perspective, he now focuses upon the physiological dimension that had previously been denied. In the section on "Morality as Anti-Nature," for example, he suggests an exhaustive series of physiological explanations for the "peace of soul" that Christianity is supposed to bring; and in a later section of *Twilight of the Idols*, he tells us that the effect of the "ugly" on one's feeling of power, on one's will to power, can be gauged with a dynamometer. In *The Antichrist*, the more explicit vocabulary of contagion comes to predominate as Nietzsche describes Christianity as the religion of the "physiologically retrograde"; and he dwells specifically on the theme of Christianity as a parasitism or vampirism, which is slowly destroying all that is estimable in humanity.[1] This physiological perspective is an important remedy for every kind of "idealism," but given Nietzsche's warnings elsewhere, it is not the "correct" alternative that he seeks to impose instead. If consciousness, with all of its values and ideals, can no longer be accepted naively at face value, then "physiology" or something like it is simply the name for that perspective that attempts to apprehend the idealizing moment in terms of the material or "bodily" reality that it expresses. "We no longer derive man from 'the spirit' or 'the deity,'" he writes, "we have placed him back among the animals. We consider him the strongest animal because he is the most cunning: his spirituality is a consequence of this." And in this sense, he concludes, "our knowledge of man today goes just as far as we understand him mechanistically" (*AC* sec. 14).

From this standpoint, however, the issue of the individual seems to be very impersonal and remote. Nietzsche's physiological perspective requires him to look at individuals in terms of the broader historical, cultural, and biological formations that have produced them. This means that sovereignty is in no sense a given, and the sovereign individual or the "free spirit" is a historical result. The most important question concerning individuals is whether they represent the ascending or declining line of humanity, and it becomes the fundamental task of a revaluation of all values to diagnose these movements of the spirit.

It is important to notice, however, that even here Nietzsche does not abandon the central position of the individual in his own thinking. With their emphasis upon grand politics and their world-historical concerns, the final writings return us to the broader cultural issues that were originally raised in *The Birth of Tragedy*. What kind of institutions or values would lead to the progressive empowerment of the individual life? How have our current values served this goal? Nietzsche laments that we no longer possess any real sense for the authentically political dimension of life. We have lost the power to build institutions that would offer an enduring framework for individual development, and instead we regard any submission to institutions as a form of slavery. "The whole of the West," he writes, "no longer possesses the instincts out of which institutions grow, out of which a *future* grows: perhaps nothing antagonizes its 'modern spirit' so much." And he adds, "One lives for the day, one lives very fast, one lives irresponsibly: precisely this is called 'freedom.' That which makes an institution an institution is despised, hated, repudiated: one fears the danger of a new slavery the moment the word 'authority' is even spoken out loud" (*TI* "Skirmishes" sec. 39). Perhaps it is in this respect that we can understand his speculative preoccupation with a morality of breeding to serve as the counterpoise to the morality of taming that has apparently driven our culture up to this point. For if it is the case that we now view our submission to the law and other institutional forms as a kind of slavery, then he will proclaim himself as an *advocate* of "slavery" and he will ask what *forms* of slavery, what caste systems, or even dietary regulations will return us to the trajectory of ascending life. Clearly, Nietzsche does not finish with an impersonal physiological critique, or with an absolute solipsism either, for in his final works he is more than ever concerned to understand the existence of the individual life within the total context of a "culture" and its dominant values.

We can now turn to the second major theme of Nietzsche's later writing. At the same time as he inaugurates the revaluation of all values he also becomes obsessed with his own individual existence, and increasingly he uses his own life as a focal point for all of his thinking. In *Ecce Homo* Nietzsche declares himself. Having confronted humanity with its most difficult project of revaluation, he wants to explain and justify himself by saying exactly who he is. *"Hear me,"* he writes, *"for I am such and such a person. Above all, do not mistake me for someone else"* (*EH* Preface sec. 1). Once again, much of *Ecce Homo* is organized around the physiological axis. Nietzsche considers his own genealogy, he writes about the weather, digestion, sickness, and all the aspects of everyday life that are usually ignored as irrelevant. In this chapter, however, I will show how in *Ecce Homo* Nietzsche presents us with the image of sovereignty, for in the very movement and progression of this text he attempts to demonstrate his own continual enhancement and attunement to life. If he is successful, then his own right to begin the revaluation of values is thereby confirmed; and indeed, the revaluation of values will actually begin with the revaluation of his own life that he offers us here.

In *Twilight of the Idols*, Nietzsche criticizes anyone who would use their own values or their own life as a prescriptive model for everyone else. "Let us finally consider how naive it is altogether to say: 'Man *ought* to be such and such!' Reality shows us an enchanting wealth of types, the abundance of a lavish play and change of forms—and some wretched loafer of a moralist comments: 'No! Man ought to be different.' He even knows what man should be like, this wretched bigot and prig: he paints himself on the wall and comments, '*Ecce Homo*'" (*TI* "Morality as Anti-Nature" sec. 6). This passage is important because it clearly alerts us that Nietzsche's own *Ecce Homo* cannot be read as a model for imitation. On the one hand, in an obvious sense, Nietzsche celebrates his life in *Ecce Homo*. Through the violation of traditional philosophical and autobiographical forms he appears to summon the unique and unrepeatable "I" that is both incommunicable and yet universally understood. *Ecce Homo* is a text that illuminates the project of sovereignty through the example of Nietzsche's own life. Insofar as it recalls individuals to themselves, however, it does not work by commanding or inspiring obedience to Nietzsche's own image, but by evoking the very possibility of the individual that had previously been forgotten.

The themes of revaluation and individual existence thus dominate Nietzsche's final writings. But we move to the very heart of his thinking once we are able to think both of these projects as equivalent to each other. In spite of everything, it cannot be a matter of imposing new values upon humanity, since any imposition of values can only depress and confine the human spirit, as in the case of Christianity, which takes its values to be the only values possible. Nietzsche makes it clear at the beginning of *Ecce Homo* that he has absolutely no use for the "improvers" of mankind; he has not come to preach new idols, for he is not concerned with teaching people anything except how to seek for themselves. In *Ecce Homo*, he attempts to enact the project of sovereignty. Insofar as he is successful, he now proclaims the revaluation of all values as a formula that has "become flesh and genius in me" (*EH* "Why I Am a Destiny" sec. 1). What all of this implies is that these two events, self-appropriation and the revaluation of values, are simply the different moments of a single project.

I will now turn to some of the more excessive themes in *Twilight of the Idols* and *The Antichrist*. For many commentators, the rancor of these final works makes them difficult to read as anything but the first expressions of madness. I want to suggest, however, that Nietzsche's condemnation of St. Paul and Christianity only intensifies the earlier performative strategy that requires us to murder God in order to reclaim the sacred character of life. Likewise, we cannot understand *Ecce Homo* without an awareness of the same performative goal. Here, Nietzsche presents himself and in so doing he calls upon the individual as such. We must now determine how all of these concerns only underline and reinforce each other.

ॐ

In *Twilight of the Idols,* Nietzsche returns to many of the arguments he had presented in earlier works in order to provide a condensed summary of his own philosophical position. In spite of its strange fragmentary character, however, *Twilight of the Idols* is held together by a physiological critique that runs throughout the text. Nietzsche claims that the philosophers have devalued the body. From Socrates on they have condemned the senses as both false and dangerous, and the result is that "philosophy" is now just another expression of nihilism and the active denial of life. As we have seen, Nietzsche's strategic corrective to this whole tendency of thinking is to emphasize the purely "physiological" dimension of existence and to treat these great cultural or philosophical questions in terms of "life" in its ascending or "decadent" forms. As he writes: "It is decisive for the lot of a people and of humanity that culture should begin in the right place—not in the 'soul' (as was the fateful superstition of the priests and half-priests): the right place is the body, the gesture, the diet, physiology; the rest follows from that" (*TI* "Skirmishes" sec. 47). In this respect, he argues that while the Greeks understood the body and knew what was needed as a remedy, Christianity only despised the body and has therefore been "the greatest misfortune of humanity so far."

According to Nietzsche, every cultural formation, every idea, and even every individual is ultimately an expression of "life" or "the will to power." Every time we make a judgment on life, that it is worthless or absolutely good, for example, we are only reflecting the type of life that we represent. Life itself forces us to posit values and "life itself values through us when we posit values" (*TI* "Morality as Anti-Nature" sec. 5). Since we can never go beyond life to make a considered judgment about its value, it follows that any final verdict on the value of life is relevant only as a symptom of the health of the one who is making it. From this perspective, of course, the Socratic and Christian attempt to overwhelm or excise the passions can be taken as a sign of their life-denying tendency; while Nietzsche's Dionysian affirmation is the deepest expression of health. The obvious problem with all of this, however, is that apart from Nietzsche's own self-avowal, there is really nothing else to suggest that his own physiological optics are correct; or that the values we have lived by for at least the past two thousand years are *really* the forms of spiritual decline. Given Nietzsche's own insistence upon perspectivism, and the denial of any absolute values that would be applicable and appropriate for everyone, how can this assertion of spiritual health be anything but an assertion that *could also* be viewed as the expression of sickness and disease? In this respect, the revaluation of all values is without any final support.

Nietzsche faces the same obvious problems and objections in *The Antichrist*. In this work he attacks Christianity by linking it to the forms of degeneration and decline, and in particular, he suggests that Christian values express nothing but nihilism. According to Nietzsche, we should not say that Christianity is overcome *by* nihilism, for in reality Christianity has always been nihilism, whatever the historical status of its ultimate ground. And it follows that the total destruction of the Christian-moral value standard is a necessary first stage in the onslaught against nihilism itself.[2]

Toward the beginning of *The Antichrist*, Nietzsche announces the physiological standard that he will use in order to determine the basic value of our ideals: "What is good? Everything that heightens the feeling of power in man, the will to power, power itself. What is bad? Everything that is born of weakness. What is happiness? The feeling that power is *growing*, that resistance is overcome" (*AC* sec. 2). In the sections that follow, he intensifies his critique of Christian values by showing how Christianity condemns every active power and affirmative instinct as an "evil" or "sinful" impulse. Christianity claims that the meaning and the justification of the world is not to be found in this life but in another order of being entirely. It therefore functions as a seduction to weakness. It supports those who cannot will their own will by placing "goodness" within the realm of passivity—as obedience and humility and the absence of strong passions and as resignation and the turning of the other cheek. So finally, instead of life empowering itself in the affirmative movement of the will to power, and instead of Dionysian celebration, there is only a longing for calm and a final release from the burden of willing.

In fact, Nietzsche claims that Christianity as we know it, with all its definite commandments and dogmas and its preoccupation with the salvation of the soul, must really be a falsification of the original Gospel message. From the few statements of the Gospels that are attributable to him, it is clear that Jesus had no "theology" and no redemptive vision to assert against the world. St. Paul and the theologians who followed him have simply used the figure of the redeemer in order to fulfill their own priestly designs.[3] But such a reversal represents nothing other than the complete domination of the slave: "Paul wanted the end, *consequently* he also wanted the means. What he himself did not believe, the idiots among whom he threw his doctrine believed. His need was for power; in Paul the priest wanted power once again—he could use only concepts, doctrines, symbols with which one tyrannizes masses and forms herds" (*AC* sec. 42). Here, then, is the *original* revaluation of all values, when Jesus as the Christ becomes the great judge who decides between eternal life and damnation for all the souls of the world. Likewise, the triumph of *this* Christianity also entails the successful devaluation of the whole of the ancient world. The Greeks, the Romans, and the entirety of ancient culture can now be reconstrued as the base accomplishments of a godless and sinful pride. "The whole labor of the ancient world *in vain*," Nietzsche writes. "I have no word to express my feelings about something so tremendous. And considering that its labor was a preliminary labor, that only the foundations for the labors of thousands of years had just then been laid with granite self-confidence—the whole *meaning* of the ancient world in vain! Wherefore Greeks? Wherefore Romans?" (*AC* sec. 59).

Insofar as it uncovers the devious strategies of St. Paul and Christianity in general, *The Antichrist* is an attempt to revalue values, to force us to a different perspective on Christian themes and values, which we tend to accept as naturally given. By focusing upon the material and corporeal elements of existence, Nietzsche is drawing our attention to what Christianity has despised and condemned. Hence, the preoccupation with smell, for example, with the "unclean breath" of the man of today, or the corrupted stench of Christian values.

Ultimately, however, Nietzsche's physiological perspective cannot be justified by anything beyond itself. St. Paul revalued the whole of the ancient world, and now Nietzsche attempts a revaluation of Christianity; but how are we to choose between the two perspectives that are offered? Presumably, both would claim to be the perfect expression of spiritual and bodily health; but what justifies the acceptance of one of them over the other? And isn't the very definition of what constitutes spiritual health something that necessarily *follows* the acceptance of a given perspective, so that it would be a circular argument to try to justify the validity of the perspective in terms of it? If *The Antichrist* is to be understood as the expression of a certain will to power, then the obvious question is, what kind of will to power speaks here? If Nietzsche admits that Christianity has successfully masked weakness as a form of strength, then how are we to know that his own philosophical position is not itself an expression of the deepest kind of rage against everything that is good?

In fact, in both *Twilight of the Idols* and *The Antichrist*, Nietzsche strives to bring us into his own philosophical orbit—particular arguments may or may not work, but the overall movement of the text challenges and breaks apart our received horizons, and so allows us to experience the validity of Nietzsche's position, at the same time that we are inspired by it.[4] In this way, the text itself overcomes the solipsistic self-concern of the reader and provides the basis for a new community through the justification of Nietzsche's authority to speak. *The Antichrist,* for example, has often been condemned as a work of incipient madness, in which Nietzsche's rancor got the better of him. For how are we to take a book seriously that calls Jesus an "idiot," or that claims as a general rule of principle that "whatever a theologian feels to be true *must* be false" (*AC* sec. 9). "I call Christianity the one great curse," Nietzsche writes, "the one great innermost corruption, the one great instinct of revenge, for which no means is poisonous, stealthy, subterranean, small enough—I call it the one immortal blemish of mankind" (*AC* sec. 62). These remain "shocking" comments, but it is also, I think, the very excessiveness of this text that makes it so effective. According to Nietzsche, the Christian idea of God is a "crime against life" that has made the world both miserable and guilty. The idea of such a God is a slander against existence, which leads in obvious ways to the desecration of the body and the denial of life itself: "Yes! God as the declaration of war against life, against nature, against the will to live! God—the formula for every slander against 'this world,' for every lie about the 'beyond'! God—the deification of nothingness, the will to nothingness pronounced holy" (*AC* sec. 18). Thus, in denying this God and casting him down with contempt, we liberate the sacred character of life that had previously been denied. "The concept of God was until now the greatest objection to existence," Nietzsche writes. "We deny God, we deny the responsibility in God; only thereby do we redeem the world" (*TI* "The Four Great Errors" sec. 8).

It is not enough, then, to offer counter-arguments against the existence of God, or to rely on philosophical persuasion. Such ordinary tactics may sow a doubt here and there, but in *The Antichrist* the important thing for Nietzsche is to communicate the experience of the death of God. Not to report an event that is still on its way, but to kill the Christian God on every page and to use every blasphemy in order to make us experience the reality of his dying. With the death of God, experienced and incorporated in this way, everything that is denied or controlled by "God" may once again affirm itself within the horizon of this life.

The very violence of Nietzsche's text is thus an attempt to liberate the sacred, or the Dionysian enjoyment and celebration of life.[5] Given all that we have argued so far, however, it is also clear that for Nietzsche, it is the individual that expresses the celebration of life and offers the point at which we may most readily glimpse the power of the sacred. Hence, his final works are filled with the images of great individuals as exemplars and models—Goethe, in *Twilight of the Idols,* and of course Nietzsche himself in *Ecce Homo;* but also the celebration of the "free spirit" or the individual with a "strong will" that runs throughout *Twilight of the Idols.* At the same time however, in these later writings Nietzsche condemns the ego and the will and anything that might *support* the traditional ideas of individuality and selfhood; so that once again we are forced to rethink the nature of the individual in the tension between these competing perspectives.

In *Twilight of the Idols,* for instance, Nietzsche argues quite persuasively that the will is just a surface phenomenon. It is not itself a "cause" of actions, but something that merely accompanies the actions, since it may or may not be present on any particular occasion. Likewise, if I decide to continue writing, it is clear that something called "willing" is present in my decision; but we cannot assume that this willing is somehow independent and separate from the rest of the world; or that when I decide to do something, I magically initiate a new causal series that is undetermined by anything that existed previously. "The 'inner world,'" Nietzsche writes, "is full of phantoms and will-o'-the wisps: the will is one of them. The will no longer moves anything, hence does not explain anything either—it merely accompanies events; it can also be absent" (*TI* "The Four Great Errors" sec. 3). In *The Antichrist* Nietzsche suggests that this triumphal conception of the will is intrinsically linked to the image of divine sovereignty, which must now be abandoned. "Formerly," he writes, "man was given a free will as his dowry from a higher order: today we have taken his will away altogether in the sense that we no longer admit the will as a faculty. The old word 'will' now serves only to denote a resultant, a kind of individual reaction, which follows necessarily upon a number of partly contradictory, partly harmonious stimuli: The will no longer 'acts' or 'moves'" (*AC* sec. 14). This is the first aspect of Nietzsche's argument. Ultimately, however, in sections like "Reason in Philosophy" and "The Four Great Errors," Nietzsche takes this discussion one step further when he suggests that *all* of our substantial concepts of "objects," "things," and even Being itself, are simply projections or displacements of the one original error of an ego substance or will. As he says, "The concept of being follows, and is derivative of, the concept of ego" (*TI* "Reason in Philosophy" sec. 5). But there is an obvious difficulty here. For Nietzsche, the total character of the world is one of ceaseless flux and becoming. Every time we use language we conceal the flux of becoming with the fixed determinations of being; and thus we falsify the world by recreating it in our own image. At the same time, however, if the very idea of the will or the subject in general is itself a fiction, it is unclear how such a falsification could ever be accomplished, since the one who is supposedly responsible for the falsification is actually a fiction to begin with. On the one hand, Nietzsche traces everything back to the anthropomorphism of the human subject; but then he also dissolves everything, including the subject, in the absolute play of becoming.

Nietzsche is bound to use both the anthropological and cosmological perspectives, because the former is the key to the latter, while the latter serves as an essential corrective to the first. In the tension between the two perspectives, all the traditional ideas of individuality, sovereignty, self, and will are radically reconstrued as particular expressions of the will to power, or as moments in the play of becoming. In the same way, his account of the self as both a fiction and as a creator of fictions produces the same self-challenging discourse that effectively deepens his own problematic of sovereignty.

In spite of his onslaught against the will and every substantial model of selfhood, Nietzsche therefore retains an account of the self-in-process. And even in these final writings, in his discussion of the free spirit, or the strong will that is capable of self-overcoming, he continues to sketch the possibility of an individual sovereign ideal. In one of his "Skirmishes" for example, Nietzsche writes of the human being who has "become free." Striking a contrast between Goethe and Kant, he argues that "Goethe" embodies the continual achievement of individual sovereignty. For he "created himself," insofar as he organized the manifold of his lived experience and sought to unify all of those aspects of existence that are normally kept separate and distinct. "What he wanted," Nietzsche writes, "was *totality;* he fought the mutual extraneousness of reason, senses, feeling and will (preached with the most abhorrent scholasticism by *Kant,* the antipode of Goethe); he disciplined himself to wholeness, he *created* himself" (*TI* "Skirmishes" sec. 49).

The discussion remains complex, however, for such strength of will, or the will to will, is not characterized by great passions or by any kind of principled fanaticism, which would entail that the individual had simply become the vehicle of a preexisting ideal. Indeed, it is interesting to note that Nietzsche explicitly dissociates his own individual ideal from the traditional conception of the great man. He calls Savonarola, Luther, Rousseau, Robespierre, and Saint-Simon "fanatics," and "the opposition-type of the strong spirit who has *become* free" (*AC* sec. 54). Thus it becomes problematic to associate Nietzsche with a typical theory of the great man, even though he uses the mask of the great man, like Napoleon and Goethe above, in order to provide a negative indication of the individual life. Insofar as he will make use of such a pose in *Ecce Homo* we are bound to question it in advance.

Nietzsche's argument, abstracted from the text, would be to emphasize that strength of will is not a matter of subjective self-assertion, nor is it marked by an unyielding set of convictions that would determine everything in terms of itself. Such a fixity of purpose could only represent a declining will to power that remains closed to everything new. In fact, as we have seen, sovereignty involves an overcoming of the self in its narrow and petty sense and an opening to life, which still maintains the strength to recuperate itself. In this respect, the affirmation of individual sovereignty is the apogee of Nietzsche's Dionysian wisdom—and the focus upon the individual is the entrance into the sacred.

For Nietzsche, perhaps the real tragedy of the modern world is that sovereignty becomes increasingly difficult, as the pressures of mass society and "democracy"—his own name for the leveling process—continually erode the possibility of difference. At this moment of the individual's obliteration, when life is characterized by weakness of the will and the inability to exist as anything more than a function of the herd, his whole philosophical enterprise becomes an urgent attempt to reawaken what has been forgotten and to uncover the genealogical trace that points us toward a different future than the one to which we are apparently doomed.

In *The Birth of Tragedy,* the dialectic of Apollo and Dionysus provides us with a key to Nietzsche's meditations upon the nature of the individual self. Likewise, Zarathustra offers a sustained meditation upon the place of the individual within the cosmos. In *Twilight of the Idols* and *The Antichrist,* in the midst of his physiological critique of decadence, Nietzsche continues to evoke the possibility of sovereignty. In these later writings, however, the discussion of the individual is made from a purely "external" perspective. "The single one, 'the individual,'" we are told, "is the whole single line of humanity up to himself" (*TI* "Skirmishes" sec. 33). Likewise, the spirit who has become free is described only in the most formal terms.

In this respect, then, Nietzsche's writings seem to move inevitably toward *Ecce Homo* as the missing part of the equation and the impossible attempt to express his own singularity from within. This may appear to change the focus from the question of what an individual is to the question of who is Friedrich Nietzsche; but in reality, these issues are joined together and illuminate the single guiding question of "How one becomes what one is." As we have seen, *Ecce Homo* is an essential work, since Nietzsche is bound to justify his own fitness to begin the revaluation of values. More than anything else, in *Ecce Homo* he presents the experience of sovereignty through the example of his own individual life. With all his swaggering and grandiose claims to greatness he points us toward the individual existence that animates his text and provokes his reader to respond.

❧

From any traditional perspective, *Ecce Homo* is not really an autobiography at all, but a fantastic piece of self-celebration that comments sporadically on Christianity, idealism, and Nietzsche's previous writings. Even the superlative titles of his chapters—"Why I Am So Wise," "Why I Am So Clever," and "Why I Write Such Good Books"—suggest in advance that in this work, whatever the "facts" are, they will be arranged to illuminate Nietzsche's greatness. This apparently precludes any honest attempt to come to grips with the meaning of his life. Thus Nietzsche explains at the outset that "the disproportion between the greatness of my task and the *smallness* of my contemporaries has found expression in the fact that one has neither heard nor even seen me" (*EH* Preface sec. 1); and at the end he asserts, "I am no man, I am dynamite" (*EH* "Why I Am a Destiny" sec. 1).

But as we have already seen, Nietzsche's textual strategy and overall position is rather more complicated than all of this might suggest, for in several passages he does his best to call such poses into question and to undermine the same heroic stance that he seems to cultivate for himself. In "Why I Am So Clever," for example, immediately after he comments that in comparison with himself, the "so-called 'first' among men" are just "the refuse of humanity," he denies any self-glorification and tells us to beware of all great poses. "There is not a moment in my life to which one could point to convict me of a presumptuous and pathetic posture," he comments. "The pathos of poses does *not* belong to greatness; whoever needs poses at all is *false*.—Beware of all picturesque men!" (*EH* "Why I Am So Clever" sec. 10). Something similar is at work when he tells us in the middle of his own book to distrust *all* books and to actively resist them, or else lose the capacity to think. In *Ecce Homo*, Nietzsche deliberately aggrandizes himself, not in order to impress us, but precisely so that we will not take his self-presentation so seriously. Through exaggeration and hyperbole, and through explicit comments like those above, he offers us a self-portrait that calls itself into question at the same time that it focuses our attention upon the continuing issue of sovereignty.[6]

At first glance, then, it may appear that *Ecce Homo* is a completely self-involved and even solipsistic work. *"How could I fail to be grateful to my whole life?"* Nietzsche asks, "and so I tell my life to myself" (*EH* untitled exergue). This sense of complete solitude becomes a major theme in *Ecce Homo*, especially in the discussion of *Zarathustra*, which dwells upon the themes of isolation and distance that are captured most poignantly in "The Night Song." Likewise, when Nietzsche begins his discussion of "How one becomes what one is," he focuses obsessively on the minutiae of his own daily existence and his own physiological condition. "My blood moves slowly," he writes, "there is altogether no sign of any local degeneration; no organically conditioned stomach complaint, however profound the weakness of my gastric system may be as a consequence of over-all exhaustion. My eye trouble, too, though at times dangerously close to blindness, is only a consequence and not a cause: with every increase in vitality my ability to see has also increased again" (*EH* "Why I Am So Wise" sec. 1). But if this total self-concern is justified by his need to declare himself and to say who he is, it is also the case that the final effect of Nietzsche's presentation is to provide an example and even an experience of sovereignty that is meant to elicit a response. Beginning with the preface, then, Nietzsche warns his readers that he does not want "followers" who will place him in the same exalted position as the very ideals that he has come to destroy. This suggests that in *Ecce Homo* his real concern is not merely with self-advertisement, but with sovereignty as such.

Significantly, the subtitle of this work is "How *One* Becomes What One Is." Nietzsche uses his own life as an example. But just in case we become too enamored of his life and forget about our own, he gives us an excessive autobiography that still provides us with a particular model of sovereignty. Nietzsche wants to be taken seriously, but since his chief target is the life-denying tendency of Christianity and every other form of idealism, he cannot portray himself as the unequivocal redeemer of mankind. In fact, he portrays himself as quite the opposite: "I *want* no 'believers'; I think I am too malicious to believe in myself; I never speak to masses.—I have a terrible fear that one day I will be pronounced *holy*" (*EH* "Why I Am a Destiny" sec. 1). The self-celebration is deliberately undercut by his ironic denial, and the text as a whole becomes a manual for sovereignty.

In the opening section of *Ecce Homo,* called "Why I Am So Wise," Nietzsche provides an account of his own genealogy. In fact, he justifies his own privileged insight in terms of his particular lineage. "The good fortune of my existence," he writes,

> its uniqueness perhaps, lies in its fatality: I am, to express it in the form of a riddle, already dead as my father, while as my mother I am still living and becoming old. This dual descent, as it were, both from the highest and the lowest rung on the ladder of life, at the same time a *decadent* and a *beginning*—this, if anything, explains that neutrality, that freedom from all partiality in relation to the total problem of life, that perhaps distinguishes me. I have a subtler sense of smell for the signs of ascent and decline than any other human being before me; I am the teacher *par excellence* for this—I know both, I am both. (*EH* "Why I Am So Wise" sec. 1)

Clearly, Nietzsche is claiming that in some sense or another his own destiny was fated by his particular genealogy, and he adds, "perhaps this is why a revaluation is possible for me alone." Once again, however, if we take such passages at their face value, then we will run into a paradox, for the very possibility of sovereignty apparently disappears if it is *all* a matter of fatedness and hereditary determination. If we bear in mind everything else that Nietzsche says about the importance of racial and hereditary features, we might conclude from the outset that the project of "becoming what one is" is really illusory, since whatever the individual does, genealogy has already determined the latter in advance.[7] Against this, however, it is also obvious that in *Ecce Homo* Nietzsche's discussion of his life and his works remains focused upon the issue of sovereignty as the most basic goal. We should therefore consider what he means by "becoming what one is," and how this emerges in the development of *Ecce Homo.* Then we may return to the problem of genealogy to determine whether this *really* is an objection to his project.

Nietzsche proclaims throughout this book that the one great enemy against life is idealism, whether this takes the obvious form of Christianity, the philosophy of Kant, or even the freethinking humanism of the nineteenth century. According to Nietzsche, the basic problem with idealism is that it cannot accept the transitory character of existence, and so it revenges itself upon life by positing the ideal as the higher and fixed form. Christian morality has condemned the basic impulses of life as sinful, and draws our attention away from material factors that effectively determine our existence, so as to focus all our attention upon an illusory hereafter. "The concept of the 'soul,' the 'spirit,' finally even '*immortal* soul,' invented in order to despise the body, to make it sick, 'holy'; to oppose with a ghastly levity everything that deserves to be taken seriously in life, the questions of nourishment, abode, spiritual diet, treatment of the sick, cleanliness, and weather" (*EH* "Why I Am a Destiny" sec. 8). Once again, Nietzsche argues that the Christian promotion of selflessness and other related virtues actually leads to the oblivion of the self as an active and affirmative power. Likewise, he also condemns the very idea of "free will" as a pernicious form of idealism, for it implies that there is a substantial part of the self that is somehow separate and set apart from all the vicissitudes of existence.

Ecce Homo can therefore be read as an attempt to root out every false ideal, including the fabrications of selfhood. Indeed, one of the most striking things about this work is that Nietzsche emphasizes the *material* and physiological basis of his own existence by dwelling upon such neglected factors as the weather, diet, and recreation. He warns us against the excesses of wine, a vegetarian diet, or tea that is too weak. He emphasizes the importance of climate upon the metabolism and the respect in which this must influence the achievements of the spirit; and in no uncertain terms, he curses "that

damned idealism" that led him to ignore this basic dimension of life. Nietzsche's discussion returns us to the body as the great blind spot of Western
philosophy. And it is significant that the one overpowering sense that per-
vades *Ecce Homo* is the sense of smell. Nietzsche writes, "my genius is in my
nostrils" (*EH* "Why I Am a Destiny" sec. 1), and he claims to have a subtler
sense of smell for the signs of ascent and decline than any other human being before him. In fact, this insistence upon smell returns us to the most basic
aspect of material existence, insofar as smell is the one sense that cannot be
idealized or consciously ignored. Our ruling ideals stink, not because they
are "wrong" or "inconsistent," but because they are the expression of a de-
generating form of life or will to power. Thus Nietzsche attempts to go beyond the level of arguments and make us experience the reality of this decomposition by breathing it along with him.

Given this emphatically materialist context, we should hardly expect an
account of selfhood or sovereignty as something that stands apart from the
absolute flux of becoming. In *Ecce Homo* there is no nostalgia for the traditional
model of the substantial self and absolutely no attempt to restore the possibility of free will. Indeed, in this respect, Nietzsche emphasizes that sovereignty,
or becoming what one is, is simply not a subjective accomplishment. It is not
the result of a tremendous self-discipline or effort of will, and in his own case,
Nietzsche denies that he ever really "willed" to become anything: "I cannot
remember that I ever tried hard—no trace of *struggle* can be demonstrated in
my life; I am the opposite of a heroic nature. 'Willing' something, 'striving' for
something, envisaging a 'purpose,' a 'wish'—I know none of this from experience" (*EH* "Why I Am So Clever sec. 9). Nietzsche's experience testifies to a
deeper truth: the achievement of sovereignty cannot be accomplished by any
rigid self-definition; for given the mutual implication of self and world, the
individual must simply remain "open" to the empowering forces of life. And
this means that in order to achieve the possibility of sovereignty one must
continually risk oneself in order to return to oneself as stronger yet different
than before. As he quotes from his own *Gay Science*: "Whoever wants to know
from the adventures of his own most authentic experience how a discoverer
and conqueror of the ideal feels, and also an artist, a saint, a legislator, a sage, a
scholar, a pious man, and one who stands divinely apart in the old style—needs
one thing above everything else: the *great health*—that one does not merely
have but also acquires continually, and must acquire because one gives it up
again and again, and must give it up" (*GS* sec. 382; and *EH* "Thus Spoke Zarathustra" sec. 2). From this it follows that sovereignty is not a fixed state of being,
since it involves a continual movement away from any fixed determination of
the self toward openness and empowerment.

Presumably this is also why Nietzsche argues, against the whole weight of tradition, that the *nosce te ipsum*, or Know Thyself, is simply a recipe for ruin. "To become what one is," he says, "one must not have the faintest notion what one is." And he comments, "From this point of view even the *blunders* of life have their own meaning and value—the occasional side roads and wrong roads, the delays, 'modesties,' seriousness wasted on tasks that are remote from *the* task. All this can express a great prudence, even the supreme prudence: where *nosce te ipsum* would be the recipe for ruin, forgetting oneself, *misunderstanding* oneself, making oneself smaller, narrower, mediocre, become reason itself" (*EH* "Why I Am So Clever" sec. 9). What Nietzsche realized was that any attempt to define oneself or to circumscribe the parameters of one's being, by asserting "I am a true Christian," or "I am a good German," is inherently dangerous since it forecloses us from the higher possibilities of our existence and denies the reciprocation of self and world. In this respect, becoming what one is must involve a continual process of self-forgetting, even at the same time as we still control and appropriate what is given to us as our life.

It is hard to comprehend this whole experience in language, but in several places Nietzsche does comment that it was the "instinct" of a deeper health that rescued him from his deepest periods of spiritual oblivion. It is quite evident from *Ecce Homo,* for example, that Nietzsche saw his break with Wagner as the most decisive event of his life; and he dwells upon his shock and sudden awakening at the first Bayreuth festival, where Wagner seemed to enjoy his new cult status and accepted himself as an emblem of the German Reich. Nietzsche came to realize, however, that the dissolution of this spiritual patrimony was only the symptom of a deeper dissatisfaction with his own life. Thus he describes how in this same period he "woke up" to discover himself as a professor of philology, buried under the books and opinions of others and living a life of the most conventional and timid "selflessness." And while he reflects on this "total aberration" of all his instincts, and the years of wasted time, he describes the uncanny summons to self-appropriation that now began to make itself known:

> What reached a decision in me at that time was not a break with Wagner. I noted a total aberration of my instincts of which particular blunders, whether Wagner or the professorship at Basel, were mere symptoms. I was overcome by *impatience* with myself; I saw that it was high time for me to recall and reflect on myself. All at once it had become clear to me in a terrifying way how much time I had already wasted—how useless and arbitrary my whole existence as a philologist appeared in relation to my task. I felt ashamed of this *false* modesty. (*EH* "Human, All Too Human" sec. 3)

We should notice the passive construction of this passage: "What reached a decision in me . . . was not a break with Wagner." Nietzsche does not view the most decisive event of his life as a choice or a simple decision that he made for himself; the choice was made for him—not because he was forced to break with Wagner, but because he allowed the deeper instinct of health to prevail.

Similarly, in "Why I Am So Clever," Nietzsche underscores the impersonal nature of selfhood from the original perspective of life. "So many dangers that the instinct comes too soon to "understand itself," he writes. "Meanwhile the organizing 'idea' that is destined to rule keeps growing deep down—it begins to command; slowly it leads us *back* from side roads and wrong roads; it prepares *single* qualities and fitnesses that will one day prove to be indispensable as means toward a whole—one by one, it trains all *subservient* capacities before giving any hint of the dominant task, 'goal,' 'aim,' or 'meaning'" (*EH* "Why I Am So Clever" sec. 9). In fact, whenever Nietzsche describes the most important events and discoveries of his own life, it is always as if "he" were continually surprised by them. "Thus it happened, for example, that one day I was a university professor—no such idea had ever entered my mind, for I was barely twenty-four years old. Thus it happened two years earlier that one day I was suddenly a philologist" (*EH* "Why I Am So Clever" sec. 9). In all of this he affirms that the individual is not self-sufficient or present to itself. Indeed, the first condition for sovereignty in its deepest sense is simply an openness to the world that would allow one to receive empowerment.

Such a formulation is still quite problematic, but in his discussion of *Thus Spoke Zarathustra* Nietzsche does offer a parallel account of artistic inspiration and creativity, which makes it clear that the process of self-creation is closely related to the original experience of the artist. "One hears," he writes, "One does not seek; one accepts, one does not ask who gives; like lightning, a thought flashes up, with necessity, without hesitation regarding its form— I never had any choice." Once again, as any artist will testify, this process is not a subjective achievement, but the result of a fundamental attunement and openness to the powers of life. Nietzsche observes correctly that at the moment of artistic creation, the myth of the independent subject collapses along with any fixed distinction between personal freedom and natural necessity: "Everything happens involuntarily in the highest degree but as in a gale of a feeling of freedom, of absoluteness, of power, of divinity. . . . This is *my* experience of inspiration" (*EH* "Thus Spoke Zarathustra" sec. 3). I would add that the experience of sovereignty belongs to this level, for it is neither a choice of the free will nor an alien destiny that is imposed from outside. The description is strange, but correct insofar as it is phenomenologically compelling. Self-appropriation is a relation of the self to itself by which the individual is attuned to the total movement of "life."[8]

In many ways, then, this discussion recalls the same basic insight that inspires *The Birth of Tragedy;* for according to the analysis in that work, the sense of empowerment that the tragic drama allows is only possible because it disengages all of our subjective willing and determinations of selfhood. Against this, any rigid self-definition would be the greatest possible obstacle to growth. The parallel with *The Birth of Tragedy* is helpful because it brings us to the second moment of how one becomes what one is. Along with Dionysus, Apollo must also be present, for if the first requirement is the disengagement of subjectivity and openness to the Dionysian forces of life, this must now be followed by an Apollinian movement of reappropriation, which secures the power that has been released and returns us to ourselves.

In fact, this movement of reappropriation is at work throughout *Ecce Homo,* and it is crucial for Nietzsche's discussion of his own life and his writings. In his account of his early life and break with Wagner, for example, he tries to demonstrate that the sickness that overcame him at this point in his life was actually the manifestation of a deeper health. He was an academic, secure in his scholarship, and a devoted friend of Wagner. When he became ill he was forced to abandon this comfortable existence; but now he revalues his own illness as the very best thing that could have happened, since it rescued him from oblivion and prepared him for his world-historical task. "For a typically healthy person," he comments, "being sick can even become an energetic stimulus for life, for living more." And he adds, "This, in fact, is how that long period of sickness appears to me *now:* as it were, I discovered life anew, including myself; I tasted all good and even little things, as others cannot easily taste them—I turned my will to health, to *life,* into a philosophy" (*EH* "Why I Am So Wise" sec. 2). In passages like this one, Nietzsche recovers his own life by calling into question the traditional opposition between sickness and health. Whereas his earlier onslaught against Christianity was charged by his ability to expose sickness masquerading as health, in *Ecce Homo* his own self-appropriation depends upon the strength that recovers every hazard, illness, or accident of existence into the horizon of personal necessity.

In this respect, Nietzsche conjoins the goal of individual self-appropriation with the task of a revaluation of values. In the passage quoted earlier, for example, he justifies his fitness for either project in terms of his ability to reverse and revalue perspectives. Referring to his "dual descent . . . from the highest to the lowest rung on the ladder of life," Nietzsche announces that he straddles the traditional opposition between health and sickness, and in so doing he claims to have gained mastery over the entire domain. This passage, though, is more than just a bold assertion, for it is itself a demonstration and a *performance* of the very revaluation that he lays claim to. There are many other examples. In *Ecce Homo,* he reserves his greatest contempt for Germany and the Germans, but he also appropriates the accident of his own birth as "a good fortune of the highest order," for it allowed his association with Wagner. In his discussion of his own writings, he reconstrues the world-historical position of Wagner and the idea of Bayreuth as a prefiguration of his own task. Similarly, he reviews *Human, All Too Human* as a prediction of the revaluation of values, which really illuminates his own genius while it apparently defers to Paul Ree. In all of these instances, Nietzsche affirms the necessity of his own intellectual progress with the momentous project of the revaluation as its goal. The very text and performance of *Ecce Homo* is itself a representation of Nietzsche's model of sovereignty. But given his own questioning of the traditional opposition between health and sickness, or even truth and falsity, *Ecce Homo* cannot be judged in any traditional terms. In fact, it can only be judged by the success of his *performance,* which is to say, the extent to which we can *experience* his strategy for becoming what one is.

In *Ecce Homo,* then, Nietzsche attempts to take charge of his own life by reappropriating every chance and accident as a necessary moment of his own becoming, not simply declaring them as such, but actively shaping them and bestowing meaning upon them. In this way he demonstrates that the individual is more than just a product of nature, for the goal of sovereignty that he or she represents and embodies can only be an achievement of those who possess the strength to order the manifold of their life. This is not to affirm an impossible doctrine of absolute self-creation *ab nihilo,* but to describe the basic structure of self-becoming that allows the individual to be an individual in the first place. Nietzsche's account is compelling; it testifies to the possibility of self-empowerment and illuminates our experience in general. In his section on *Human, All Too Human,* when he discusses the meaning of his subtitle, "A Book for Free Spirits," he describes this ideal of sovereignty, which remains his philosophical focus. "The term 'free spirit,'" he writes, "is not to be understood in any other sense. It means a spirit that has *become free,* that has again taken possession of itself" (*EH* "Human, All Too Human" sec. 1). This is the ideal of self-appropriation that now directs the performance of *Ecce Homo.* Elsewhere, Nietzsche understands it as the key to *Zarathustra* and the meaning of his own life.

We can now return to the problem of genealogy that confronted us earlier. At the start of *Ecce Homo,* the unavoidable heredity of race and family seemed to refute the possibility of any genuine sovereignty. Whatever one does one will always remain the child of one's parents. However, I think it is now clear that Nietzsche's attention to genealogy is not necessarily an objection to the possibility of sovereignty. For in *Ecce Homo* the genealogy that Nietzsche describes belongs to the same past that he has actively constituted for himself: in creating himself he has also created his own history. In this sense, genealogy can no longer be viewed as the passive inheritance of the past—which characterizes every form of racism or the simple appeal to blood—but as an active forging of roots. This is not to say that Nietzsche makes up the past or tries to avoid an unexceptional family history. On the contrary, in *Ecce Homo* he *recollects* his genealogy and actively uncovers his own line of descent by selecting and cultivating that genealogical line that best accounts for his own existence.

In fact, at this point, *Ecce Homo* links up perfectly with the historical task of *On the Genealogy of Morals:* for both are attempts to seize hold of the past—to redeem what is fragment and riddle and dreadful accident—by forging a new perspective that would illuminate the nature of our existence so far. In the *Genealogy,* the Christian-moral value standard is reappraised from a higher perspective as the "slave" morality that promotes weakness and the oblivion of the individual as such. Through the celebration of his own life in *Ecce Homo,* Nietzsche achieves a perspective that allows him to revalue and repudiate the concepts of "God," "the beyond," "the immortal soul," and "free will" as lies that slander life and secretly promote a declining form of humanity. Indeed, he relates this achievement as his own particular destiny. "I have chosen the word *immoralist* as a symbol and badge of honor for myself," he writes,

> I am proud of having this word which distinguishes me from the whole of humanity. Nobody yet has felt Christian morality to be beneath him: that requires a height, a view of distances, a hitherto altogether unheard-of psychological depth and profundity. Christian morality has been the Circe of all thinkers so far—they stood in her service.—Who before me climbed into the caverns from which the poisonous fumes of this type of ideal—slander of the world—are rising? Who even dared to suspect that they are caverns? Who among philosophers was a *psychologist* at all before me, and not rather the opposite, a "higher swindler" and "idealist"? There was no psychology at all before me.—To be the first here may be a curse; it is at any rate a destiny; *for one is also the first to despise.*—Nausea at man is my danger. (*EH* "Why I Am a Destiny" sec. 6)

Earlier, in *On the Genealogy of Morals,* Nietzsche had discussed the nature of language and the power of those who first pronounce the names of things. "The lordly right of giving names extends so far," he comments, "that one should allow oneself to conceive the origin of language itself as an expression of power on the part of the rulers: they say, 'this *is* this and this,' they seal every thing and event with a sound, and, as it were, take possession of it" (*GM* I sec. 2). This comment now becomes very relevant, for in *Ecce Homo* Nietzsche himself, as the "immoralist" and free spirit, seizes hold of the world in pronouncing the terms of a new language. Here the "good" man is revealed to be weak, while the "evil" free spirit is revealed to be strong. Idealism is called anti-nature, and selfishness is now "becoming what one is." The revaluation of all values is thus at work in the account of Nietzsche's own life. Nietzsche-Dionysus declares war and proclaims himself master. But since he challenges every ordinary philosophical perspective, his text cannot simply be "judged," but only received or incorporated as a total experience.

All of which brings us back to our earlier account of *Ecce Homo* as a kind of performance. Certainly, Nietzsche is very selective in the facts that he provides, and he uses these facts as so many cues and stage directions that help him to demonstrate how one becomes what one is. *Ecce Homo* is an autobiographical performance in which Nietzsche enacts a particular strategy of self-appropriation.[9] But as an excessive and self-conscious performance, it makes it clear that the "self" that is thereby presented only exists in the moment of the performance itself. *Ecce Homo* challenges all fixed and substantial notions of selfhood. It is not the uncovering of the "real" Friedrich Nietzsche, but an act of self-presentation that refuses to consider itself definitive. This leads us, however, to a final paradox. In *Ecce Homo,* as I have argued, Nietzsche deliberately makes use of the mask and the great pose. "I am no man," he comments, "I am dynamite"; and in this sense he presents himself as a great example and as a type. But in the end such a strategy only serves to remind us of what has been left out of this account: which is to say, nothing other than the real individual, Friedrich Nietzsche himself. Nietzsche's mask and his great pose offer a negative indication for that which can never be appropriated or said. For it is the individual as such that haunts this text and even presents itself as an imperative. In *Ecce Homo,* Nietzsche offers us a trace of the individual through the representation of sovereignty, and he still evokes this possibility though he cannot speak its name.

~

"I know my fate," Nietzsche writes at the end of *Ecce Homo.* "One day my name will be associated with the memory of something tremendous—a crisis without equal on earth, the most profound collision of conscience, a decision that was conjured up *against* everything that had been believed, demanded, hallowed so far. I am no man, I am dynamite" (*EH* "Why I Am a Destiny" sec. 1). Standing at the beginning of a section called, "Why I Am a Destiny," such portentous claims only seem to underline the world-historical mission of Nietzsche's philosophy. For here he explicitly rejoins the account of his own life to the overall project of a revaluation of all values, analyzing modern life in terms of the logic of nihilism. *"Revaluation of values,"* he continues, "that is my formula for an act of supreme self-examination on the part of humanity, become flesh and genius in me. It is my fate that I have to be the first decent human being; that I know myself to stand in opposition to the mendaciousness of millennia.—I was the first to *discover* the truth by being the first to experience lies as lies—smelling them out.—My genius is in my nostrils" (*EH* "Why I Am a Destiny" sec. 1). The relationship between the individual and the revaluation of values is not, however, an incidental one. In *Ecce Homo* Nietzsche is supposed to justify his own fitness to perform the revaluation of values, but what becomes clear, both in this text and in his other final writings, is that the revaluation is bound to begin with the individual as the only proper point of application for value itself. This forces us to question whether Nietzsche's project is intended to be world-historical in any massive cultural sense. And it requires us to think the relationship between the revaluation of values and the sovereignty of the individual as such.

In this regard, *Ecce Homo* is the most important text; though even in the titles of his other final writings, *Nietzsche Contra Wagner*, or *The Antichrist*, Nietzsche draws attention to himself as the particular point of origin. And this, upon reflection, seems particularly strange, for the claims that are made in these works are presumably not dependent on Nietzsche having made them.[10] Similarly, in the preface to *The Antichrist*, Nietzsche dwells upon his own untimeliness, and he repeats Zarathustra's motif of loneliness upon the mountains. "The conditions under which I am understood, and then of *necessity*," he writes,

> —I know them only too well. One must be honest in matters of the spirit to the point of hardness before one can even endure my seriousness and my passion. One must be skilled in living on mountains—seeing the wretched ephemeral babble of politics and national self-seeking *beneath* oneself. One must have become indifferent; one must never ask if the truth is useful or if it may prove our undoing. The predilection of strength for questions for which no one today has the courage; the courage for the *forbidden;* the predestination to the labyrinth. An experience of seven solitudes. New ears for new music. New eyes for what is most distant. (*AC* Preface)

He concludes, "Such men alone are my readers, my right readers, my predestined readers: what matter the *rest?* The rest—that is merely mankind." Once again, however, this is a very strange admission, for if *The Antichrist* is meant to inaugurate the revaluation of all values, as Nietzsche intends, then such a work must be supremely relevant and important to humanity. Given the world-historical moment of the revaluation, why does Nietzsche declare in advance that his words will only resound in the silence of individual solitude, and then only for those who have the courage to hear them? What this suggests is that the revaluation is actually focused on the self-transformation of the individual life, and that all of its cultural, political, and historical perspectives may actually be secondary to this.

If we return to his comments in "Why I Am a Destiny," for example, Nietzsche sustains his world-historical pose by affirming a declaration of war against the lies of millennia and promising convulsions, upheavals, and more. "For all that," he comments,

> I am necessarily also the man of calamity. For when truth enters into a fight with the lies of millennia, we shall have upheavals, a convulsion of earthquakes, a moving of mountains and valleys, the like of which has never been dreamed of. The concept of politics will have merged entirely with a war of spirits; all power structures of the old society will have been exploded—all of them are based on lies: there will be wars the like of which have never yet been seen on earth. It is only beginning with me that the earth knows *great politics*. (*EH* "Why I Am a Destiny" sec. 1)

The problem with such passages, however, is that they are easily misconstrued and given a straightforward reading, which is plainly at odds with Nietzsche's other comments in *Ecce Homo* itself. Nietzsche declares war at the end of *Ecce Homo*, but in his earlier discussion of *Human, All Too Human*, for example, he insists upon "war" without powder and smoke, "without warlike poses and strained limbs." And he comments that "all that would still be 'idealism'" (*EH* "Human, All Too Human" sec. 1). It is also significant that in the preface to *Ecce Homo*, he denies that he is any kind of a prophet with a message for mankind; and he recalls Zarathustra, who counsels us not to be misled by the frenzy of great causes and great events, since in fact "it is the stillest words which bring on the storm," and "thoughts that come on dove's feet guide the world" (*EH* Preface sec. 4). All of this seems to imply that the great politics that he opposes to the petty politics of contemporary nations and states is really not apocalyptic in any ordinary sense. Nietzsche explicitly disdains the pathos of such poses, and this suggests instead that he is really concerned with the politics of the individual soul as the highest tribunal of all.[11]

A closer look at the nature of values will lead us to a similar conclusion. Behind Nietzsche's demand for the revaluation lies the basic insight that the essential feature of all values is to inspire and enhance human existence in some sense.[12] In *The Antichrist*, as we have seen, Nietzsche comments, "What is good? Everything that heightens the feeling of power in man, the will to power, power itself. What is bad? Everything that is born of weakness" (*AC* sec. 2). Using this criterion, he then argues that the Judeo-Christian values that we have inherited only depress and diminish the individual life, and as such they are "symptomatic of decline, *nihilistic* values . . . lording it under the highest names" (*AC* sec. 6). A value, we might say, only functions as a value for as long as it promotes the "will" or the principle of individual life in the project of its own empowerment. This is why Nietzsche insists that everyone invent their own categorical imperative, since attention to duty without any deeply personal choice is "just a recipe for decadence."

From this basic conception of value we are therefore referred to an ideal of self-appropriation or sovereignty, which would represent the most complete self-commandment and disposal over the individual life. In this respect, the revaluation of values cannot be taken as an attempt to prescribe new values, for wherever values are imposed on life they can only depress and confine it. Nietzsche makes it clear at the beginning of *Ecce Homo* that he has absolutely no use for the "improvers of mankind"; he has not come to preach new idols, for he is not concerned with "teaching" people anything except how to seek for themselves. *Ecce Homo* is the representation of sovereignty, which makes its appeal to the individual as such.

At its deepest level, then, the revaluation of values is collected into the individual moment of existence. In spite of all the obvious political, cultural, and ethical consequences of Nietzsche's thought, it seems that his philosophy only fully resounds within the solitude of the individual life. Such a conclusion may initially suggest the total despair of solipsism. In fact, he specifically argues in *Twilight of the Idols* that the most important experiences cannot be communicated, since they have no name. "We no longer esteem ourselves sufficiently when we communicate ourselves," he writes,

> Our true experiences are not at all garrulous. They could not communicate themselves even if they tried. That is because they lack the right word. Whatever we have words for, that we have already got beyond. In all talk there is a grain of contempt. Language, it seems, was invented only for what is average, medium, communicable. With language the speaker immediately vulgarizes himself. Out of a morality for deaf-mutes and other philosophers. (*TI* "Skirmishes" sec. 26)

Thus, language and the concept must mean the *end* of the individual and the unique; and here the underlying paradox of Nietzsche's project, the *philosophical articulation of sovereignty*, becomes completely apparent.

8 ∾

Nietzsche and the Philosophy of the Future

In this book I have tried to show how all of Nietzsche's writings, from *The Birth of Tragedy* to *Ecce Homo,* are concerned with the issue of the individual. From the very beginning, Nietzsche is "astonished" by the fact of individual existence, and although he is well aware that language can never directly communicate what is most singular and unique, he attempts, in spite of this, to inspire and evoke the individual life that had previously been abandoned. Nietzsche's discussion of the individual is thus more than simply descriptive; his texts have a performative dimension, and we can only begin to grasp his writings once we have understood the particular strategy that directs them. Nietzsche's preoccupation with the individual also leads directly to a discussion of sovereignty, for in sovereignty individuals recover themselves. "Sovereignty" represents the achievement of the individual as such, and in one way or another it is a major theme in all of his writings, even if the idea of self-appropriation or "becoming what one is" only becomes completely explicit in his final work.

Even so, Nietzsche's concern with the individual should not be viewed as the key to the philosopher's labyrinth. There is no final "secret" to Nietzsche— he himself would reject such a simplistic account of the "truth"—and the very nature of Nietzsche's writing, fragmentary and overdetermined as it is, repels in advance any attempt at total critical control. In this book, I have simply tried to describe Nietzsche's concern for the individual and his preoccupation with sovereignty, for his work makes a lot of sense if it is understood as a sustained response to this problem.

It is here, however, that Nietzsche's philosophy both rejoins and fulfills a tradition of thought that began with Christianity and its absolute concern for the individual life. In the first chapters of this book I sought to retrieve this "Christian" tradition of thinking. Following Nietzsche's own practice, I illuminated a genealogy that spans St. Paul, Kant, Schopenhauer, and Nietzsche as its most significant moments. Thus we may recall St. Paul's attempts to provoke a new will, and the description of his inmost self struggling against the desires and thoughts that seem to overwhelm him from without. In early Christianity this urgent demand for self-appropriation is directed toward the salvation of the individual soul. Later, in Kant, the autonomy of the individual becomes the basis of morality and the highest expression of willing; and indeed, there is a deep respect in which the whole of Kant's critical system depends upon the possibility of autonomy, which first calls the subject into being. On the face of it, Schopenhauer's philosophy represents a complete break with this concern for the individual life. He seems to regard individuality as an illusion, and he continually denies the meaning or value of individual existence. But as Nietzsche pointed out, Schopenhauer's philosophy is still essentially "Christian," and it finishes, in spite of everything, with the redemption of nature through the turning of the will against itself, and the achievement of the individual life. Nietzsche rejects the traditional account of free will; he challenges the accepted conventions of morality; and he ridicules the religious hypothesis, with its denial of this life and its focus upon the hereafter. But despite all this, Nietzsche still retains a "vision" of individual sovereignty as something that is absolutely important. In the main part of this book we have seen how Nietzsche continues to support this ideal even while he attacks and condemns every corresponding construct, including the idea of a fixed and substantial self.

In the terms of this tradition, then, I have tried to show how Nietzsche's engagement with the problem of individual sovereignty remains illuminating. St. Paul abandons the project of sovereignty in favor of self-dispossession in the grace of God; Kant circumscribes autonomy with a specific account of "rational nature" that only constrains and denies the individual as such; and Schopenhauer's account of individual "salvation" misapprehends the individual as an objection, and places the latter in a position of conflict and antagonism with nature. Nietzsche, on the other hand, develops an account of sovereignty that suggests, both in broad outline, in his discussion of Apollo and Dionysus, for example, and in some detail, as in *Ecce Homo*, how the individual can take charge of existence to become what he or she is.

In opposition to St. Paul, Nietzsche continually unmasks the various forms of self-abandonment, and he has a "nose" for all of the values and routines of thinking that promote individual oblivion. In opposition to Kant, he refuses to legislate sovereignty, or to prescribe any universally binding precepts, for he understands that sovereignty is effectively destroyed once it is reduced to a set of rules. In fact, Nietzsche is completely aware of the "problem of education," and much of his philosophical strategy may be viewed as an attempt to provoke and inspire sovereignty without fixing its form. Like

Schopenhauer, Nietzsche also tries to comprehend the place of the individ-ual within the total scheme of things, and in response to the traditional philo-sophical prejudice of idealism, he focuses his inquiry on both the material and historical dimensions of human life. In this respect, he can show how the individual subject is actually a product and a construction of forces that lie outside of itself. Even so, Nietzsche claims that individual sovereignty is still possible as a moment of this total process; and in opposition to Schopen-hauer's version of the individual, Nietzsche's own presentation testifies to the complex interrelationship of sovereignty, the world, and others. For Nietz-sche, the moment of self-dispossession is an essential feature of sovereignty and a necessary supplement to the insistence on self-appropriation.

If it is the case that Nietzsche represents the "end" of this tradition, it is therefore in the double sense of both a termination and a goal. In the first place, he terminates the tradition as a Christian tradition by exposing and attacking the treatment of the individual within this theological context and by showing how every metaphysics is really a disguised theology. He argues that such accounts have actually devalued individual existence by reducing it to an inferior moment of some higher realm of truth or Being. While Paul and other Christians may urge us toward sovereignty as the highest task, the theological basis of their concern actually reflects a prejudice against life and the valorization of another kind of existence that is supposedly beyond this one. But further, as the goal or culmination of this tradition, Nietzsche of-fers us a discussion of individual sovereignty that is not compromised by the quest for redemption or transcendence. In Nietzsche, the sovereignty of the individual life is esteemed as the very touchstone of value, and as that in terms of which value takes its value in the first place. Likewise, in Nietzsche, the focus upon the individual, through stratagems like the eternal recurrence, becomes the means whereby we enter into the "sacred." God is dead, but unlike his rationalist counterparts, Nietzsche attempts to recover the sacred character of existence—the "Dionysian"—which had previously been aban-doned. In this sense, his deep preoccupation with the individual as unique and unrepeatable and impossible to "say," underlies the experience of the sacred that he attempts to communicate.

I have argued that Nietzsche attempts to provoke sovereignty. Through various philosophical and literary strategies, he tries to force us into that mode of willing that is the only possible remedy for the "nihilism" that still besets our age. And yet, Nietzsche's account of the individual will and the will to power does not promote a willful self-assertion or celebrate domination and control—for as we have seen, this could only be a slavish interpretation of the meaning of empowerment that falsely assumes that the subject remains self-contained and separate from everything that is outside itself. Nietzsche suggests that the most essential feature of nihilism is will-lessness and the yearning for individual oblivion. To provoke the individual will in its authentic sense and secure sovereignty is thus to effect a counter-movement against nihilism. In this respect, his reflective encounter with sovereignty is itself a celebration of the individual life.

◆

All of this may suggest that Nietzsche is a thinker of some historical interest, and it may lead us to revise some of our basic conceptions about "the tradition" and our history of ideas. But it can also be argued that this very tradition is now a dead tradition, for as structuralism, poststructuralism, and postmodernism continue to inform us, the whole language of "sovereignty" and "autonomy," with the associated ideas of "individuality" and selfhood in general, is deeply suspect and reflects a mythology of mastery and self-presence that it would now be better to abandon. In both structuralism and poststructuralism, for example, the self is nothing more than a surface effect whose meaning must forever lie outside of itself in the various systems and codes, including language, which precede and maintain it. In a very famous passage, Lévi-Strauss comments that the ultimate goal of his own research was "not to constitute man but to dissolve him,"[1] and the whole tendency of contemporary Continental philosophy is to agree. From this perspective, any recourse to the idea of individual sovereignty is deeply problematic and may have to be reconstrued as an attempt to achieve an imaginary plenitude and mastery (following Lacan); as the impossible desire for an immediate self-presence that somehow escapes the differential system of meaning in language (following Derrida); or as an effect of power that creates responsible "subjects" as the bearers of its effects (as in Foucault). Beginning, perhaps, with the later Heidegger, what all of these discussions in recent Continental philosophy affirm is the fragmentary character of selfhood and the sense in which any attribution of mastery or even identity is really an impossible fiction.

In this respect, Foucault's interpretation of the death of God, which appears at the end of *The Order of Things,* may be read as a symbolic manifesto for much of recent Continental thought, since it really encapsulates the attack on "man," humanism, and every ordinary account of self-appropriation. In this passage, Foucault reads the death of God as a prediction of the end of our anthropocentric age. Nietzsche *is* an untimely thinker, because he envisioned the death of the subject and the dispersion of "the individual" in the basic regularities of life. "In our day," Foucault writes, and once again Nietzsche indicated the turning-point from a long way off, it is not so much the absence or the death of God that is affirmed as the end of man . . . is it not the last man who announces that he has killed God, thus situating his language, his thought, his laughter in the space of that already dead God, yet positing himself also as he who has killed God and whose existence includes the freedom and decision of that murder? . . . Rather than the death of God—or rather, in the wake of that death and in a profound correlation with it—what Nietzsche's thought heralds is the end of his murderer; it is the explosion of man's face in laughter, and the return of masks; it is the scattering of the profound stream of time by which he felt himself carried along and whose pressure he suspected in the very being of things; it is the identity of the Return of the Same with the absolute dispersion of man.[2]

According to Foucault, the final meaning of the death of God is the death of "man," in the sense of the final passing of that episteme or order of things that has focused upon man, human experience, and human history as the locus of all meaning and truth. And if it is allowed that such "humanism" has frequently defined itself in opposition to the religious hypothesis, then the surpassing of the latter must ultimately lead to its own demise. "To all those who still wish to talk about man," Foucault writes, "to all those who still ask themselves questions about what man is in his essence . . . who refer all knowledge back to the truths of man . . . [and] who refuse to mythologize without demystifying . . . we can answer only with a philosophical laugh—which means, to a certain extent, a silent one."[3]

Foucault's interpretation of Nietzsche is compelling. In his own notebooks, for example, Nietzsche explicitly condemned all the varieties of bourgeois humanism as so many forms of "incomplete nihilism," which merely substitute "man" in place of God within the same Christian-nihilistic schema.[4] This is the point of the madman's warning: "What did we do when we unchained this earth from its sun? Whither is it moving now? Whither are we moving now? Away from all suns? Are we not plunging continually?" As I have already argued, the death of God implies the death of all fixed centers of meaning (all suns, such as man, ego, subject, or atom, etc.) that could provide a foundation from which we might derive a final account of the world. Once God is removed, every other substantial unity must be challenged as a displacement of this central pole. So that with the death of God, the self is effectively decentered and the traditional goal of self-possession becomes entirely problematic as we find ourselves straying through an infinite void.

Recent Continental philosophy has in this way seized upon Nietzsche's proclamation of the death of God and his explicit accounts of the subject as a multiplicity. Indeed, Nietzsche's original problematic of the self makes him both the forerunner and the contemporary of Foucault, Derrida, Lacan et al. And yet, such a reading of Nietzsche remains incomplete since it is completely silent about the possibility of sovereignty, when it is clearly *this* that Nietzsche insists upon, even in the same texts where he comments on the disarticulation of the self. From this revised perspective, then, Nietzsche is apparently both a "modernist" and a "postmodernist," a reactionary and a progressive at the same time. And while his critique of traditional conceptions of the self is well taken, it may also be argued that his final insistence upon sovereignty is symptomatic of his attachment to the discredited ideology of individualism.[5]

᠊ᢨ

The later Heidegger, Foucault, and Derrida offer three complementary approaches to the problem of sovereignty. This is not to say that their work somehow circumscribes all of the available positions in Continental thought. But with their explicit rejection of humanism and their deep suspicion of the traditional category of the subject, they are profoundly representative of the Continental turn away from the possibility of autonomy. According to the later Heidegger, the individual project of self-mastery is inextricably bound up with the domination and violation of Being as a whole; for Derrida, the goal of autonomy can be viewed as an illusory attempt to achieve total "self-presence"; and in Foucault, the very idea of autonomy is a self-serving myth that only justifies the creation and subject-ification of "responsible" citizens for the forces of oppression and control. Altogether, these are perhaps the three most important moments of recent anti-humanism; and as such, I think we are obliged to consider their claims before we determine the contemporary relevance of the philosophy of sovereignty.

Heidegger's discussion of authenticity in *Being and Time* reflects his original emphasis on self-assertion and resolve as the only appropriate manner in which Being may be grasped in its truth. In his later writings, however, Heidegger is at pains to distance himself from such a "subjectivist" position. In the *Letter on Humanism,* for example, he opposes his own thinking to Sartre's existentialism by insisting that "humanism" of any kind has to be rejected, since it "does not set the humanitas of man high enough."[6] Heidegger claims that in the most original sense, before he is ever determined as a subject, "man" ek-sists in the openness of being as neither subject nor object, but as *Da-sein,* or the one who is claimed by Being in order to speak its truth. This primordial imperative of attendance to Being undermines the subjective imperative of self-mastery: henceforth, the individual is to relinquish all willful and self-assertive attitudes, since the latter can only prevent the individual from attending to the original disclosure of Being.

In Heidegger's later writings, the attack on subjectivism directs his reading of the history of philosophy as the record of humanity's violent suppression of Being. This is held to culminate in the rise of technology, and Nietzsche's explicit avowal of the will to power (or the "will to will," as Heidegger often refers to it), as the basic character of everything that is. This "will to will," Heidegger comments, "forces the calculation and arrangement of everything for itself as the basic forms of appearance, only, however, for the unconditionally protractible guarantee of itself." And he explains, "The basic form of appearance in which the will to will arranges and calculates itself in the unhistorical world of completed metaphysics can be stringently called 'technology.'"[7] For Heidegger, the will to will has triumphed insofar as technology now secures and arranges everything with a view to its own continuation and enhancement. Against the ravages of this objectification, he proposes the stance of *Gelassenheit* (or releasement) as the only appropriate remedy. *Gelassenheit* is a form of openness in which the individual resolves not to will any more. It is the resolve *not* to appropriate either oneself or the world, but to exist in a "patient noblemindedness [that] would be pure resting in itself of that willing which, renouncing willing, has released itself to what is not will."[8]

Thus, Heidegger uses the "will to will" to describe the epochal determination of Being. And yet, the "will to will" might also be construed as an excellent determination of the essential nature of autonomy itself. Heidegger would say that "man" is *willed* by the will to will. At the same time, however, I think it also follows that the project of individual autonomy represents the highest fulfillment of the will to will, since it achieves the most complete incorporation of this epochal determination at the level of the individual self. In an epoch of subjectivism, the project of autonomy may be regarded as an attempt to grasp the subjectivity of the subject, or the individuality of the individual, insofar as the latter can support and direct itself against everything that lies outside. From Heidegger's perspective, the ideal of self-appropriation may therefore represent the final achievement of the will to power, and thus the final blasphemy against Being and the mark of its most complete oblivion.

Heidegger in no way regrets the loss of the "subject" or bemoans its subordination to the order of technology. In fact, the self-assertion of the subject is itself the corollary and accomplice of object-ification. So if our task is, somehow, to think outside of the essence of technology, then the subjectivism or humanism that makes "man" the lord over beings must accordingly be abandoned. This means that Heidegger *must* view sovereignty as an entirely selfish project, in which individuals can only command themselves as individuals by denying or dominating the world or the other. This is certainly the main thrust of his interpretation of the will to power in his writings on Nietzsche. What Heidegger does *not* recognize, however, is that in Nietzsche's work the will to power is simply not construed as a unitary principle. In *On the Genealogy of Morals,* as we have seen, Nietzsche makes a clear distinction between the will to power of the master and the will to power of the slave. Whereas the latter can only understand power as domination and control, the former experiences it as a joyful self-affirmation and celebration of strength that does not presuppose the subjection of the other. Heidegger interprets the will to power in purely slavish terms—as calculation, ordering, and control—and as a result, the only solution he can offer is one of quietism, where we must wait patiently for the "grace" of Appropriation (or *Das Ereignis*), the "event" of Being.[9] This suggests a monolithic critique that refuses even to recognize the possibility of an individual ideal that would not reduce to individualism. In opposition to Heidegger, it may therefore be argued that the most important task today is to *rethink the nature of sovereignty.* For while Descartes or Kant may be criticized for their inherent subjectivism, this does not mean that *every* version of autonomy must be predicated upon a slavish self-assertion.

Perhaps a similar critique may also apply to Derrida, who has developed a more sustained argument, which may be used to support Heidegger's proclamations. In *Speech and Phenomena,* Derrida rejects Husserl's account of the Transcendental Ego by demonstrating the incoherence of a pure consciousness that is supposed to grasp its own identity prior to language. For Derrida, there can be no such realm of "phenomenological silence" in which one could be directly related to oneself, since the determination of any object of knowledge, including one's own self, will always be mediated by the differential system of language. Moving beyond this specific critique, Derrida has generalized his argument to show how any philosophy that seeks to comprehend the final nature of things is inevitably thwarted by its dependence on "writing," or the materiality of the signifier, which it is bound to suppress and deny. His deconstructive readings expose the logic of this suppression within particular texts and, in general, they force us to reconsider language as the very fabric of meaning rather than its incidental cover. In this respect, the "subject" is not simply the one who *uses* language, since its very position is itself an effect of textual dispersion and difference.

In fact, Derrida seems to reject any substantive conception of the human "subject," since he holds that the latter must always rely upon the notion of self-presence that he has shown to be incoherent. In his essay on "Freud and the Scene of Writing," for example, he is quite unequivocal: "The last part of the lecture concerned . . . erasure of the present and thus of the subject, of that which is proper to the subject and of his proper name. The concept of a (conscious or unconscious) subject necessarily refers to the concept of substance—and thus of presence—out of which it is born."[10] In a text like "Limited Inc.," Derrida actively performs this erasure of the subject and the subject's proper name, by showing how the author's claim to (legal or textual) mastery cannot be sustained. In this case, John Searle is singled out for signing and copyrighting his response to Derrida. Derrida shows that such ordinary claims of identity and propriety are deeply problematic. For given Searle's own admission of his indebtedness to others, as well as his final inability to fix and control the meaning of his own discourse, Derrida can argue that his proper respondent is not the singular Searle but "SARL," an abbreviation for the French "*Societé à la Responsabilité Limitée*" or Limited Inc.[11] In other texts, Derrida plays similar tricks with his own name, transforming the proper into the common, and thus generating an anonymous multiplicity of the self as an antidote to all dreams of self-appropriation and mastery.

Derrida's work effectively destroys the myth of the self-present subject that could create itself *ab nihilo* and thus mirror the activity of God. On the other hand, he seems to use this particular critique to dispense with *any* discussion of the subject or autonomy. And when he argues, as above, that every account of subjectivity relies upon an illicit notion of presence, this leads to some false alternatives, where we are obliged to accept *either* the self-legislating enthroned subject of consciousness *or* the disintegration of the self in infinite textuality. Like the later Heidegger, Derrida cannot countenance alternative models of autonomy or sovereignty that would recognize the thrown character of human existence and reject self-presence. The radical dispersion of the self leaves him no way to distinguish between the various levels and degrees of self-possession. One suspects, in fact, that from Derrida's perspective *any* investigation into the forms of subjectivity is bound to use the outmoded categories of the "philosophy of presence." And hence, despite some later texts that seem to offer an evocation of singularity that *could* provide us with the space for sovereignty, Derrida's position obliges him to reject every articulate version of autonomy in advance.[12] It is another "monolithic" critique.

Finally, let us consider Foucault as the third pillar of recent Continental thought. In a profound respect, Foucault's work represents a sustained illustration of Heidegger's claim that humanism must be rejected "since it does not value the humanitas of man high enough." In an early discussion with

Foucault, for example, Noam Chomsky argues that a humanistic social theory would have to be based "on some firm and humane concept of the human nature or human essence."[13] Foucault responds that the concept of human nature is really dispensable, since all it describes are the products of various economic, technological, and political regularities—a position that he argues for most fully in *The Order of Things*. As well as questioning the theoretical status of "human nature," Foucault also insists that the very idea of some fixed human essence is inherently dangerous, since it can be used to dominate and control individual men and women by foisting some ideal model upon them. And in a much later interview he repeats this claim: "What we call humanism has been used by Marxists, liberals, Nazis, Catholics. I think that there are more secrets, more possible freedoms, and more inventions in our future than we can imagine in humanism as it is dogmatically represented on every side of the political rainbow."[14]

In his writings on madness, sexuality, and the prison, Foucault describes various disciplines and technologies of power that control individuals and reproduce them as docile utilizable "subjects." In effect, Foucault shows how the concept of human nature—especially as it accompanies the growth of the human sciences in the nineteenth century—is fundamentally repressive; for it has always sanctioned a particular vision of "man" to serve as the norm, against which all deviations may be corrected and punished or reduced to silence. In the case of sexuality, for example, Foucault points out that the idea of perversion did not exist in the Middle Ages: intercourse during Lent, sodomy, and bestiality received equal condemnation as simple violations of canon law; the sexual life of children was not a matter of concern. Yet in the nineteenth century, as a result of specifically bourgeois values becoming the focus of all humanism, the "perverted" homosexual "personality" was incarcerated and cured, while the campaign against child masturbation achieved an intensification of familial surveillance and control. All of this was justified and directed by a dominant version of "normal" or "natural" sexuality that could be supported, in turn, by the findings of "experts."

On the basis of this brief sketch it might be supposed that Foucault's work is intended as a philosophy of liberation that seeks to uncover all of the ruses of power that have dominated and controlled us for so long. The problem with this, however, is that Foucault himself insists upon the complete and mutual implication of knowledge and power, and he is therefore bound to reject, as hopelessly naive, any argument that reduces to the simple assertion that "the truth will make you free." At the beginning of *Discipline and Punish*, for example, the horrendous account of Damiens's execution in 1757 does not allow us to congratulate ourselves for our humanitarian "advances," since it is followed by the daily timetable of a nineteenth-century reformatory, which demonstrates that while power has changed its forms it is now perhaps even more efficient in controlling individuals and populations than it ever was before.[15] The very idea of a "liberation" from power remains deeply problematic. Foucault cannot assume any privileged position for his own work, and as a result he seems open to charges of fatalism and even nihilism.[16]

Marxist critics pointed out the existence of this theoretical impasse in *The Order of Things*, where the unequivocal emphasis on systems and regularities seems to deny the possibility of individual agency and any suggestion that human beings might "make their own history."[17] Foucault's later work on the relations of power examines various practices of surveillance and control that developed in institutions like schools, factories, and prisons in the course of the nineteenth century. Once again, though, Foucault's claim is that these techniques of power do not so much capture as *constitute* human subjects, who therefore exist only within the relations of power by which they have been produced.[18] Such a view seems to make all "resistance" impossible. And indeed, Foucault is at pains to point out that at the very moment the subject rebels against the system, he or she is always already constrained by the system in another respect. To return to our previous example, in volume one of *The History of Sexuality* Foucault seems to argue that the whole discourse of sexual liberation is just as constrained by the "prison" of sex as prudish Victorian morality. For both pornography and prudery force us to think of ourselves as primarily sexual beings. This implies that power is the only subject and that individual agency or autonomy is merely an illusory projection of power itself.

This brings us, then, to an apparent paradox in the tension between Foucault's theoretical position and the practical orientation of his work. On the one hand, Foucault, the anti-humanist, seems to rule out any possibility of individual sovereignty. And yet, as a spokesperson for the oppressed of history—the mad, the criminal, the deviant, and so on—Foucault's work is directed by an obvious revolutionary praxis. It is a discourse of liberation that has inspired various dispossessed groups, such as prisoners and women; and a thoroughly anti-authoritarian project that seeks to undermine the "givenness" of the present order by recollecting the forms of violence and oppression through which it has achieved its hegemony. Exactly as in the case of Heidegger, Foucault's attack on "man" and "humanism" is motivated by a profound humanistic impulse. And though he challenges theoretical constructions and models of subjectivity, it is only in order to liberate individual men and women from whatever controls and represses them, so that the real sovereignty of the individual may be restored, at least as a possibility.

In fact, in Foucault's final writings, on the classical and early Christian problematic of sexuality, he opens up a theoretical space for the *possibility* of sovereignty by returning to the "subject" as a basic field of analysis. He argues that the *rapport à soi* that constitutes subjectivity is to be studied, along with "power" and "knowledge," as the basic object of a "historical ontology."[19] And while he continues to specify the workings of power upon the *rapport à soi*, his final account of subjectivity does not reduce it, as in earlier work, to the simple *effect* of power or discursive formations. Clearly, Foucault sought to understand the possibility of a genuine resistance and freedom within the economy of power itself. Following the lead of Nietzsche, his renewed meditation upon the *rapport à soi* does not give us a theory of sovereignty, but it does allow us to think the individual as a "fold" within the field of power that may cultivate itself so as to resist power's control.[20]

◦

Recent Continental philosophy has demonstrated the inadequacy of conceiving the subject as the center of all meaning, and has shown the absurdity of "autonomy," if this is construed as the complete and god-like self-presence of the subject. It is at this point, though, that Nietzsche's complicated discussion of sovereignty becomes both timely and relevant. For he has demonstrated in his own work that not *all* conceptions of sovereignty are founded upon an absolute self-presence, and this conforms to our commonsense understanding that there are different degrees of sovereignty—something that would be impossible if sovereignty was an all-or-nothing affair.

Instead of abandoning the goal of sovereignty, what we now need is a renewed discussion of the individual that might allow us to articulate the nature of sovereignty in its non-absolutist form. After proclaiming the "death of man," recent Continental philosophy has tended to avoid this issue as anathema; but through its account of the Apollinian and the Dionysian, the eternal recurrence, the will to power, and how one becomes what one is, Nietzsche's philosophy still offers a very powerful and compelling discussion of individual sovereignty and the self-in-process, which is aware of the pitfalls and excesses that have plagued traditional accounts of autonomy and the individual life. Nietzsche's call for "new versions and refinements of the soul hypothesis" remains profoundly relevant. In contemporary feminism, for example, the question of the subject and the need to rework traditional conceptions of selfhood have remained at the forefront. But if Nietzsche is even partially correct in his diagnosis of contemporary life, a more sustained account of individual sovereignty and empowerment is still urgently needed.[21]

There is a similar point of confrontation between Nietzsche and contemporary Continental philosophy in regard to the issue of the sacred. In recent years, postmodernist thinking has tended to define itself in specifically anti-apocalyptic terms. So that, with all the "goals" and results of history sufficiently demystified, it seems that we may no longer look forward to anything, and all that we can ever expect is the continual return of the same. At the beginning of our age, the age of the last man, Nietzsche proclaimed the death of God to wrench us out of our wretched contentment. But while he apparently believed that it would only be a matter of time before we became aware of the consequences of this deed—"for they have done it to themselves"—today we are aware of the implications of this catastrophe and yet we are untroubled by them. The death of God suggests the profanation of modern life and the death of the sacred. But far from resisting this conclusion, postmodernist thinking has actively embraced it. The death of God has become unremarkable. It has been followed by the death of the death of God, and the call to sovereignty that Nietzsche's original proclamation entails is now re-visioned as the nostalgia for an impossible mastery.

Perhaps postmodern or poststructuralist thinking is bound to reject the very notion of the sacred, insofar as the latter usually implies a privileged region of being that somehow escapes the material play of differences. And this would even apply to a thinker like Nietzsche, who reverses the traditional account by forswearing otherworldliness and the existence of God in order to consecrate the "deep, deep eternity" of every present moment. As we have seen, however, Nietzsche's evocation of the sacred is bound up with the thought of the individual; for if "God" is the ultimate desecration of the world, then for Nietzsche it is the sovereign individual or the experience of the individual as such that allows us to reclaim the world as a sacred region of being. At this point, then, we may choose: for we can either reject every discussion of the sacred in advance and follow our deepest suspicions concerning this privileged concept; or else, we can admit that Nietzsche's account of the sacred actually articulates something that attunes with the deepest reality of our own experience. In fact, we might say that Nietzsche's philosophy really is a liberation of the sacred, which recovers the absolute value of the individual even though it does not commit us to the existence of any "supernatural" principle.

I suggested earlier that when Nietzsche wrote, he saw humanity poised at a kind of crossroads: either things will continue to go down until we reach a point of absolute leveling and spiritual decline, or else, with "the return of the master" we will finally appropriate an alternative and affirmative type of individual existence. Today, I think that we are in a similar place, if not the same place, for the continued dissolution of individual existence in modern mass society is only supported and sustained by the death of the subject in contemporary philosophy. Postmodernism has correctly gauged the anonymous character of contemporary life, and the apparent oblivion of sovereignty. And as Nietzsche himself predicted, the complete acceleration of all the ordinary rhythms of existence must now threaten everything that subtends the sacred.

But is the oblivion of the individual and the obliteration of the sacred simply the final truth about the human condition, and something to be celebrated for its own sake? Or is this now to be diagnosed as a symptom of something deeper—in terms of "nihilism" perhaps, or the historical triumph of a certain modality of the will to power that could be overcome? Through the example of Nietzsche's own work, it is at least clear that the criticism of postmodern perspectives does not necessarily return us to a discredited account of the subject. Nietzsche affirms the dispersion of the self, but for all that he still articulates the countervailing possibility of self-appropriation. His account of the individual pays homage to both the Apollinian and the Dionysian aspects of selfhood. So that, in opposition to the self-definition of our age, Nietzsche's reflection upon the problem of sovereignty still suggests the possibility of an alternative future, through the recollection of the individual and the evocation of the sacred.

Afterword

This book has offered a specific way of reading Nietzsche through the whole problematic of sovereignty. Through the analysis and discussion of particular texts, I have tried to elaborate Nietzsche's philosophical and performative strategy; and any general conclusions which now follow from these readings derive as much from what he was trying to *do* as from what he was trying to say. Thus, Nietzsche engages in a very sustained meditation upon the significance of the individual. Within the broader context of his reflections upon "higher humanity," his discussion of sovereignty is also an attempt to provoke the future and to bring about the very sovereignty that he describes. This means that there is both a descriptive and a performative dimension to his work. Even if his theoretical discussion of sovereignty remains unresolved or philosophically incomplete, there is still a sense in which he forces the reader to experience the possibility of sovereignty and to incorporate it as one of the most urgent requirements of life.

On the theoretical level, Nietzsche examines the nature of selfhood, and he clarifies how the latter must contain both the elements of self-appropriation and self-abandonment. Following the initial dialectic of Apollo and Dionysus in *The Birth of Tragedy,* he develops a philosophical account of the individual in the rest of his writings, specifically through concepts like the eternal recurrence, the sovereign individual, and the master and slave. We have seen how such figures as the sovereign individual or the free spirit also imply an *ideal* of sovereignty that signifies the fulfillment of the individual as such. In the course of this book I have tried to unpack some of these ideas to show how they function strategically within Nietzsche's writings as a whole.

And yet, the discussion must remain incomplete. Nietzsche does not want to prescribe the content of sovereignty. Wherever he offers an account of the sovereign individual or the overman in his work, it is always evocative and fragmentary; and it works alongside his ongoing criticism of established ideals like Kantian autonomy, or the traditional conception of freedom as the "property" of a self-contained subject. Nietzsche does not make anything easy for us. And given his powerful arguments against free will, it might actually be tempting to conclude that he came to regard sovereignty as an impossible goal. For after the urgent summons to the individual in *Schopenhauer as Educator,* the mature thinker of *Ecce Homo* seems to challenge the importance of self-assertion when he reads his own life as something for which he never had to struggle at all.

From this point, then, some serious philosophical problems begin to emerge concerning Nietzsche's conception of sovereignty. On the one hand, he seems to value sovereignty as an important ideal and as something that can be attained: the sovereign individual is said to be "free" and capable of complete self-disposal. But if everything is the product of nature, or if we must refer everything back to the will to power as a play of forces that underlies every substantial existence, then in what sense could sovereignty be an "achievement," as opposed to a necessary outcome? Either Nietzsche's arguments against freedom and free will are successful, in which case there is no one who is both sovereign and free in any strong sense; or else, if we allow that freedom is possible, and we do choose ourselves, then Nietzsche is at odds with himself and nature is apparently overcome. Such issues are raised but never satisfactorily answered on the theoretical level of his work.

In fact, it is only when we move to the performative level of the text that things become clearer, once we open up the total context of Nietzsche's theoretical discussions and his own self-understanding of what it means to be a philosopher. In *Beyond Good and Evil,* he proposes a new way of thinking about philosophy. According to him, philosophy is not just a matter of reconstruction or the rationalization of an existing content. It is an attempt to command and control the future. In this regard, philosophy is essentially transformative; and the genuine philosophers are those who re-create the world in the image that they describe:

> *Genuine philosophers, however, are commanders and legislators:* they say, "*thus* it *shall* be!" They first determine the Whither and For What of man, and in so doing have at their disposal the preliminary labor of all philosophical laborers, all who have overcome the past. With a creative hand they reach for the future, and all that is and has been becomes a means for them, an instrument, a hammer. Their "knowing" is *creating,* their creating is a legislation, their will to truth is—*will to power.* (*BGE* sec. 211)

I have argued that in spite of the world-historical tone of these remarks, they can serve to illuminate Nietzsche's own relationship to the individual soul.

For the discussion of sovereignty is itself the provocation of sovereignty. And the underlying intention of Nietzsche's writing is always to transform the individual life by forcing it out of its "wretched contentment" and toward the experience of the sacred.

From the "human" or "anthropological" perspective, the successful achievement of this project would be a very real accomplishment. It would entail the intensification of existence, and what in other contexts might be called the "perfecting of nature," through the celebration of the individual life as a "work of art." Through his own insistence upon it, Nietzsche implies that such a degree of sovereignty and self-commandment is possible—it is the intended effect of his philosophical intervention—and this remains true, even if from the alternative "cosmic" perspective that he describes everything must still take place within the horizon of necessity. Thus, sovereignty becomes the latest achievement of nature, although it is not something that is simply given and received. For we are ourselves a part of nature, and so we are bound to experience sovereignty as an inner imperative that we must actively come to terms with. Viewed in this way, the project of sovereignty does not pit us *against* nature. And even Nietzsche's admission of his own nonheroic life is perhaps only a projection of this final goal of attunement, in which the sovereign self remains sovereign while it is fully inscribed within nature itself.

Are we then to say that freedom is completely contained and circumscribed by nature, or that freedom is just another aspect or mode of necessity? The language that we use is probably unimportant. For especially if we remember that Nietzsche criticizes both the traditional conceptions of free will and determinism, we may conclude that his goal is not to offer a theoretically adequate account of sovereignty, but to suggest a meaningful and compelling image of the sovereign ideal that would follow from both the "human" and "cosmic" perspectives that his thinking describes. These two perspectives continually challenge and supersede each other at different levels within Nietzsche's texts. The tension that arises from these shifting horizons forces us to experience the problem of sovereignty within ourselves. For these same reasons of strategy, Nietzsche's theoretical philosophy *must* remain open and undecidable, such that any attempt to return his thought to "nature" or any other final principle must always be foreclosed.

All of this shows how Nietzsche is connected to the tradition and how he problematizes the received idea of autonomy, although he never disdains it as an impossible goal. Even if the theoretical underpinnings of sovereignty remain undefined, his intense meditation upon this theme is still compelling for an age in which "the individual" has apparently withdrawn as a rel-

evant category of everyday life. What does it mean to be a subject? What is
the relationship between the self and the world? And in what sense is autonomy still a meaningful possibility? Nietzsche's philosophy contains vast reserves for thinking through these issues. The present work has been an attempt to map out some of the preliminary terrain. We may not have reached
a final set of answers, but our primary task has really been to articulate the
nature of this problem that challenges Nietzsche's thought.

In this book I have argued that from the very beginning Nietzsche is most
concerned with the nature of individual existence—the individual as such—
and that he sought to elaborate the possibility of sovereignty. Nietzsche understood, however, that the latter cannot be described or even experienced
in any active or direct way. The reflection on sovereignty therefore calls for a
deliberate and oblique strategy that might evoke the possibility of sovereignty
and suggest a new attunement, even if it cannot articulate the meaning of
the individual life. In this regard, Nietzsche provokes and seduces us to his
projected goal, and his writings test us like a tuning hammer. In a key passage from *Beyond Good and Evil,* later repeated in *Ecce Homo,* he comments
on this philosophical strategy, which is meant to reawaken the individual and
summon us to the project of sovereignty. "I forbid any surmise about whom
I am describing," he writes; but it is clear that the subject of this passage can
only be Nietzsche himself.

> The genius of the heart, as that great concealed one possesses it, the tempter god
> and born pied piper of consciences whose voice knows how to descend into the
> netherworld of every soul; who does not say a word or cast a glance in which there
> is no consideration and ulterior enticement; whose mastery includes the knowl-
> edge of how to seem—not what he is but what is to those who follow him one
> *more* constraint to press ever closer to him in order to follow him ever more in-
> wardly and thoroughly—the genius of the heart who silences all that is loud and
> self-satisfied, teaching it to listen; who smooths rough souls and lets them taste a
> new desire—to lie still as a mirror, that the deep sky may mirror itself in them—
> the genius of the heart who teaches the doltish and rash hand to hesitate and reach
> out more delicately; who guesses the concealed and forgotten treasure, the drop
> of graciousness and sweet spirituality under dim and thick ice, and is a divining
> rod for every grain of gold that has long lain buried in the dungeon of much mud
> and sand; the genius of the heart from whose touch everyone walks away richer,
> not having received grace and surprised, not as blessed and oppressed by alien
> goods, but richer in himself, newer to himself than before, broken open, blown
> at and sounded out by a thawing wind, perhaps more unsure, tenderer, more frag-
> ile, more broken, but full of hopes that as yet have no name, full of new will and
> currents, full of new dissatisfaction and undertows. . . . (*BGE* sec. 295; and *EH*
> "Why I Write Such Good Books" sec. 6)

On the face of it, Nietzsche's celebration of the individual and his continual warnings against self-abandonment and the lures of morality, pity, and even neighbor-love, have helped to characterize him as a "selfish" thinker who is oblivious to the claims of the Other. At the same time, however, it must not be forgotten that Nietzsche's thinking is also directed *toward* the Other in the most immediate way. He does not want to prescribe or legislate in the manner of traditional philosophers. But in the very movement of his texts, he creates a context that allows the reader to appropriate the possibility of sovereignty; and this is the source of the great joy that reading Nietzsche provides. In the end, it might even be asked whether there could be a more profound commitment to the Other as an Other. For through this philosophical activity, Nietzsche frees the individual to become what he or she is.

⌁

Nietzsche's philosophy of sovereignty is necessarily incomplete, since it was from the outset an "impossible" project, in the sense that no set of words or theories can ever articulate that which is singular and unique. On the other hand, Nietzsche does offer a thoughtful and sustained meditation upon the essential moments of sovereignty; and the very performance of the text points us toward the individual as such. Read in this way, Nietzsche's difficult and apparently unreconcilable texts cohere in a way that makes good and important sense, at the same time as they release the life-transforming power with which he sought to endow them.

Notes

Introduction

1. See Heidegger's discussion of this interpretation at the beginning of volume 1 of his monumental work on Nietzsche, *Nietzsche,* 4 vols., trans. D. Krell et al. (New York: Harper and Row, 1979).

2. See, for example, the important collection edited by D. Allison, *The New Nietzsche* (New York: Dell Publishing Company, 1977). Also, Jacques Derrida, *Spurs,* trans. B. Harlow (Chicago: University of Chicago Press, 1979); and J. Derrida, *The Ear of the Other,* trans. P. Kamuf (New York: Schocken Books, 1985).

3. Karl Jaspers, *Nietzsche,* trans. C. Wallraff and F. Schmitz (Chicago: Henry Regnery Company, 1965).

4. Nietzsche's rejection of mechanism is consistent. See, for example, *GS* sec. 373.

5. See, for example, Jacques Derrida, "Structure, Sign, and Play in the Human Sciences," in *Writing and Difference,* trans. A. Bass (Chicago: University of Chicago Press, 1976).

6. Nietzsche views the sovereign individual as a masculine figure in this passage. In order to conform to this usage, reflected by the translation, I have therefore referred to the sovereign individual as "he" throughout. On the other hand, especially given the "mobility" of Nietzsche's terms, I am not convinced that such an ideal has to be gender specific.

7. Most notably, Walter Kaufmann's study, *Nietzsche: Philosopher, Psychologist, Antichrist* (Princeton, N.J.: Princeton University Press, 1968), which influenced a whole generation of Nietzsche studies.

8. See Kaufmann, *Nietzsche,* p. 307ff.; also B. Magnus, "Aristotle and Nietzsche: Megalopsychia and Uebermensch," in *The Greeks and the Good Life,* ed. D. Depew (Indianapolis: Hackett Publishing Company, 1980).

Chapter 1: On the Value of the Individual

1. Of course, this requires a very long argument, especially since Foucault, among others, has discussed the various ideals of "self-cultivation" that existed in the *pre*-Christian world. I would not deny that such ideals existed, but with Christianity the task becomes a universal one. If God counts every hair on our heads, then the dra-

ma of every individual existence becomes absolutely important. Historians of auto-biography—such as K. Weintraub in *The Value of the Individual* (Chicago: Universi-ty of Chicago Press, 1978) and G. Gusdorf in "The Conditions and Limits of Auto-biography," in J. Olney, ed., *Autobiography: Essays Theoretical and Critical* (Princeton, N.J.: Princeton University Press, 1980)—have also shown how in classical times, self-cultivation was usually in accordance with some *impersonal* principle of reason or nature. With Christianity, however, it is the *uniqueness* of each individual that be-comes the very focus of concern and the cause for celebration.

2. See A. MacIntyre, *After Virtue* (Notre Dame, Ind.: University of Notre Dame Press, 1981), p. 122. In this chapter, "The Virtues in Homeric Societies," MacIntyre makes his case very strongly: "In such a society a man knows who he is by knowing his role in these structures; and in knowing this he knows also what he owes and what is owed to him by the occupant of every other role and status" (p. 115).

3. Homer, *The Iliad*, books 6 and 18. See C. Brinton's discussion of the latter passage in *A History of Western Morality* (New York: Harcourt Brace, 1959), p. 65.

4. Plato, *The Republic*, trans. A. Bloom (New York: Basic Books, 1966) p. 123 (443d).

5. Aristotle, *Nicomachean Ethics* 1113a. See H. Peters, *Greek Philosophical Terms* (New York: New York University Press, 1967), p. 163, for a translation and discussion.

6. Hannah Arendt offers an excellent discussion of *proairesis* in *The Life of the Mind*, vol. 2, "Willing" (New York: Harcourt Brace Jovanovich, 1978), pp. 60–62.

7. Epictetus, *Discourses*, bk. 1, chap. 1. I have used Kahn's translations (see note 12).

8. Epictetus, *Discourses*, bk. 4, chap. 7.

9. See M. Foucault's discussion of humanism at the end of *The Order of Things* (London: Tavistock Publications, 1970).

10. See Weintraub, *Value of the Individual* and Olney, *Autobiography*.

11. J. J. Rousseau, *The Confessions*, trans. J. Cohen (Harmondsworth: Penguin Books, 1977), p. 17.

12. An excellent overview of this issue in historical perspective is offered by C. Kahn in "Discovering the Will: From Aristotle to Augustine," in *The Question of "Eclecticism": Studies in Later Greek Philosophy*, ed. J. Dillon and A. Long (Berkeley: University of California Press: 1988). See also, A. Dihle, *The Theory of the Will in Classical Antiquity* (Berkeley: University of California Press, 1982).

13. St. Augustine, *Confessions*, trans. R. Pine-Coffin (Harmondsworth: Penguin Books, 1989), bk. 8, sec. 5.

14. Ibid., bk. 5, sec. 2.

Chapter 2: The Genealogy of Sovereignty

1. Luther, for example, interpreted the text as a straightforward autobiographi-cal account of St. Paul's failure to achieve God's will. "It is a great consolation to us," he writes, "to learn that such a great apostle was involved in the same grievings and

afflictions in which we find ourselves when we wish to be obedient to God." Quoted by P. Achtemeier in "Some Things in Them Hard to Understand: Reflections on an Approach to Paul," in *Interpretation* 38, no. 3 (July 1984).

2. Important philosophical commentaries on the "Letter to the Romans" include H. Arendt, *The Life of the Mind;* H. Jonas, "The Abyss of the Will: Philosophical Meditation on the Seventh Chapter of Paul's Epistle to the Romans," in *Philosophical Essays* (New York: Prentice Hall, 1974); T. Altizer, *History as Apocalypse* (Ithaca: State University of New York Press, 1983), chap. 4; R. Bultmann, "Romans 7 and the Anthropology of Paul," in *Existence and Faith* (Cleveland: World Publishing Company, 1966), pp. 147–57; A. Van Den Beld, "Romans 7:14–25 and the Problem of Akrasia," in *Religious Studies* 21 (1985):495–515.

3. *New English Bible* (Oxford and Cambridge: Oxford and Cambridge University Press, 1970).

4. Here I follow Jonas, "Abyss of the Will," in his interpretation.

5. Quoted in Achtemeier, "Some Things."

6. St. Augustine, *Confessions,* trans. R. Pine-Coffin (Harmondsworth: Penguin Books, 1989), bk. 8, sec. 9

7. Immanuel Kant, *Foundations of the Metaphysics of Morals,* trans. L. Beck (Indianapolis: Bobbs-Merrill Company, 1959), p. 83 (463). The first reference is to Beck's translation, the second is to the standard Akademie edition. Hereafter this work will be cited in the text as *F.*

8. Immanuel Kant, *Critique of Practical Reason,* trans. L. Beck (Indianapolis: Bobbs-Merrill Company, 1956), p. 48 (47). The first reference is to Beck's translation, the second is to the standard Akademie edition. Hereafter this work will be cited as *CPR.*

9. Thus, in later work, Kant distinguishes between the legislative and executive aspects of will, between the will as *Wille* and the will as *Willkür.* To put it briefly, the will as *Willkür* is the faculty of choice or the elective will that is quite capable of choosing evil as well as good. The will's legislative function, or *Wille,* is simply the expression of our rational nature, and by its very existence it pronounces the law that we must follow in order to achieve autonomy as the most complete appropriation of ourselves. Thus the imperative of morality requires us to act in such a way that our *Willkür* becomes identical with our *Wille.* Kant argues (though this is surely open to question), that the *Willkür* that rejects the law of its rational nature is simply a deficient mode of willing. See B. Carnois, *The Coherence of Kant's Doctrine of Freedom,* trans. D. Booth (Chicago: University of Chicago Press, 1987), p. 52. In writing this chapter I have greatly benefited from this book, and also from H. Allison, *Kant's Theory of Freedom* (Cambridge: Cambridge University Press, 1990).

10. Kant, *Religion Within the Limits of Reason Alone,* trans. T. Greene and H. Hudson (New York: Harper and Row, 1960). "We cannot rightly call the idea of the moral law, with the respect which is inseparable from it, a predisposition to personality; it is personality itself (the idea of humanity considered quite intellectually)" (p. 23).

11. As Kant writes, "Freedom itself thus becomes in this indirect way capable of enjoyment . . . at least in origin, it is analogous to the self-sufficiency which can be ascribed only to the Supreme Being" (*CPR* p. 123;118).

12. This is the interpretation that R. Kroner offers in his excellent work, *Kant's Weltanshauung,* trans. J. Smith (Chicago: University of Chicago Press, 1956).

13. Arthur Schopenhauer, *The World as Will and Representation,* 2 vols., trans. E. F. J. Payne (New York: Dover Publications, 1969), vol. 1, pp. 321–22. Henceforth, this work will be referred to as *WWR.*

14. Cf. *GS* sec. 99; also *TI* "Skirmishes" sec. 37.

15. Schopenhauer, *On the Foundation of Morality,* sec. 20. This is quoted by P. Gardiner in his excellent study, *Schopenhauer* (Harmondsworth: Penguin Books, 1967). Gardiner gives a particularly lucid account of Schopenhauer's ethics.

16. For a very clear statement of this problem, see T. Sprigge, *Theories of Existence* (Harmondsworth: Penguin Books, 1984), chap. 4.

Chapter 3: The Individual and the Birth of Tragedy

1. For the fullest discussion of scholarly reaction to *The Birth of Tragedy,* see M. Silk and J. Stern, *Nietzsche on Tragedy* (Cambridge: Cambridge University Press, 1981).

2. This point is also made very convincingly by D. Allison in "Nietzsche Knows No Noumenon," *boundary* 2 (Spring/Fall 1981).

3. My reading of the Dionysian is influenced by the work of Georges Bataille. See, for example, the collection of essays, *Visions of Excess,* ed. A. Stoekl (Minneapolis: University of Minnesota Press, 1985), and *Eroticism,* trans. M. Dalwood (London: Marion Boyars Publishers, 1987). For Bataille, the suspension of the everyday world of "project"—in sacrifice, eroticism, and festival—is what brings us back to the realm of the sacred. The latter is thus associated with the self-dispossession that is an anticipation of death.

4. On the meaning of the "tragic" experience of life, see Gilles Deleuze, *Nietzsche and Philosophy,* trans. H. Tomlinson (New York: Columbia University Press, 1983), chap. 1.

5. This is discussed by Paul de Man in *Allegories of Reading* (New Haven, Conn.: Yale University Press, 1979).

6. See *EH* "The Birth of Tragedy" sec. 1

7. Schopenhauer's relationship to Nietzsche is discussed by I. Soll in "Reconsiderations of Nietzsche's *Birth of Tragedy,*" in *Reading Nietzsche,* ed. R. Solomon and K. Higgins (Oxford: Oxford University Press, 1988); see also F. Copleston, *Friedrich Nietzsche* (New York: Barnes & Noble Books, 1975), chap. 7.

8. For a very insightful account of how this artistic metaphor could be worked out, see Alexander Nehamas, *Nietzsche: Life as Literature* (Cambridge, Mass.: Harvard University Press, 1985).

9. For more on this theme, see Gilles Deleuze, "Nomad Thought," in *The New Nietzsche,* ed. D. Allison (New York: Dell Publishing Company, 1977).

10. The essay by R. McGinn, "Culture as Prophylactic: Nietzsche's *Birth of Trag-edy* as Cultural Criticism" (*Nietzsche Studien*, vol. 4 [1975]), contains an interesting discussion of Apollinian versus Dionysian modes of being, as well as a careful over-view of *The Birth of Tragedy* as a whole. Another excellent discussion of *The Birth of Tragedy* is offered by Richard Schacht in *Nietzsche* (London: Routledge, 1983), chap. 8.

11. See B. Russell's discussion of Nietzsche in *A History of Western Philosophy* (New York: Simon and Schuster, 1945), p. 760ff; also, J. Dewey, *German Philosophy and Politics* (New York: E. P. Dutton, 1915).

12. L. Thiele, in his book, *Friedrich Nietzsche and the Politics of the Soul* (Prince-ton, N.J.: Princeton University Press, 1990), focuses much of his discussion on what Nietzsche might mean here and how this ideal is implicit in all of his writings.

13. On this theme, see the excellent essay by W. Hamacher, "'Disgregation of the Will': Nietzsche on the Individual and Individuality," in *Reconstructing Individual-ism: Autonomy, Individuality, and the Self in Western Thought*, ed. T. Heller et al. (Stan-ford: Stanford University Press, 1986).

Chapter 4: Against Idealism

1. Along these lines, see Terry Eagleton's critique of Nietzsche in *The Ideology of the Aesthetic* (Oxford: Basil Blackwell, 1990), chap. 9.

2. *HH* I, sections 126, 150, 220, 223.

3. *HH* I, for example, sections 5 and 17.

4. Even though Nietzsche's discussion of freedom and the free will would seem to be absolutely central to an understanding of his philosophical position, in fact very little has been written on this subject. But see R. Schacht, *Nietzsche* (London: Rout-ledge, 1983), chap. 5, for a thoughtful discussion.

5. For an interesting account of the rhetorical strategies of *The Gay Science*, see R. Kuenzli, "The Signifying Process in Nietzsche's *The Gay Science*," in *Nietzsche: Literature and Values*, ed. V. Durr et al. (Madison: University of Wisconsin Press, 1988).

6. This reading of *The Gay Science* is influenced by Georges Bataille's discussion of laughter. See, for example, *Guilty*, trans. B. Boone (Venice, Calif.: Lapis Press, 1988).

7. See *GS* sec. 143.

8. On this point, see René Girard, "Dionysus Versus the Crucified," in *Modern Language Notes* 99:4 (1984). Girard's work is in part a response to Bataille's eleva-tion of transgression (in *Eroticism*, for example).

9. Following the lines of this critique of autonomy, see J. Bernstein, "Autonomy and Solitude," in *Nietzsche and Modern German Thought*, ed. K. Ansell-Pearson (Lon-don: Routledge, 1991).

10. Of course, it is precisely this absolute distinction between the "inside" and the "outside" that contemporary philosophy has called into question. See, for example, Jacques Derrida, *Margins*, trans. A. Bass (Chicago: University of Chicago Press, 1982).

Chapter 5: Zarathustra and the Teaching of Sovereignty

1. Until quite recently there were relatively few philosophical interpretations of *Thus Spoke Zarathustra*. Now, however, this situation is changing. See H. Alderman, *Nietzsche's Gift* (Athens: Ohio University Press, 1977); L. Lampert, *Nietzsche's Teaching: An Interpretation of "Thus Spoke Zarathustra";* R. Pippin, "Irony and Affirmation in Nietzsche's *Thus Spoke Zarathustra,*" in *Nietzsche's New Seas,* ed. M. Gillespie and T. Strong (Chicago: University of Chicago Press, 1988); G. Shapiro, *Nietzschean Narratives* (Indianapolis: Indiana University Press, 1989); and G. Shapiro, *Alcyone: Nietzsche on Gifts, Noise, and Women* (Ithaca: State University of New York Press, 1991). These works have all influenced my own reading of *Zarathustra*.

2. See M. Heidegger, "Who Is Nietzsche's Zarathustra?" in *The New Nietzsche,* ed. D. Allison (New York: Dell Publishing Company, 1977).

3. Ibid., p. 76.

4. See, for example, E. Bertram, *Nietzsche: Versuch einer Mythologie* (Berlin: G. Bondi, 1918); and A. Baeumler, *Nietzsche der Philosoph und Politiker* (Leipzig: P. Reclam, 1931). An excellent discussion of these works can be found in the "Analysis" by D. Krell that accompanies his translation of Heidegger's four-volume *Nietzsche* (New York: Harper and Row, 1979).

5. Helpful discussions of the overman are included in W. Kaufmann, *Nietzsche: Philosopher, Psychologist, Antichrist* (Princeton, N.J.: Princeton University Press, 1968). B. Magnus, *Nietzsche's Existential Imperative* (Indianapolis: Indiana University Press, 1978); and D. Conway, "Overcoming the Übermensch: Nietzsche's Revaluation of Values," in *Journal of the British Society for Phenomenology* 20:3 (1989).

6. On the possible relationship between the overman and Aristotle's "great-souled man," see Kaufmann, *Nietzsche,* pp. 382–90; and B. Magnus's essay in D. Depew, ed., *The Greeks and the Good Life* (Indianapolis: Hackett Publishing Company, 1980).

7. For an excellent discussion of the "gift-giving virtue," see G. Shapiro, *Alcyone: Nietzsche on Gifts, Noise, and Women* (Ithaca: State University of New York Press, 1991); and L. Hunt, *Nietzsche and the Origin of Virtue* (London: Routledge, 1991).

8. See Pippin, "Irony and Affirmation," on this point.

9. On this point, see Magnus's interpretation in his *Nietzsche's Existential Imperative.* Also see M. Sterling, "Recent Discussions of Eternal Recurrence," in *Nietzsche Studien* 6 (1977).

10. In "Nietzsche, Zarathustra, and the Status of Laughter" (*British Journal of Aesthetics* 32:1 [1992]), J. Lippitt discusses the significance of the various types of laughter that are to be found in *Zarathustra*.

11. The first interpretation is supported by Nehamas in *Nietzsche: Life as Literature* (Cambridge, Mass.: Harvard University Press, 1985); the second is defended by Shapiro in his *Nietzschean Narratives.* I want to suggest that in a sense *both* interpretations are correct.

12. In this respect, see Gilles Deleuze's reading of the eternal recurrence as a "selective" thought in *Nietzsche and Philosophy,* trans. H. Tomlinson (New York: Columbia University Press, 1983), chap. 2.

13. This ideal of self-integration or self-appropriation is spelled out very well in Nehamas, *Nietzsche,* who offers a very important chapter on "How One Becomes What One Is."

14. As well as Shapiro, *Alcyone,* see P. Klossowski, "Nietzsche's Experience of the Eternal Recurrence," in Allison, ed., *New Nietzsche,* on this point.

15. Perhaps it is inappropriate to talk of a Nietzschean "theodicy," but this is a very relevant area of concern. See, for example, G. Goedert, "The Dionysian Theodicy," in *Studies in Nietzsche and the Judeo-Christian Tradition,* ed. J. O'Flaherty et al. (Chapel Hill: University of North Carolina Press, 1985).

16. See the discussion by E. Fink, "Nietzsche's New Experience of World, in *Nietzsche's New Seas,* ed. Gillespie and Strong.

17. See F. A. Lea, *The Tragic Philosopher* (London: Methuen, 1957), and R. Hollingdale in *Nietzsche: The Man and His Philosophy* (London: Routledge and Kegan Paul, 1985). Both dismiss part four in this way. For two very affirmative readings of part four, see Shapiro, *Alcyone,* pp. 53–107, and K. Higgins, *Nietzsche's Zarathustra* (Philadelphia: Temple University Press, 1987).

18. On this idea of a "self-deconstruction," see R. Kuenzli "Nietzsche's Zerography: *Thus Spoke Zarathustra,*" *boundary 2* (Spring/Fall 1981).

Chapter 6: The Return of the Master

1. For example, in his first volume on Nietzsche, Heidegger points out that "Only he can truly command—and commanding has nothing to do with mere ordering about—who is always ready and able to place himself under command." See Heidegger's *Nietzsche,* vol. 1, p. 41.

2. This follows A. Lingis, "The Will to Power," in D. Allison, *The New Nietzsche* (New York: Dell Publishing Company, 1977).

3. Heidegger's interpretation of the will to power runs throughout his published writings on Nietzsche. But his most illuminating and focused comments can be found in the early chapters of the first volume of his *Nietzsche.*

4. See N. Davey, "Nietzsche's Doctrine of Perspectivism," in the *Journal of the British Society for Phenomenology* 14:3 (1983). Also, A. Nehamas, "Immanent and Transcendent Perspectivism in Nietzsche," in *Nietzsche Studien* 12 (1983).

5. See *BGE* sec. 230. "That commanding something which the people call 'the spirit' wants to be master in and around its own house and wants to feel that it is master; it has the will from multiplicity to simplicity, a will that ties up, tames, and is domineering and truly masterful."

6. A very full account of Nietzsche's problematic account of the self is offered by D. Booth in "Nietzsche on 'The Subject as Multiplicity,'" *Man and World* 18 (1985). See also S. Corngold, "The Question of the Self during Nietzsche's Axial Period (1882–1888)," *boundary 2* (Spring/Fall 1981).

7. Once again, Nietzsche's discussion stands behind the "death of the subject," which has become a very important theme in recent Continental thought. See, for example, the essays in D. Allison, ed. *The New Nietzsche* (New York: Dell Publishing

Company, 1977); also L. Ferry and A. Renaut, *French Philosophy of the Sixties: An Essay on Anti-Humanism* (Amherst: University of Massachusetts Press, 1990).

8. See *GM* II sec. 12. "One places . . . 'adaptation' in the foreground, that is to say, an activity of the second rank, a mere reactivity; indeed, life itself has defined itself as a more and more efficient inner adaptation to external conditions. . . . Thus the essence of life, its *will to power* is ignored."

9. From a passage that Nietzsche intended for inclusion in *Ecce Homo,* but which was later suppressed, he writes: "I don't understand it, but Julius Caesar could have been my father—or Alexander, this embodied Dionysus." A full translation of this passage may be found in T. Strong, "Oedipus as Hero: Family and Family Metaphors in Nietzsche," *boundary 2* (Spring/Fall 1981).

10. This comparison is forcefully made by W. Hamacher in his essay, "The Promise of Interpretation," in *Looking After Nietzsche,* ed. L. Rickels (Ithaca: State University of New York Press, 1990).

11. This is pointed out by Gilles Deleuze in *Nietzsche and Philosophy* (New York: Columbia University Press, 1983), p. 111ff.

12. See ibid., especially pages 114–16, for an account of Nietzsche's typology and the possibility of such a transformation.

Chapter 7: *Ecce Homo,* or the Revaluation of Values

1. On Nietzsche's obsession with contagion and disease in these final texts, see M. Serres, "Corruption—*The Antichrist:* A Chemistry of Sensations and Ideas," in *Stanford Italian Review* 6:1–2 (1986).

2. This discussion of nihilism is influenced by R. Schacht, "Nietzsche and Nihilism," and R. Solomon, "Nietzsche, Nihilism and Morality." Both are included in *Nietzsche: A Collection of Critical Essays,* ed. R. Solomon (Notre Dame, Ind.: University of Notre Dame Press, 1980).

3. See G. Shapiro's important essay on *The Antichrist,* which is incuded in his *Nietzschean Narratives* (Indianapolis: Indiana University Press, 1989).

4. H. Alderman, in *Nietzsche's Gift* (Athens: Ohio University Press, 1989), also argues strongly for the importance of the *experience* of reading Nietzsche, something that must be distinguished from Nietzsche's particular philosophical ideas.

5. This is to follow Bataille's account of sacrifice. See, for example, the early chapters of *Eroticism,* trans. M. Dalwood (London: Marion Boyers Publishers, 1987).

6. To follow this idea of *Ecce Homo* as an ironic autobiography, see H. Silverman, "The Autobiographical Textuality of *Ecce Homo*"; and R. Gasché, "Autobiography as *Gestalt:* Nietzsche's *Ecce Homo.*" Both texts are in *boundary 2* (Spring/Fall 1981). See also, J. Derrida, *The Ear of the Other,* trans. P. Kamuf (New York: Schocken Books, 1985).

7. This is the problem that T. Strong addresses in his essay, "Oedipus as Hero: Family and Family Metaphors in Nietzsche," in *boundary 2* (Spring/Fall 1981).

8. In this respect, I think that while Nehamas's account of "how one becomes what

one is" is very illuminating, it seems to make self-appropriation into a matter of personal choice and individual artistry; but this "voluntaristic" reading is not completely warranted by the text.

9. On this idea of *Ecce Homo* as an autobiographical performance, see M. Ryan, "The Act," in *Glyph* 2 (Baltimore: Johns Hopkins University Press, 1977).

10. For further discussion of this point, see T. Harrison, "Have I Been Understood? The Eternal Nowhere of Nietzschean Existence," in *Stanford Italian Review* 6:1–2 (1986).

11. D. Conway makes this point very clearly in "Overcoming the Übermensch: Nietzsche's Revaluation of Values," *Journal of the British Society for Phenomenology* 20:3 (1989).

12. Heidegger's discussion of value is very important here. See "Nietzsche's Word: God is Dead," in *The Question Concerning Technology,* trans. W. Lovitt (New York: Harper and Row, 1977). Heidegger's discussion focuses on sec. 715 of *The Will to Power,* where Nietzsche writes: "The standpoint of 'value' is the standpoint of conditions of preservation and enhancement for complex forms of relative life-duration within the flux of becoming."

Chapter 8: Nietzsche and the Philosophy of the Future

1. See Claude Lévi-Strauss, *The Savage Mind* (Chicago: University of Chicago Press, 1966), chap. 9.

2. Michel Foucault, *The Order of Things* (London: Tavistock Publications, 1974), p. 385.

3. Ibid., pp. 342–43. Foucault argues that the "modern" period is characterized by an impossible attempt to "think the unthought" and to ground all of our knowledge of the world upon the being who knows. "Man" is regarded as the active subject of knowledge; but paradoxically, his very activity is then esteemed as the final *object* of all inquiry—thus ensuring the continual removal or "retreat" of the origin as thinking attempts, impossibly, to step behind itself.

4. See especially the first part of *The Will to Power,* "European Nihilism."

5. For a recent collection that considers this issue, see *Nietzsche as Postmodernist: Essays Pro and Contra,* ed. C. Koelb (Ithaca: State University of New York Press, 1990).

6. M. Heidegger, "Letter on Humanism," in *Basic Writings,* ed. D. Krell (New York: Harper and Row, 1977), pp. 209–10.

7. M. Heidegger, "Overcoming Metaphysics," in *The End of Philosophy,* trans. J. Stambaugh (New York: Harper and Row, 1973), p. 93.

8. M. Heidegger, *Discourse on Thinking,* trans. J. Anderson and E. Freund (New York: Harper and Row, 1966), p. 85.

9. Heidegger's discussion of Nietzsche may be found in his *Nietzsche,* 4 vols., trans. D. Krell et al. (New York: Harper and Row, 1982); and in "The Word of Nietzsche," in *The Question Concerning Technology,* trans. W. Lovitt (New York: Harper and Row,

1977), pp. 53–112. In the latter work, for example, he writes of a univocal will to power in essentially negative terms: "in deliberately willing the will to power as the being of whatever is; and . . . in rebelliously withstanding and subjugating to itself every necessary phase of the objectifying of the world [willing as will to power makes] secure the stably constant reserve of what is for a willing of the greatest possible uniformity and equality" (p. 102). Here, Heidegger is simply oblivious to any affirmative account of the will to power as a principle of individual sovereignty and difference.

10. Jacques Derrida, "Freud and the Scene of Writing," in *Writing and Difference,* trans. A. Bass (Chicago: University of Chicago Press, 1976), p. 229.

11. Jacques Derrida, "Limited Inc.," in *Glyph* 2 (1977). My discussion of Derrida has benefited from P. Smith, *Discerning the Subject* (Minneapolis: University of Minnesota Press, 1988), and from P. Dews, *Logics of Disintegration* (London: New Left Books/Verso, 1987).

12. Consider the following passage from Derrida's essay, "Shibboleth," in *Midrash and Literature,* ed. G. Hartman and S. Budick (New Haven: Yale University Press, 1986), p. 314 (also cited by Dews). "This you, which may be an I, like the '*er als ein Ich*' of a moment ago, always figures an irreplaceable singularity—one which is thus replaceable only by another irreplaceable singularity which takes its place without substituting for it." Surely there is quite a distance between such "irreplaceable singularity" and the complete dispersion of the subject and its proper name.

13. The discussion appears in *Reflexive Water,* ed. F. Elders (London: Souvenir Press, 1974), p. 135ff.

14. See the interview with Foucault in *Technologies of the Self,* ed. L. Martin, H. Gutman, and E. Hutton (Amherst: University of Massachusetts Press, 1988), p. 15.

15. Michel Foucault, *Discipline and Punish: The Birth of the Prison,* trans. A. Sheridan (New York: Vintage, 1979).

16. See C. Taylor's discussion of this point in *Foucault: A Critical Reader,* ed. D. Hoy (Oxford: Basil Blackwell, 1986), pp. 69–102.

17. For example, see D. Lecourt, *Marxism and Epistemology* (London: New Left Books, 1970).

18. Consider, for example, Foucault's comments in *Power/Knowledge,* ed. C. Gordon (New York: Pantheon Books, 1980): "The individual is not to be conceived as a sort of elementary nucleus, a primitive atom, a multiple and inert material on which power comes to fasten or against which it happens to strike, and in so doing subdues or crushes individuals. In fact it is already one of the prime effects of power that certain bodies, certain gestures, certain discourses, certain desires come to be identified and constituted as individuals" (p. 98).

19. See the interview with Foucault, "On the Genealogy of Ethics," included in H. Dreyfus and P. Rabinow, *Michel Foucault: Beyond Structuralism and Hermeneutics,* 2d ed. (Chicago: University of Chicago Press, 1982), p. 237.

20. The idea of the subject as a fold within power is Gilles Deleuze's formulation in his book, *Foucault,* trans. Sian Hand (Minneapolis: University of Minnesota Press, 1988).

21. This is not the place for a survey of recent feminist thinking. However, it does seem that there is at least a possibility of a creative interchange between the two "wings" of contemporary feminism. On the one hand, the (primarily Anglo-American) approach that tends to emphasize *women's* experience and *women's* history, and so on; on the other hand, the (Continental) approach, which is informed by deconstruction and psychoanalysis and remains deeply suspicious of all "essentialist" accounts of "woman." Perhaps the conjunction of these two moments could provide us with a critically renewed conception of the self. See P. Smith, *Discerning the Subject,* and L. Alcoff, "Cultural Feminism Versus Post-Structuralism: The Identity Crisis in Feminist Theory," *Signs* 13:3.

Index

Achilles, 14
akrasia, 15, 29, 33, 34
Alcoff, L., 205*n*21
Alderman, H., 200*n*1, 202*n*4
Allison, D., 195*n*2, 198*n*2, 201*n*7
Allison, H., 197*n*9
Altizer, T., 197*n*2
Apollo/Apollinian, 21, 23, 24, 50, 54–77,
    86, 87, 95, 96, 116, 160, 167, 175, 187,
    189
Arendt, H., 196*n*6, 197*n*2
Aristotle, 10, 15, 16, 17, 200*n*6
Arnold, T., 8
art, 56–77, 166–67, 191
autobiography, 16, 17, 196*n*1
autonomy, 5, 7, 8, 9, 12, 26, 34, 36–44, 52,
    96, 98–99, 122, 141, 145, 175, 179, 182,
    185, 190, 191, 192

Baeumler, A., 200*n*4
Bataille, G., 198*n*3, 199*n*6, 202*n*5
Being, 179–81
Bernstein, J., 199*n*9
Bertram, E., 200*n*4
body, 2, 13, 164
Booth, D., 201*n*6
Brinton, C., 196*n*3
Bultmann, R., 197*n*2

Calvin, J., 33
Carnois, B., 197*n*9
categorical imperative, 26, 40, 42, 43, 134,
    140, 173
Chomsky, N., 183

Christ, 142. *See also* Jesus
Christianity, 10, 11, 17, 18, 25, 28–36, 45,
    47, 52, 78, 93, 105, 120, 125, 136–49,
    150–60, 161, 162, 163, 167, 169, 174,
    175, 176, 178, 195*n*1
Conway, D., 200*n*5
Copleston, F., 198*n*7
Corngold, S., 201*n*6

Davey, N., 201*n*4
death of God, 10, 91–96, 100, 103, 105,
    121, 157, 176, 177, 186
death of man. *See* death of the subject
death of the subject, 10, 16, 24, 95, 177–
    78, 185, 201*n*7
deconstruction, 1, 2, 3, 181, 205*n*21
Deleuze, G., 198*nn*4,9, 200*n*12, 202*nn*11–
    12, 204*n*20
De Man, P., 198*n*5
Derrida, J., 177, 181–82, 195*nn*2,5,
    199*n*10, 202*n*6, 204*n*12
Descartes, R., 181
Dewey, J., 199*n*11
Dews, P., 204*n*4
Dihle, A., 196*n*12
Dionysus/Dionysian, 8, 21, 22, 23, 24, 50,
    54–77, 86, 88, 96, 116, 117, 118, 130,
    135, 144, 146, 154, 155, 160, 167, 175,
    185, 187, 189

Eagleton, T., 199*n*4
education, 75, 79, 175
egoism, 80, 136
Epictetus, 16, 17

eternal recurrence, 1, 3, 9, 24–25, 51, 96, 100, 108–18, 122, 127, 148, 176, 185, 189
Euripides, 61
existentialist, 9

feminism, 185, 205*n*21
Ferry, L., 202*n*7
Fink, E., 201*n*16
Foucault, J., 16, 24, 177–78, 182–85, 195*n*1, 196*n*9, 203*n*3, 204*nn*18–19
freedom, 2, 9, 21, 24, 36, 38, 41, 43, 46, 49, 78–88, 99, 118, 130–35 passim, 152, 158, 163, 164, 168, 169, 175, 185, 190, 191
free spirit, 6, 19, 21, 24, 78–88, 95, 98, 118, 158, 159, 168, 170, 189
free will. *See* freedom

Gardiner, P., 198*n*15
Gasché, R., 202*n*6
Gelassenheit, 180
genealogy, 4, 11, 26, 136–49, 162, 163, 169
gift-giving virtue, 106–8, 116
Gillespie, M., 200*n*1
Girard, R., 199*n*8
God, 16, 146, 157, 169, 182, 186. *See also* death of God
Goedert, G., 201*n*15
Goethe, J., 20, 43, 158, 159
Greece/Greeks, 10, 54–77
Gusdorf, G., 196*n*1

Hamacher, W., 199*n*13, 202*n*10
Harrison, T., 203*n*10
Hegel, G., 52
Heidegger, M., 3, 101, 117, 177, 179–81, 182, 184, 195*n*1, 200*n*2, 201*nn*1,3, 203*n*12, 203*n*9 (chap. 8)
Higgins, K., 201*n*17
higher humanity, 4, 7, 11, 149, 189
Hollingdale, R., 201*n*17
Homer, 196*n*3
Hunt, L., 200*n*7
Husserl, E., 181

idealism, 2, 79–99, 151, 162, 163–70, 172, 176

Iliad, 14
individual, 6, 7, 13, 14, 15, 16, 45, 47, 67, 69–73, 79, 97–99, 126, 153, 160–73, 174, 184, 189, 192, 193
individualism, 11, 13, 35, 52, 56, 179

Jaspers, K., 2
Jesus, 155. *See also* Christ
Jonas, H., 197*n*2

Kant, I., 7, 8, 11, 20, 26, 27, 36–44, 52, 53, 56, 63, 76, 96, 98, 135, 140, 159, 175, 181, 197*n*9
Kahn, C., 196*n*12
Kaufmann, W., 195*n*7, 200*nn*5–6
Klossowski, P., 201*n*14
Krell, D., 200*n*4
Kroner, R., 198*n*12
Kuenzli, R., 199*n*5, 201*n*18

Lacan, J., 177
Lampert, L., 200*n*1
language, 97–98, 158–59, 169, 173, 181
last man, 4
laughter, 88, 89, 90, 92, 95, 96, 113, 121
Lea, F., 201*n*17
Lecourt, D., 204*n*17
Lévi-Strauss, C., 13
Lingis, A., 201*n*2
Lippitt, J., 200*n*10
Luther, M., 196*n*1

MacIntyre, A., 196*n*2
Magnus, B., 195*n*8, 200*nn*5–6,9
master and slave, 3, 26, 129, 133, 134, 135, 136–49, 169, 181, 186, 189
materialism, 2, 81, 91, 130, 163. *See also* physiology
McGinn, R., 199*n*10
morality/moral ideals, 75, 133–49

Napoleon, 159
Nehamas, A., 198*n*8, 200*n*11, 201*n*4,13, 202*n*8
nihilism, 5, 27, 35, 50, 51, 52, 53, 66, 78, 105, 111, 113, 144, 146, 150, 153, 155, 171, 176, 177, 178, 184, 187

overman, 1, 4, 9, 19, 100–113, 116, 117, 118, 127, 189

performative, 3, 86, 138, 146, 147, 168–70, 174–75, 189, 193
perspectivism, 128, 155
pessimism, 2, 27, 53, 65
philosopher of the future, 23, 144–47, 148, 190
physiology, 2, 151, 153, 161. *See also* materialism
Pippin, R., 200*nn*1,8
Plato, 15, 16, 128, 148
postmodernism, 1, 10, 177, 186, 187
poststructuralism, 9, 177, 186
power, 183–84
proairesis, 15, 17

race, 168, 169
Renaut, A., 202*n*7
ressentiment, 138, 141, 147, 150
revaluation of values, 5, 52, 145, 150–73
Rousseau, J., 17
Russell, B., 199*n*11
Ryan, M., 203*n*9

sacred, 7, 21, 22, 58–59, 60, 62, 69, 94, 95, 107, 157, 176, 186–87, 191
Sartre, J., 179
Schacht, R., 199*n*10 (chap. 3), 199*n*4, 202*n*2
Schopenhauer, A., 26, 42, 44–52, 53, 56, 59, 63, 64, 65, 66, 76, 129, 175, 176, 198*n*7
science, 90, 143
Searle, J., 182
selfhood, 21, 23, 86, 130–36, 163, 166, 175, 187
Serres, M., 202*n*1
Shapiro, G., 200*nn*1,7,11, 201*n*16, 202*n*3
Silenus, 66–67
Silk, M., 198*n*1
Silverman, H., 202*n*6

Smiles, S., 7
Smith, P., 204*n*11, 205*n*21
Socrates, 54, 55, 61, 62, 145, 154
Soll, I., 198*n*7
Solomon, R., 202*n*2
sovereign individual, 4, 5, 6, 7, 23–24, 49, 55, 86, 144–45, 189, 190, 195*n*6
Sprigge, T., 198*n*16
St. Augustine, 17, 18, 19, 26, 28, 33, 34, 36
Sterling, M., 200*n*9
Stern, J., 198*n*1
stoicism, 16, 17
St. Paul, 11, 18, 19, 26, 27, 28–36, 52, 53, 132, 150, 153, 155, 174, 175, 176, 196*n*1
Strauss, D., 74
Strong, T., 200*n*1, 202*n*7,9
structuralism, 177

Taylor, C., 204*n*16
Thiele, L., 199*n*12
tradition, 5, 10, 25, 26, 27, 176, 177, 191
tragedy, 54–77
truth, 89–91, 128, 143, 146

value, 173, 203*n*12. *See also* Christianity
Van den Beld, A., 197*n*2

Wagner, R., 27, 54, 63, 64, 76, 77, 165, 166, 168
Weintraub, K., 196*n*1
will/willing, 15, 17, 18, 20, 24, 28, 32, 34, 39, 43, 65, 82, 84, 85, 104, 105, 106, 115, 123, 126, 127, 129, 130–36, 145, 148, 155, 158, 159, 164, 175, 180
Wille and *Willkür,* 197*n*9
will-lessness, 8, 35, 66, 141, 143, 146, 177
will to power, 1, 3, 9, 118, 123, 124–36, 140, 146, 155, 156, 159, 164, 173, 176, 180, 181, 185, 187, 190
will to will, 18, 19, 34, 123, 144, 180

Zarathustra, 8, 100–123, 124–27, 160

Richard J. White is an associate professor of philosophy at Creighton University in Omaha, Nebraska. He has written widely on recent Continental philosophy, the philosophy of love and sex, and the relationship between philosophy and literature.